anta Cruz Etla

W9-CJI-228

El Arroyo

Main Ditch (Zanja)

Augustina

Martín

Rosario

Dam

Trail to Sierra

Casimiro

Bartolo

arcelino

Zanja

Amado

Joel

Pantéon

San Lorenzo Ditch

San Lorenzo Trail

Estefana

Sofía

Florenzio

Dry Arroyo Bed

Melitón

San Lorenzo Loma

Paula's Garden

Ceferino

Paula

Chico

Félíz Jiménez

na

His Garden

San Lorenzo Ditch

Dry Season Well

San Lorenzo People

Ramírez Brothers

Dry Arroyo Bed

Ox cart Road

Helen Miller Bailey 1958

SANTA CRUZ
OF THE
ETLA HILLS

SANTA CRUZ
OF THE
ETLA HILLS

BY Helen Miller Bailey

UNIVERSITY OF FLORIDA PRESS
GAINESVILLE
1958

A UNIVERSITY OF FLORIDA PRESS BOOK

COPYRIGHT, 1958, UNIVERSITY OF FLORIDA

Library of Congress Catalogue Card Number: 58-11099

ROSE PRINTING CO., INC.
TALLAHASSEE, FLORIDA

Contents

Illustrations

The People of Santa Cruz Etla

THE FAMILIES

Don Amado, the sage of Santa Cruz Etla, three times its president; Doña Rufina, his wife; Cassiano, Martiniano, and Margarito, his sons.

Doña Estéfana, leader of the women, Amado's cousin, hostess to the author, 1944; Doña Sofía, her daughter; Joel, Sofía's son by her first husband; Don Pablo *el Bracero*, Sofía's second husband; Inocencio and Leopoldo, their sons; Don Ignacio, Estéfana's son; Aurelio, his son.

Don Martín, the baker, three times municipal president; Doña Pastorcita, his wife; Miguelto, their son; Chabella, his wife; Margarita, Artemio, Adela, Lupita, Graciela, Jesús, and Guillermo, their children; Doña Enriqueta, Don Martín's sister-in-law; Don Pedro, her husband; Ordón, their son; Doña Margarita, Pedro's mother; Doña Rosario, Chabella's mother; Adelita, Rosario's other daughter.

Doña Patrocina, the cure woman, hostess to the author, 1945; La Abuelita, her mother; Don Fausto, Patrocina's brother; Doña Buenaventura, his second wife; Chico, Patrocina's older son; Esperanza, his wife; Ramón, their son; Nico, Patrocina's other son; Doña Manuela, his wife; Eloisa, their daughter; Eostolia, cousin to Chico and Nico; Elijeo Ramírez, her husband; Eliseo, her brother-in-law; Don Melitón Arroyo, Esperanza's father; Hipólito, his son.

Don Julio, the miller, municipal president, 1938; Doña Fecunda, his first wife; Eduardo, Juanita, and Susana, their children; Rafaela, Eduardo's wife; Doña Refugio, Julio's second wife.

Don Bartolo, goat farmer, municipal president, 1945; Doña Sista, his wife; Timoteo and Luisa, their children.

Don Marciano, chairman of public works, 1945; Doña Clara, his wife; Panfilo and Juanito, his sons; other children; Adolfo Soto, his son-in-law.

Doña Paula, gardener, householder next to the school; Doña Nobarra, her mother; Máximo, Paula's oldest son; Elodia, his wife; Esteban, Paula's second son, municipal president in 1944; María, his wife; Crescencio and Alicia, Paula's other children.

Don Féliz Jiménez, horticulturist, municipal president, 1954.

Don Ceferino, leader of the band.

Don Féliz León, former chairman of public works; Doña Angélica, his wife; Francisco and Felicito, their sons.

Don Casimiro, raiser of hogs; Doña Beatriz, his wife; Gerónomo, their son.

Don Florenzio, owner of the orchard; Doña María Teresa, his wife.

Don Féliz Mendoza, farmer on San Sebastián ridge.

Don Marcelino, municipal president, 1951; Perfecto and Teresa, his children.

Don Lalo; Aurelia, his daughter, school pet in 1934.

Doña Carmen, a deaf old widow; Carmita, her daughter.

Isaías Pérez, fourth-grade leader, 1945.

Augustina, "slavey" at the school, 1934; Juan López, her husband.

San Pablo People: Doña Socorro, godmother to Chico; Don Bernabé, her husband; Don Enrique *et Alto*, a *bracero*.

THE OUTSIDERS

Rosita Arrieta, the first teacher; Doña Rafaela, her mother; Doña Mercedes, Rosita's aunt; Don Octaviano, Rosita's uncle; Doña Elena, *la profesora americana*, the author; Don Enrique, her husband (his Mexican name); El Maestro, Don Solomón, Doña Ofelia, Doña Ester, Don Alfredo, and Estella, his wife, later teachers; Señor Ximello, Don Luis Varela, and Señor Gómez, Oaxaca State school officials.

Through the Decades

PART ONE

Santa Cruz Etla IS a Town

1. DON AMADO: *This "Sage of Santa Cruz Etla" created a municipality.*
2. DON MARTÍN: *The "first modern man" ran the town's funerals and became a wheat-bread baker.*
3. DON JULIO: *This hard-headed businessman who brought in a corn mill was able to find little personal happiness.*
4. DON BARTOLO: *The town comic had a chance to run the local government.*
5. DON MARCIANO: *The owner of the only horse was chairman of public works.*
6. DON FÉLIZ: *This shy horticulturist supervised the building of a chapel.*

~~ I ~~

Don Amado, Mexican Indian farmer, wisest and best educated man in the village of Santa Cruz Etla, spoke earnestly. I, the American visitor whom he knew as Doña Elena, sat with him on the hard earthen floor of the little adobe house, sleepily trying to listen to his long harangue and to keep up my end of the conversation. It was July of 1944.

"Santa Cruz Etla *is* a town, Doña Elena, a *municipio* of itself. It is not a ward, a *barrio* of San Pablo Etla."

"Does it matter so much, Don Amado? San Pablo is a nice enough village, larger than your *municipio* here in Santa Cruz," I argued for the sake of something to say.

He was offended. "All my life I have struggled to make Santa Cruz Etla a separate town. I went to Mexico City myself to arrange it, Doña Elena. I went on the train in 1923, when the train ran

2

seldom. For then the Indian towns were being given charters by Obregón, when the Revolution was hardly yet won."

"And you got a separate charter? What did the people of San Pablo think about that? Often enough you and I and many Santa Cruz people go to weddings and funerals in San Pablo Etla, and your own cousins are married to San Pablo people," I said. I don't know why I kept on extolling San Pablo. As I remember back to that visit in my second decade of friendship for Santa Cruz Etla, I can't excuse myself. Surely I should have known by then how much it meant to Don Amado to insist on the independence of his own community.

"True, the San Pablo neighbors did not love me for it," he answered to my objections. "But since that time we have been a town. What does it take in your country to make a municipality, a chartered village? We have our school, which through the years will surely bring so much good for *la gente*, the people here. We have our president, our public affairs committees. We have our water supply, of which the San Pablo people are so jealous. My sons and my sons' sons will keep Santa Cruz Etla a separate town. Who knows what great good may come out of Santa Cruz?"

So prophesied the sage of Santa Cruz Etla, Don Amado Méndez, while light from the pine-bough torch flickered on the faces of a handful of neighbors and cousins who had drifted in to listen. I had been sitting there with him since sunset, both of us guests for the evening in the large adobe house of his elderly cousin. I had plied him with a hundred questions about the thirty or so families who lived near him there in the Etla Hills, and always he had come back to the insistence on the town's independence. To weld the families into a unit, to raise their standards, to provide them a school, to inspire their children to serve the community in their turn; in these efforts he had spent his life—he of the small Vandyke beard, the faraway eyes and the manner of a college professor—while he himself remained the poorest man in town as far as material prosperity was concerned, and his land was untilled, and his own sons went uneducated. Sad to say, no son of his today lives in Santa Cruz Etla at all.

But Don Amado's interest in his hillside town helped buoy up my own interest, and it was one reason I kept coming back there through the years, from 1934 to 1944 to 1954, until I knew and loved all the houses and the people who lived in them, a love that has lasted more than two decades.

It takes love and enthusiasm to call Santa Cruz Etla a town. As the visitor comes by train or by car into the valley of Oaxaca, nearly four hundred miles south of Mexico City, he can see the small church of San Pablo Etla, that smug, self-righteously superior town, up near the timber on the sierra to the left. It is beyond the large valley market center called Etla, a name given also to the entire hill region behind that city. There is a jagged oxcart and truck trail leading up to the San Pablo church from a flag stop on the railroad. If the visitor has sharp eyes, he can make out the burros coming down the trail, dragging behind them the hand-cut railway ties which the hill people bring down to pile at the Hacienda Blanca station. In the fold of the hills three miles above the San Pablo church, and just below the dark line of the sierra forest, are the homes of Don Amado and his neighbors of Santa Cruz Etla.

There are thirty families in the Santa Cruz municipality, living along three ridges, or *lomas,* and in the ravines between. Up the center ridge runs the burro and oxcart road; a brook from the higher sierra has been canalized to run down the top of this ridge to provide the town's water supply. In a level cleared space on this central ridge are the school and the municipal building, built by volunteer labor under Don Amado's leadership, and by the mid-1950's a neat new chapel. Most of the thirty families live along the brook in adobe huts a hundred yards or so apart and set in little cleared spaces, the houseyards in which the cattle and other livestock are tethered.

The fields farmed by the families stretch down either side of the ridge. From every house in Santa Cruz Etla there is a breath-taking view of the valley of Oaxaca, twenty miles wide, with valley villages and the river bed below, the ancient ruins of Monte Albán across on the other side, and around the bend out of sight, the state capital, the city of Oaxaca de Juárez with its 30,000 people, a

4

bustling metropolis compared to the hill villages. Between Santa Cruz in the hills and the parallel lines of the Pan American Highway and the narrow-gauge railway that run the length of the valley floor lies that "sophisticated" rival, San Pablo Etla, with its three hundred or more people, its cobbled plaza, its centuries-old church and burial grounds, its acceptance by valley authorities, both lay and religious, as a true municipality of longstanding and unquestioned authenticity.

Up behind Santa Cruz Etla are the wooded hills, forest which belongs in community holding to all the people, to which the young men have gone for four generations to cut wood for cash sale in the city, wood for pottery kilns in valley villages, wood for the charcoal fires of the city household kitchens, wood for the railway ties which first helped to bring "modernism" into Oaxaca State. For generations the sierra provided the cash income of the people, though by 1957 many young men had left the increasingly treeless and eroding hillsides to seek wage work in the city. The older men plow the lower hillsides with oxen and homemade plows, planting corn and beans in the rainy season and harvesting them in the dry. Each family has about five acres of land (two hectares) and grows enough so that few have to buy food. The little gardens around the houses produce mangoes and avocados and squashes and tomatoes; chickens, turkeys, and pigs in the houseyards provide occasional meat for fiestas. Every yard has its trees, its roses and hibiscus bushes, and its bougainvillea vines and jasmines blooming the year around.

To Santa Cruz Etla in 1934 came my husband and I, sociologically-minded young enthusiasts, prepared to spend a summer photographing one of Mexico's new rural schools, those products of Mexico's Indian Revolution which were being founded in the early 1930's to "Mexicanize" and modernize remote, illiterate communities and to raise the standard of living. Dr. Rafael Ramírez, Director of Indigenous Education, had given us letters of introduction to a Mr. Ximello, the Director of Rural Education for the state of Oaxaca, asking him to locate us in a model community. I wrote in a 1934 diary:

Mr. Ximello already knew of our arrival and had made plans for us. He was most delightfully cordial, suggested that we go to a small town called Santa Cruz Etla and stay there during our study of rural schools. He thought the little town was one of surpassing beauty, and had made a special trip on horseback to plan for our coming. He called it our *pueblecito* and has arranged for us to stay in a vacant part of the school house.

The day after that first arrival in Oaxaca City we all went in Mr. Ximello's official car as far as Hacienda Blanca. Dramatically, the driver stopped the car below the San Pablo church and said: *En esta vía no puede andar El Cristo* (Christ himself couldn't drive on this road). The town council of San Pablo sent a runner up to the Santa Cruz Etla community to tell the people that the education director and his guests were stranded down below on the edge of the valley. That first time the Santa Cruz people sent burros to get us. We have since been in by oxcart, by mule, on foot, in latter years by station wagon, and finally in 1954 in our own car (with the aid of a team of oxen through the bad mudholes). Getting to Santa Cruz Etla is still a transportation problem, however.

How could I ever have been disappointed in Santa Cruz Etla? Yet, that first time with Mr. Ximello, I was. My diary notes, written as I prepared for the trip, constantly referred to the "village," the "little town." I expected a crisscross of streets, probably cobbled, a church, a plaza bigger than San Pablo's, perhaps a market. "Rural" schools that we had visited during studies made in 1933 near Mexico City were often in good-sized provincial towns. I did not know the mountain communities above Oaxaca City. For Santa Cruz Etla is to a village near Mexico City what a Kentucky mountain rural school district is to a county seat.

I was never disappointed in Santa Cruz Etla again after my first few days there. It is the people, even more than the view, that make me love to go back; my deep regard for them has taken me into Oaxaca Valley and up the hills when I had no other excuse at all to go—in 1938 again briefly, and for a two weeks' stay in

6

1944; for a long whole summer in 1945, then for a day's picnic in 1951, and for a ten-day visit in 1954, two decades after my first.

If I had "anthropological and sociological" interest in the people of Santa Cruz, if I hoped to write learned reports on them for credit in university graduate work, the people never knew or cared. I never classified them by type, nor measured their heads for anthropological data, nor considered them interesting specimens of anything. I had come to them an honored guest, I had stayed with them rather than with other villagers because Mr. Ximello thought they had such a fine school, and the school was their own pride and joy. Their town sage and wiseman considered me a fellow spirit, even though I spoke his native Spanish haltingly, and still do. I was a guest in their houses; I danced at their weddings and at their funerals; I took scores of photographs of them and their children through the years, seldom for my own purposes but to send back to them as gifts. Because these snapshots are their only family photographs, the photos are enshrined above their home altars inside the rough adobe huts, and often my husband and I appear in the photographs. When any current town president knew beforehand of our coming, he hastened to plan a fiesta for us, with turkey dinner and music and rockets. By accepting me as an equal, these people taught me a deep lesson in the equality of all mankind, and I have done little for them in return through the years.

Everyone visiting Mexico has seen the poor, ragged, country Indians in the markets of the larger towns. Their hair is uncut; their ill-fitting, white cotton clothes are ragged and dirty; the men have scraggly beards and torn straw hats with high crowns and wide brims. The women wrap themselves in dark blue shawls, the familiar *rebozo*, and sit on the ground in the market streets with their bare feet tucked under them. They offer a few tomatoes, or some embroidery, or a basket of beans, or two or three clay water jars, or a burro-load of firewood or charcoal for sale. They are always sitting in the market place when the city visitor gets up in the morning, and they have suddenly disappeared when market is over in the middle of the afternoon. The visitor is told

7

that they come on foot from many miles away, that they are *peones,* or *paisanos,* or *campesinos,* or *inditos,* or whatever word is used locally. They all look alike except for the different wares they sell. Even in an Indian center like Oaxaca, where many different costumes and types are seen, they appear almost identical in the market place. Such as these are the people of Santa Cruz Etla when they come to market in Oaxaca City.

But not so at home in the hills. There they are people of great dignity and importance. They are "householders." They call each other by their first names, with the title *Don* for men and *Doña* for women. To this day I know few last names in the village, and I checked Don Amado's own last name only when I very recently undertook correspondence with his son. To call a person Don Juan or Doña Isabella, in the days when the Spanish language was first brought to the valley of Oaxaca in the sixteenth century, was the same as calling an English person Sir John or Lady Isabel. It is still the sign of great respect and courtesy. They have always called me "Doña Elena," the Spanish word for Helen. When the grown men introduce themselves, they say, "Don Martín García, at your service, señora," and say it so fast, like a ritual, that you must ask them to repeat in order to catch their names. Greeting each other on the ravine trails, they shake hands all around with the deepest courtesy. Everyone assumes responsibility in the town government, entertains guests in his houseyard with dignity, and carries on his affairs with the poise of a well-to-do farmer in the United States. This for five days of the week. Then on Saturday he takes firewood or charcoal and farm products to market to get cash for his few store-bought necessities. There in the market of Oaxaca he is suddenly a poor, ragged Indian, indistinguishable from all the other ragged Indians of Mexico.

Don Amado, he who cut the least firewood and had the least cash, had determined that Santa Cruz people should not be "indistinguishable," that they should be citizens of an outstanding, separate community. He was not an old man, though when I first saw him in 1934 I was in my early twenties and anyone over forty seemed old to me. My first mention of him in my diary notes describes him as "that very ragged old man with the Van Dyke beard who makes those long, dignified speeches at fiestas." I had difficulty following the speeches in Spanish in those days, and I did not think to question him carefully and at length about the history and growth of the town until I was there on a leisurely visit just a decade later. At that time I was the guest of his respected older first cousin, his *prima hermana,* his "cousin-sister" as they say in Oaxaca, the matriarch Doña Estéfana, and he had come to chat with us in the evening as we all sat at twilight helping Doña Estéfana shell corn. They were pleased that my Spanish was better, that I could converse with them more freely than on my previous two visits; and Doña Estéfana was asking me about that *idioma,* that "dialect," the English language, the existence of which they had not known until they had heard the talk between my husband and me on our first visit. Many things about the United States are hard to explain to them, and one of them is that we do not speak Spanish at home, also that our language is not just another Indian dialect from the remote sierra, such as those spoken by Santa Cruz Etla's more primitive neighbors, the Mixes and the Zapotecs of the higher hills and the farther valleys. Then I wondered out loud why Santa Cruz, almost entirely of Indian blood, spoke no Indian dialect itself.

"Why, Don Amado," I asked, "does no one in the whole Etla region speak an *idioma?* Everyone, the oldest people know the *castellano,* the Spanish. Why is this? In the large town of Mitla, thirty miles away only, everyone speaks the *idioma,* the Zapotecan."

"We are of the Mixtecs, Doña Elena; our ancestors built the monuments at Monte Albán across the valley. We never knew Zapotecan. How could we speak it now?"

Thus spoke Don Amado, the history professor. Surely no other person in all the Etla Hills knows anything of Zapotecs, or Aztecs, or Mayas. The great ruin of Mitla, which brings so many tourists to Oaxaca, is unknown to these people. The huts in the far sierra where live *los tontos,* as the ignorant ones who speak *idiomas* are called in Santa Cruz, are spoken of as "the houses of the primitives." But Don Amado did not scorn these *tontos.*

"Of such Zapotecs came Benito Juárez," said Don Amado, speak-ing of his hero, the famous Indian president of Mexico who defeated Maximilian in the 1860's. "In Juárez' day, his town Ixtlán was no bigger than San Pablo Etla. The Zapotecs were proud people; they fought the Spaniards. Our people in this part of the valley were perhaps never so independent. They bowed to the conquerors."

Don Amado, ragged, unread hill farmer, knew almost as much of the history of Oaxaca as the archeologists who work in the ruins of Monte Albán and Mitla. Students of the ancient peoples of Mexico know that there were the two groups of civilized Indians here in the south, Mixtecs and Zapotecs, that they warred against each other, perhaps in the twelfth and thirteenth centuries, that they both built elaborate cities of stone. When the Spaniards came, most of the common people were living much as Santa Cruz Etla lives today. The customs and dances and ways of eating remained. The Zapotecs kept their language, since few Spaniards went into their region where the land was less fertile. The Mixtecs lost their fertile lands to the Spanish soldiers. The city of Oaxaca was built in their territory, and the soldiers took wives among the valley people. Then the valley villagers forgot the old language and spoke the language of their conquerors. They learned to use burros and oxen from Spain, to hitch their oxen to Spanish peasants' wheeled carts, to raise chickens, to put tiles on their roofs. These things, though not the Spanish blood, spread to the nearby hills. They remained the only changes, the only way Don Amado's village differed in his childhood from a village of his ancient ancestors.

"But we have never been slaves of the landowners; we were always free municipalities here in the hills," he told me as the dark descended that night at Doña Estéfana's, and we lit the pine-wood torch. I was startled at these words, for I had known that the history of many Indian villages was the sad story of lands worked by peons around a privately owned hacienda. There was a ruined hacienda, a typical Spanish colonial house, as the only landmark at the railway flag stop of Hacienda Blanca. The school authorities with whom I first came to Santa Cruz Etla had told

me that the lands around the large valley town of Etla had once
been part of this hacienda. I had taken it for granted that the hill
land had also belonged to *el patrón,* the hacienda owner, and that
the revolutionists of 1910 had freed the lands when they burned
the building. And now Don Amado was telling me that the lands
of Santa Cruz Etla had always been free. "The Spaniards took only
the level lands near the river; under Carlos IV charters were given
to the mountain villages," he went on.

"Is there such a charter here? Do you have it?" I asked, eager
for historical documents.

"It was lost at our first village, Santa Cruz Salinas, Doña Elena,
long before the days of my grandfather."

Santa Cruz Salinas? Don Esteban, the serious young man who
was town president in 1944, had told me that very day to ask Don
Amado about Santa Cruz Salinas. "We only know our grandfathers
lived there. Don Amado knows all those things for us," he had said.
So Don Amado told me all those things, coming back to Doña
Estéfana's two more evenings.

The Mixtecs called all the ridges and the upper valley "Etla."
The Spaniards found Mixtecan grass-hut villagers living near a
place where rock salt was found on a ridge near Etla town. A salt
mine is a *salina;* the Spaniards first saw the village on Holy Cross
Day; they called it "Santa Cruz Salinas de Etla." From this Santa
Cruz Salinas Don Amado's grandfather went to fight the French,
joining a young lieutenant named Porfirio Díaz (born in Oaxaca
City) against Maximilian's army in the 1860's. The French drove
his grandfather back to the gates of Oaxaca, but then many others
from Santa Cruz Salinas went to fight with him for Benito Juárez.
In the armies they got the cholera, the only "booty" from the long
war that they brought back to the hills. For two years people in
Santa Cruz Salinas had cholera occasionally; then suddenly cholera
was very bad. People in every family died; nothing could stop it.
There was only one solution, to move away what was left of the
town. The ancient Mixtecan rights applied to the uncleared ridges
farther from Etla. The leading citizens got a new charter from the
governor of Oaxaca, who granted it on San Pablo Day. The families

with most possessions went to the new San Pablo Etla, near an abandoned hillside shrine which they made their church. About sixty or more families live there today. The men of this new site had never held lands from the hacienda. Their fathers had often been "rounded up" during harvest seasons by riders who came into the hills. Then they were forced to leave their own harvests and to gather the harvests of the *patrón*. Because of this forced labor, they were "glad to help the valley people burn the hacienda in 1915." Don Amado implied that he was talking about the families who had settled in San Pablo Etla.

Don Amado's grandfather went farther up the ridges. Above San Pablo Etla he picked another spot. He worked out a plan for bringing water to the site. He planted mangoes and avocados and oranges. He built the house in which Doña Estéfana, the old cousin-sister, lived in 1944 and where we were her guests when Don Amado told me this history. The grandfather cleared about eighteen acres of land. Others followed him; they all called their new village a ward, a *barrio*, of San Pablo Etla. Since Don Amado's grandfather had had the idea of moving, he himself brought the name "Santa Cruz" to his *barrio*, changing it from "Salinas" to "Etla." Here they had always had a *pueblo sano*, a healthy town.

"My grandfather came to build on the *loma*, the ridge of Santa Cruz Etla, where the devils of the cholera were not in the virgin ground," Don Amado said in concluding one evening's "lecture." Before that particular night, I had been walking and talking and visiting all day; I was so tired I could hardly listen. Much of the time that he was talking about Santa Cruz Salinas, I was dozing in the torchlight. His voice went on and on in a soft, musical cadence. I ceased translating the Spanish words to myself; he might have been reading a church sermon aloud in Medieval Latin for all I understood. But I could piece together the story the next day, and I had occasion many times in my later relations with Santa Cruz Etla to remember about the *pueblo sano* and the words *tierra virgen*, the virgin ground.

Maybe Don Amado told me—and I didn't like to ask him if he didn't, though his sons have recently wondered if I would know—

12

what happened among the children of his grandfather, how it was that Doña Estéfana, daughter of his grandfather's older son, should then have eight hectares of land and a strong adobe house, while Don Amado had only one and a half hectares and lived in a hut of thatch and wattle. He had never spoken of his father—only of his grandfather. "My grandfather served as a secretary to the municipality of San Pablo." "My grandfather had learned to read and write from his captain while in the armies of Juárez." "My grandfather taught me my letters." (All this reading and writing in an otherwise completely illiterate community.) "He sent me for a year to the priest at Etla to study books and history." "He sent me on a trip to Mexico City with a soldier friend of his when I was not yet eighteen years old." "He wanted me to be a second Benito Juárez." How often those of us who had hopes for Santa Cruz Etla were to think of the hopes of Don Amado, and of his grandfather before him, in connection with "a second Benito Juárez."

Benito Juárez had been pure Indian. Don Amado looked something of an aristocrat, for he had lighter eyes and more beard than any full-blooded Mixtec. Doña Estéfana and her children and her children's children are completely Indian, but she it was who inherited the good house and the good land. Was Don Amado a favored grandchild, son of the younger son who did not inherit house and land, but who passed the brains and soul of the grandfather, perhaps through a valley wife with Spanish blood, into the spirit of Don Amado?

He was satisfied with what his grandfather had done for him. "The finest years were in the priest's school in Etla," he said. "Thanks to the blessed saints and my grandfather that I went there. I came back from Mexico City and many other wanderings determined to make this a better municipality for the people." Surely he succeeded. He got a charter for their town; he arranged to build their school; he kept their records; in intermittent years he served as their *presidente municipal.* He went to council meetings in San Pablo to give advice; he helped the *tontos,* the Indians in the remote sierra, get clear titles to their land. Of course, his own land went often to weeds, and he was always late planting corn. I remember hearing him curse at the slow oxen as he urged them through the neglected fields, and I thought to myself: "How much he hates the farm work!" But his public service brought him no corn crop, and his wife and children had to eat. He was too idealistic to live off other people as a fat politician; anyway, there is no place for such a person in the scheme of life in Santa Cruz.

Doña Rufina, his patient and hard-working wife, was an Indian woman, sweet and smiling of face, though frail of body. Twenty years his junior, she was perhaps a sudden love of his middle age, when he paused between community welfare projects. She had borne him a daughter whom we knew as a child in school in 1934, but who had died of typhoid by 1944, and then three fine sons, all still living. But Doña Rufina never understood what went on in his mind, for she could neither read nor write; and when I came back for my long visit in 1945, the year after the twilight history lectures, she could do little to help answer my questions.

When I arrived at the school steps of the village in 1945, heralded by school authorities, riding in a school director's station wagon, prepared to spend a summer asking Don Amado more questions as a part of a "history of a village" project of mine, the first words I heard from the people were of the death of Don Amado in March. The municipality was still trying to rearrange its affairs and to recover from the shock. One of his projects in 1944 was to secure title to land on which to build a graveyard, a *Panteón* for the dead of Santa Cruz, so that they could lie in Santa Cruz ground away from the church of San Pablo. Now he himself filled one of the first graves there. Doña Rufina urged me to go visit him in the graveyard, the second day of my visit, to pay my respects to him at his high, new grave.

"He would want you to come, Doña Elena. He spoke of writing you letters in other years, but there was always the matter of the strange country and the postoffice money. There were questions he wanted to ask you, why there was a war in your country and who was fighting. He would have wanted you at the funeral, such a large funeral at the church in San Pablo, and then a procession from San Pablo back up here to our own graveyard in Santa Cruz. Imagine how pleased he was at that, Doña Elena, after the years we have taken funeral processions from up here down to the graveyard in San Pablo. All San Pablo came to the funeral, and many men in black suits, wearing shoes, came from Oaxaca City. They knew of his death without our sending word. Some of them walked up from the bus road; they came to show respect for him." She was still in awe about it months after the occasion. "Go to see him in the *Panteón,* Doña Elena, you will not be here to talk with his spirit when it comes on All Saints' Day in November."

So I went. I sat under the giant wild-fig tree at the graveyard and looked down the valley for an hour; and I determined that some day, for his memory, I would write this little story, perhaps in one decade, or perhaps in the next. Then I came back to sit on a straw mat, a *petate,* in Doña Rufina's house, and ask about his last days. He had died in March, after three months of "sickness of the stomach." He had been unable to eat anything, he was in great pain and lost weight rapidly. Perhaps he had a cancer. For all his "book learning," all his concern for the *pueblo sano,* and all his interest in progress, Don Amado clung to the old ways in medicine. When Doña Patrocina, our dear old cure woman in Santa Cruz, had been unable to help him, it had not occurred to him to go to a modern doctor in Oaxaca. *¡Qué lástima!* "What a pity, for myself and my sons, that you did not take more pictures of him before, Doña Elena. I have only this one taken in the shadow." She took from her old bridal chest, the only furniture in the house, a bad print of the picture of Don Amado shown here. I had taken it in 1944 as a typical shot of a Santa Cruz farmer going to plow— a poor choice by a poor photographer. Don Amado was not a typical farmer and he never went willingly to plow. I have since had a careful photography shop in the United States make good enlargements of this weak negative, one each for Don Amado's sons, so that more portraits of him are now in existence.

With the poor little photo in the chest, Doña Rufina had rolls and rolls of papers and correspondence carried on by the "sage" of Santa Cruz Etla. "Tell me what these things all are, Doña

Elena," she said wistfully, for the letters were then just so many scratches to her. I myself started to teach her to read that same summer in the campaign against illiteracy; her oldest son carried her on. But even if she had learned to read better than any other woman in the Etla Hills, still she would never have understood all that went on in the mind of Don Amado, or all that was explained in his papers.

First there was the legal founding of the independent town. Don Amado had been in great sympathy with the Mexican Revolution of 1910 to 1920. Naturally he was an "armchair" revolutionist who did not go out burning haciendas with the San Pablo men, but he read the proclamations posted in Oaxaca City and heard the speeches on market days. He knew that the Indian villages from the hacienda lands were being urged to incorporate and to make their local governments and their land holdings legal. In 1923 he had written to the authorities in Mexico City asking how Santa Cruz Etla could become an independent town. Doña Rufina had the brief, legalistic answer suggesting a charter, a municipal head-quarters. He had gone to Mexico City about it, his first visit since his youth. This time he went on the train.

My husband and I had been often to Mexico in the 1930's on the second-class native trains, in years of low budgets and ambitious study projects; and we thought of those bare coaches as the hardest part of hard trips—the crowds, the fleas, the hard benches, the dirty toilets. To Don Amado who loved crowds, who came from a community where there are fleas in every grass-mat bed, where the town council itself sits on the hard ground for meetings, where in his day there was no toilet of any kind, outdoor or indoor, clean or dirty, but only the hedgerows and the cornfields—to Don Amado the second-class train was doubtless the whole outside world. But I can see him lost in the maze of officialdom in Mexico City, where in 1923, even more so than now, long lines of poor barefooted Indians waited and waited to see some official or to ask for help about a problem in some distant village.

Anyway, Don Amado got the papers, which I have never seen, and came back successfully with them and with the plan for the municipal building. I would like to have asked Don Amado about all this: what the other Dons of Santa Cruz thought and said, whether there was a fiesta. If only he had shown me these papers when we were talking the year before at Doña Estéfana's! But now I saw only the letters, three altogether, that Don Amado received from Mexico City about it. Anyway, after the letters were sent, Santa Cruz was a town!

There was more correspondence about the school. Don Amado had heard about the plans for rural schools after the Revolution, and in 1929 he had started the idea of building the Santa Cruz school. In order to get federal government funds for the school, he had sent the papers of incorporation of Santa Cruz Etla as independent of San Pablo to Mexico City. They had never been returned. I am the one who asked to see them in 1944 in order to show them to the rural education director who urged the town council members to get them back and to keep them in their own municipal building. Evidently, at a later council meeting after I left that year, Don Amado volunteered to go to Mexico City himself and get them during the dry season.

Such a journey costs twenty-five pesos round trip. Don Amado himself had told me, in speaking of his 1923 trip: "I would prefer to spend my twenty-five pesos in that manner, Doña Elena, than to save for a tile roof on my house. When I go again, I will take my Cassiano [his oldest son, then fifteen years old] to see the cathedral of Guadalupe, the great markets, the Aztec museum." Cassiano was to wait ten years, finally to go under much more tragic circumstances; and as of 1958 he had never yet moved back to Santa Cruz. But in the fall of 1944 Don Amado was short of money. He went alone and stinted himself on the trip. He was ailing when he left. He came back to find his dear and only daughter dead of typhoid. He took the charter for some sort of recording into Oaxaca City and left it with authorities there. Then he came home to the hills, lay down on his *petate* and slowly died. No one else has ever got the papers back; no one knows for sure, as far as I was able to find out in 1954, in just what official bureaucratic department of the state government Don Amado had left them. Perhaps if Don Amado

17

had not gone on that last, unnecessary trip to Mexico City? Perhaps if no one had suggested that the documents should be back? Perhaps if *I* had not come in 1944 and fussed to see the documents, there would not have been that first big grave in the *Panteón* in 1945.

But Don Amado would have exhausted himself, anyway, trying to raise the village by its sandal straps. Nothing less than death would ever have stopped him. Doña Rufina had letters about his attempt to found a *Cooperativa*. As early as 1934 we had called a small empty building near the San Pablo boundary *La Cooperativa;* I had often wondered why. A whole package of letters in Doña Rufina's collection helped me to piece together the story. I could see then why Don Amado never had time to write to me; he had handled so many letters all his life, going to the general delivery window to ask for answers every time he was in Oaxaca City.

The *Cooperativa* was his idea to start a gasoline mill. In the 1920's all the people of Santa Cruz Etla were equally poor. No one had capital to run a mill to grind the corn for the tortillas, the daily bread of every Mexican rural family. The women ground it by hand through many, many hours of hard handwork, bending over a stone grinder as had their remotest ancestors in Aztec and Mixtecan times. In most Mexican villages a corn-grinding mill has been the first machinery introduced. Mechanical corn grinding was listed as a "must" for rural improvements by the school authorities under whose sponsorship we first came to Santa Cruz. Don Amado knew of such machinery. Perhaps it cost a hundred or two hundred pesos; the letters about it did not say the cost. After many speeches and much persuasion, Don Amado got thirty householders in Santa Cruz and on the upper trails of San Pablo to join his *Cooperativa*. They paid seven pesos apiece. The machinery was purchased, the *Cooperativa* shed was built in the dry season when farm work was slack. *Cooperativa* members were to get their corn ground free, non-members would pay enough to buy the gasoline. It was a fine idea.

Unfortunately, Don Amada was a dreamer, a planner—a social engineer, but not a mechanical engineer. He did not know anything about the machinery. Doña Rufina said a *joven*, a youthful one, ran it, but she did not say what *joven*. Anyway, he was too *joven*, and when the machinery broke he could not fix it. When a mechanic had to walk in to make repairs, all the members of the *Cooperativa* had to pay again. The mill ran for two years, while Don Amado worked on the idea about the school building. Finally, the machinery stopped altogether, and a man from the valley bought the broken engine. In 1934 lazy women walked to a new mill in San Pablo Etla; industrious women ground their own corn. Then a Santa Cruz Etla farmer named Don Julio (he will be often a character in this account) who had much mechanical ingenuity and hard-headed practical sense, but who looked scornfully at the *Cooperativa*, sold some corn land and bought a mill. Thus private capital triumphed over socialism. How unfortunate for Santa Cruz Etla that Don Amado did not have Don Julio's love of machinery, that Don Julio did not have Don Amado's love of Santa Cruz Etla! How unfortunate for all of us that the Don Julios and the Don Amados of the world are not oftener combined in the same person!

After the failure of the mill, Don Amado's correspondence showed that he was trying to found a chapter of the *Confederación de Obreros y Campesinos*, a workers' and farmers' union active during the Calles regime. He was appointed the organizer for the region; a letter from the Mexico City headquarters in 1930 told him to go ahead and start a group. Another letter urged him to come to a big meeting in Mexico City, unfortunately held in June, the busiest planting season. Evidently he didn't go. There was a whole package of literature this organization had sent him, many fine things about fertilizing, irrigating, improving seed corn, about founding cooperatives to buy farm machinery or to put in electric power lines, and about electing certain people for local and national offices who would do all these things for the hill farmers.

But no other man in Santa Cruz Etla who owned land, only Don Amado himself, could read at that time; and he knew about all these things already. No one in Santa Cruz Etla, not even Don Amado, ever went to Oaxaca or to Etla to vote in any state or national election, to help choose any farmers' candidate. Doña Rufina, when I tried to explain these letters to her, shook her head sadly. "I remember this thing, this *Confederación*. He was disappointed in it. He said many times, 'We must all have more education before we can use these ideas!'"

Anyway he lived long enough to see elementary education come successfully to Santa Cruz Etla, to see the first teacher he helped to hire become in her turn a leader in Santa Cruz. But that is another part of the story.

Another set of "official correspondence" among Don Amado's papers which interested and amused me was an account of the *guerrita* with San Felipe de Agua in 1934. We had been at Santa Cruz Etla when that happened, and it had seemed to us then a "tempest in a teapot," an "interesting small-town economic problem." Now here were all the documents to prove how important it had been to Don Amado and to the town. Perhaps from the ancient Mixtecs, perhaps from early Spanish law, it had been established that charcoal burners could cut wood in the forests of the sierra, the public forests. Santa Cruz Etla is a woodcutting town, Teotitlán del Valle makes *sarapes*, Santa María Asumpa makes pottery. Without the forest Santa Cruz Etla would have had no cash crop. Always our men had used the wood "to the top of the divide." I have been up there on horseback; it is perhaps fifteen miles away from the village.

But San Felipe de Agua, a mountain town directly up out of Oaxaca City, also has charcoal burners; they also work up to the "top of the divide." Suddenly in the spring of 1934, they said, "The top of the divide means *this* divide," the one in Santa Cruz Etla territory. When the young men of Santa Cruz cut wood, the San Felipe cutters took it in the night. Such a thing is never heard of there between individuals. A feud developed between the towns. The people of the two towns seldom cross each other's paths, going into market by different routes. Few families of one are related to those of the other; no one even knows anyone else except among the woodcutters. But all the men of Santa Cruz Etla had been woodcutters in their youth. The town council called a meeting.

Hot-blooded young men asked for action. I remember, when my husband and I were sleeping in the school, being awakened at

20

dawn by the bell madly tolling. All grown men were to come and bring weapons to the school porch, said the council president. The men came wrapped in *sarapes* to their eyes; it is cold at that altitude in the early morning. One is more likely to see Mexicans wrapped up like that painted on pottery or carved on bookends, souvenirs of a Mexico that never existed, than to see such at work in the fields or at the market. But the Santa Cruz men looked that way that morning. And the "weapons" of Santa Cruz Etla! One man had a muzzle-loader made to shoot game, another a deer rifle, a third a shotgun. All the other men had machetes, the long knives they use to cut corn and alfalfa. We stood on the school porch and watched them file off on the three-hour hike to the sierra, the older men going up for the first time in fifteen or twenty years.

My husband had a small telescope. Through it we could see the trees on the high hills, each tree standing out individually; but we could not see beneath the trees because the undergrowth was too thick. Wisps of smoke continued to rise where wood was burning into charcoal. Doubtless we would not have seen or heard any shots fired, but everyone left at home wanted to look through the telescope; and my husband had a tiring day adjusting it for the wives and children the "warriors" had left behind. In the evening they all came down again. There had been an armed truce all day in the hills, they said. Now there was another council meeting, held on the school porch in the fading light, but I could not speak Spanish then well enough to follow the intricacies of meetings. We did know, though, that Don Amado went to Oaxaca City to see the governor, that two "armed men" went to the hills with the young woodcutters every day. This went on for three weeks. The dispute came to be called *la guerrita*, the little war.

At the end of the fourth week, Don Amado had received three letters from the forestry supervisor, evidently, for Doña Rufina had the correspondence dated July, 1934. One letter, couched in the elaborate language of Mexican official correspondence, announced that inspectors sent by the forestry supervisor would come and survey the ridge. I remember the day they came—two mounted

21

inspectors with high-stepping horses and a pack animal carrying surveying instruments. They stopped at the school, chatted with us and the teacher, and went ceremoniously off up the hill. When they came down the next day, they had driven the San Felipe men from the Santa Cruz sierra. From that time on, the top of the divide has meant the *top* of the divide. I came to realize, in long conversations in 1954 with the "no longer young" men who had been the hot-headed woodcutters in 1934, how important this negotiation of Don Amado was to Santa Cruz. Twenty years later the sierra on the Santa Cruz side had begun to be depleted, and hot-blooded young men were having to look elsewhere for a cash income. Winning the *guerrita* by arbitration kept Santa Cruz men busy at home for another two decades.

I did not translate all of Don Amado's other correspondence—the plans for the school, the legal title to two acres of fertile farm land to be held in the name of the school and worked by the school committee for a cash crop to buy supplies for the children, the plans for the graveyard and for the municipal building. All these records are now kept by Cassiano, Don Amado's oldest son and one of those young men who sought work elsewhere, in a sad, slum-area rooming house in Mexico City; but Cassiano reveres the memory of his father, he can read well, he has Santa Cruz Etla in his blood, and he still hopes to go back. Other writing in Don Amado's fine hand is kept in the records of the municipal building, since Don Amado served as municipal secretary when he was not president.

Zealous young Mexican reformers, after the stormy days of the Revolution had subsided, were organized into "cultural missions" which were sent into remote villages to found schools, spread public health ideas, teach illiterates, and raise the rural standard of living. So successful were these missions in the late 1920's and early 1930's that other backward nations took up their ideas, and rural communities throughout the world profited. No such cultural mission ever came to Santa Cruz, although some correspondence implied that Don Amado and the Santa Cruz council had asked for one. However, when the long-term goals of the cultural missions

22

program were standardized and published, after twenty years of success in many other backward parts of Mexico, it was evident that Don Amado himself had accomplished a good part of the "long-range goals." "Secure legal title to community lands. Guarantee legal incorporation of local governments. Construct adequate public buildings. Build modern schools." These things high on the "must list" Don Amado had done in Santa Cruz Etla.

"Assure practice in local self-government by guiding the choice of wise community leaders," say the instructions to the cultural missions. But the slogans of revolutionary Mexico since 1920 have included "no re-election." Only one term per president—in succession, that is. Thus, Don Amado, local president for two years, 1925 and 1926, alternated the post with other community leaders every two years. And of course, Don Amado had not given Santa Cruz such fine "town" status singlehanded; a group of other men, now the grandfathers of Santa Cruz, were behind him in most of what he did.

⌇ 2 ⌇

A TOWN ELECTION had been held in January, 1933, beginning one of Don Amado's "out" terms, and Don Martín García had been elected Santa Cruz Etla's *presidente municipal.* When we arrived with Mr. Ximello the next year for our first visit, it was Don Martín who welcomed us to the school. Even then a trifle plump and bald, but with fine white teeth flashing a bright smile in his dark, pockmarked face, Don Martín sang to the guitar by torchlight on the school steps that night. Not only his position as president, but his big heart and high integrity endeared him especially to my husband, and they spent many days together under the portico of Don Martín's hut that first summer, even though neither understood the other's language. Don Martín was willing to make special trips into Oaxaca to see my husband at a city boardinghouse two other summers, when I made the long hike into Santa Cruz alone.

23

When I came to spend the entire summer of 1945 and to work in the campaign against illiteracy, my husband, a teacher of science with only mild interest in teaching illiterates, chose to stay at Mexico's west-coast beach resorts. I had to lie to Don Martín about the bad health of Don Enrique, as they called my husband, and explain to him that Don Enrique needed to bathe in the ocean. No one in Santa Cruz Etla had then seen the ocean, perhaps not even pictures of it; they knew only that the dear Don Enrique was in bad health *¡qué lástima!* and I have been explaining about the medical properties of ocean bathing on every visit since. When I left Santa Cruz in 1945, Don Martín sent my husband a big *abrazo,* an embrace and a plea to come the next year and spend the entire summer in his house. "Don Enrique will like it then," he said, "as I will have it whitewashed inside."

It was not until 1951 that we, either of us, were to see the whitewash in Don Martín's house. We drove down the Pan American Highway into Guatemala and Honduras that summer, and coming back, we brought our own car up to San Pablo. Roads had been so bad in Central America that no oxcart trail could frighten us. Don Martín and the then president, Don Marcelino, sent an oxcart to bring us the rest of the way. We stayed all day at Don Martín's, admiring his whitewashed house and his grandchildren, complimenting him on the progress of the town in his two terms as president after 1934, and above all on the progress of his family, and his venture into "business." His daughter-in-law had been one of my favorites in the school in 1934, his house was always my house, *es su casa* as the good host says in Mexico; so when I went to Santa Cruz Etla in 1954, two decades after Don Martín's first presidency, I slept in his house, with his granddaughters, on a real bed set up on a tile floor in a whitewashed house, not on a straw mat, a *petate,* in a floorless adobe house. Santa Cruz *was* really a town then. It had a "grocery store" and a "bakery," both created by Don Martín.

Before he was ever president Don Martín had delivered loads of firewood to a bakery in Oaxaca City. There he had watched the bakers mix the wheat dough, for even in 1930 well-to-do city

24

people in Oaxaca ate wheat rolls for breakfast in preference to the common Mexican corn cake, or tortilla. These city bakers used Santa Cruz charcoal, heated large adobe ovens which had been constructed easily enough, and put the wheat dough into the oven as rolls. One time Don Martín had taken home rolls of wheat bread as part payment for wood, when it had been a bad corn year; it was at the end of the dry season, and corn tortillas were getting scarce at home. His family had eaten the rolls with wonder and enthusiasm; his wife, Doña Pastorcita, a keen, intelligent woman, compared the process of their preparation to the long labor of making tortillas. The flour was already ground; the mixing was done with large ladles; the rolls were quickly shaped; eighty of them were in the oven at once. They cost ten centavos apiece in any bakeshop.

Don Martín remembered the rolls when he retired from being municipal president the second time, in 1942. Since he had served the community well, both as official and as public-spirited citizen, he had incurred debts for funerals and fiestas. Miguelito, his only child, was thin and slight to work up at the woodcutting, but he had a strong right hand to shape rolls. Don Martín went again with a load of charcoal to visit the bakeshop in Oaxaca City. The proprietor gave him the recipe: so many kilograms of flour, so many packages of dry yeast, so much water, so much salt. Mix it in a large wooden trough, roll it out into long rolls as big as a man's leg, let it set overnight, knead it again the next day. Then with a sharp knife cut it into two-inch lengths; work each length into a saucer shape, two at a time, one in each hand. It was certainly simple.

In return for more loads of charcoal, Don Martín took home five sacks of flour on burro-back. He baked first for his family and his daughter-in-law's family in a crude mud oven his wife, Doña Pastorcita, had sometimes used for meat. Others heard about the bread; they came to look, to taste, to buy. He taught the corn-and-tortilla-loving people of Santa Cruz Etla to eat wheat rolls in spite of themselves. "Today they ate one hundred fifty rolls," he told us in 1951. "I use up fifty-four kilograms of flour every week."

25

In back of his house he built another room in which the ovens were situated and the bread was made. The oven was just a big hole surrounded by adobe bricks. The rolls were placed in it on a long, hand-hewn plank, charcoal was piled all around, and the fire was fanned through vents in the adobe. The rolls got done before the planks caught fire; the bread came out brown and gnarled-looking, because the flour used was of the cheapest Mexican grade, a sort of unscreened wholewheat; and the dry yeast and primitive baking methods made the center of each roll come out one big hole. But the fame of these rolls spread even to San Pablo Etla.

Monday, Wednesday, and Friday Don Martín's family baked, four ovenfuls a day. The rolls were sold right at his house, which was a half-mile up the ridge from the school. Each family sent up a child, or a young girl, to buy them in the evening, one, two, or three rolls at a time. Don Martín sometimes took things in trade, but usually wanted cash; he had to pay for the flour in cash when he bought it in Oaxaca every two weeks. "No Sunday has ever come that we were not out of bread on Saturday night," said Doña Pastorcita proudly. There was only one old lady in Santa Cruz Etla who would not eat Don Martín's bread: Doña Estéfana, the cousin of Don Amado. Not that she had any enmity against Don Martín, quite the contrary; she had stood up as godmother at the baptism of his only child and thus was his *comadre*, a relationship as close as blood. But she would not touch anything but handmade tortillas; she even thought corn ground in a mechanical mill tasted bad. However, the family with whom I lived all summer in 1945 knew I sometimes tired of tortillas, and often the new little bride went up to Don Martín's to buy rolls for supper. They were good on Monday, Wednesday, or Friday nights, but dry by Tuesday or Thursday and uneatable by Sunday night, unless dunked in cocoa. In 1954 I lived in Don Martín's enlarged house, right next to the ovens, and so had the rolls fresh and hot. It would have been nice to try them with butter sometimes, but such a luxury article as butter had never been seen in Santa Cruz!

With errand runners from every houseyard coming up the trail to Don Martín's, and with actual cash money in his pocket every time he went to Oaxaca City, how easy it was for Don Martín to buy in the city things which his neighbors might want. No Mexican city dweller would have said that Don Martín ran a grocery store any more than he ran a bakery; but how about a community where there had been no way to buy candles, or cigarettes, or tequila, or the rice and macaroni all housewives like to cook when they can afford something more than beans and tortillas, or even the strawberry pop so necessary for fiestas? And now, right in Don Martín's house on the main ditch and oxcart trail, one could get such things for cash—well, surely that was a store. When I was amazed in 1954 to find pop being sold right in the community like that, with no trip to Oaxaca seventeen miles away necessary, I thought that Don Amado would have been pleased and would have said, "Santa Cruz Etla *is* a town."

Pastorcita, the wife, and Miguelito, the son, did the work of the bakery in the busy planting and plowing season. Don Martín, as a man of honor and integrity in the community, had to till his own fields; he could hire a worker in the bakery, but never a man to do the farm work, if he was himself physically able to do it. In 1954 business in the bakery was so heavy right at planting time that he got a young man from the sierra, a green *tonto* who had never seen bread, to come and take Doña Pastorcita's place in the bakeshop. It is better that a man's wife plant the corn behind him as he plows than that a paid man do it; and Miguelito had to stay and run the "store."

I was there one day when this Indian from the sierra was learning the job. He was a great, rawboned, bigmouthed fellow, bold and jolly, standing high above the small-boned Santa Cruz Etla men, even though barefooted when they wore sandals. Since the *tonto* knew little Spanish, Miguelito, who was in those days a shy, wistful person himself, dominated by his father, had to show him over and over how to judge the size of the chunks of dough, how to knead it, how to put it in the oven.

Don Martín was a modern man. He branched out in business, he hired help, and he also improved his real estate. The last day of my 1954 visit, in order to honor the fact that I was there, he was building cement steps from the brook into his houseyard. This was a revolutionary idea in Santa Cruz Etla; no one else there would think of steps. The cement alone cost fourteen pesos, which though little over a dollar in today's exchange, is a good deal in terms of ten-centavo rolls or three-peso loads of charcoal. His house was whitewashed inside, and above the new brick tile on the floor there was a stripe of bright blue color all round, up two feet from the floor. Would he have whitewashed the outside after that? There are two houses whitewashed on the outside in San Pablo Etla; they have stripes of pink and red around the bottom. In 1954 Don Martín's house looked as nice inside as any house I was ever in in San Pablo Etla, but it would have to be whitewashed inside and out to beat those two San Pablo houses on all counts. "Whitewashing houses inside and out" is one of the things on that cultural missions list.

However, in spite of the warm feeling we had for Don Martín and our admiration for his progressive ways, his memory was for years connected in our minds with funerals. Not that funerals are unhappy times in Santa Cruz Etla—quite the contrary. But he officiated at so many, and put on such grand parties for them, that I would have liked to have Don Martín run my funeral for me.

The first one we attended, in 1934, was that of his own old Aunt María, who lived in his household. She was nearly eighty and suffered from no one knows what complaints. Doña Patrocina, our herbwoman, could not prescribe anything to help the old lady. But Aunt María had land in her own right. She asked Don Martín to sell this land for cash in San Pablo Etla, during the last days of her illness. She made three hundred pesos on the sale. Don Martín, progressive and practical, took some of the money to a doctor in Oaxaca for advice. There was then no active department of health for the rural areas, and advice from a private physician was an unusual thing in Santa Cruz Etla. Don Martín gave the doctor ten pesos—three-for-a-dollar pesos in those days—and received in return two doses of sedatives to be given in hypodermic injections. Don Martín knew nothing of giving hypos, and he sadly made a visit to the coffinmakers. There he ordered a hundred-peso coffin, silk ruffles, silver handles, and all. Coming back by the school, he asked advice of the enthusiastic young teacher, schooled in the art of "health for rural communities." She found a hypodermic needle among her "health supplies" in the enema can with the school chalk, washed the chalk dust out of it in the brook, and went with Don Martín to give the old lady the shots.

It was too late. Next day Don Martín and Miguelito went to Oaxaca City to get the coffin. They did not take the oxcart for fear the coffin would get scratched. Instead they walked into the city in the morning and caught the bus out to Hacienda Blanca in the afternoon. I knew that bus, which covered the valley run from Oaxaca City out to Etla town and back in those days; you could carry anything on it as long as the driver did not have to help you put your load on and off. Hence, even live pigs could be carried if other passengers helped you get them up on top. Undoubtedly the coffin traveled its first ten miles in style, with Miguelito sitting on top with it to watch that it came to no harm. It had a triumphant march up the hill trail, too; even the sophisticated people of San Pablo Etla had seldom seen so fancy a coffin. After many stops, Don Martín and Miguelito got it to the school porch and sat down to rest. We were living in the school building that year, and we joined the children in a long admiration of such a fine honor for Aunt María. Many children followed it the half-mile farther up to Don Martín's house, just to touch the silver handles.

A really religious funeral, with a priest officiating, should be held for such a dignified older person. Parties and dances are for the funerals of children. But a priest, even today, comes to the church at San Pablo Etla only one Sunday morning a month, and no other time; when he next came, he would say a prayer for the soul of Aunt María, a very faithful member of his flock. To speed her soul till then, Doña Pastorcita, her sister Doña Enriqueta, and all the other grown women of Don Martín's family spent the night praying and burning candles at the San Pablo church. The next day, Don Martín held open house, serving pulque and tequila to all who came and sat awhile with him on the dirt floor of his portico.

We went ourselves with the schoolteacher, one of my first formal visits to Don Martín's, to pay our respects to the withered old Indian lady in her beautiful coffin. The women brought ten large religious banners home with them to be carried in the procession. At sundown on the second night, the members of the town council, carrying the coffin, led the whole village down to the San Pablo Etla churchyard. The people all had on clean, starched clothes, washed and ironed for the occasion. Banners, flowers, and candles were in everyone's hands. We could hear the echo of rockets, made with black powder by Don Martín himself, as the coffin was lowered into the San Pablo burial ground.

The funeral party given in 1934 by Don Martín for his little godchild was the most elaborate funeral he arranged during his years as a leading citizen. For an aged aunt there is dignity; candles, banners, prayers, but no music, no dancing. For a child under ten there is merriment and festivity. This custom follows logically a very happy philosophy. The people of Santa Cruz Etla used to lose so many little children—to the "water sickness," the "dry season's sickness," the "coughing sickness," and so on. Doña Estéfana had two survive out of six born; Pastorcita saved only Miguelito out of I don't know how many; her sister Enriqueta had only one grow to maturity out of five. If they had observed the traditional Spanish Catholic ideas of mourning, every family would have been in black all the time. Instead, they reasoned it out. A little child just come to earth is still an angel. In the first ten years of its life it has no chance to sin. Therefore, when the saints call it home to heaven it automatically becomes an *angelito*, a little angel without stain. How fortunate that it died before life spoiled it! How fortunate is the family that the saints so choose to grant it such honor! So, hold a party, hire the best musicians, and entertain the town.

Don Martín's little godchild was three years old. He and his wife had stood up at his baptism in the San Pablo church; now they were obligated by custom to give his funeral. Pastorcita, joined by other women whom she had helped at such "parties" during the past year, spent the day after the child's death grinding chiles for *mole,* their favorite sauce, dressing turkeys, and preparing chocolate. Next morning they were up early to make tortillas for everyone. I had refused to go to the child's funeral, expecting great sorrow and unhappiness; hence, I did not get in on any of the turkey because it was all gone by noon.

But the schoolteacher went to the dance in the afternoon, and when I heard there was music and dancing, I followed along. The child was sitting up inside Don Martín's house, in front of the Virgin on the adobe altar. He was dressed all in white with a paper crown on his head and red and white roses entwined in his fingers. Flowers banked the coffin on both sides; Don Martín and the child's own father, Don Marcelino, stood on each side of the altar to give the latecomers a drink of pulque from a gourd. Don Martín received our congratulations on how beautiful the *angelito* looked. Then he put long chains of hibiscus flowers, like leis from Hawaii, over our heads. Such a crowd had come to the municipal president's *angelito* that none of the festivity could be held inside the house. The band alone, sitting down on the floor, would have filled every inch of space. The four Santa Cruz musicians and six San Pablo musicians sat on a hill slope behind Don Martín's house. There were two bass viols. Women and children sat around on the ground, on Don Martín's sleeping *petates* (he had no beds until after several years of prosperity in the bakery) while the men stood near the door or drank inside the house.

There had been a lull in the proceedings just as the teacher and I got there. Then Doña Pastorcita stood up in the center of the open space, holding under her dark blue *rebozo* a basket of hard, store-bought candies. The musicians struck up a lively tune, and she began to throw candy out of the basket into the crowd. She jigged up and down and tossed the candy in time to the tune. Soon her sister joined her with another basket of candy. While the children and young men scrambled for the candy, the crowd called for the godfather, yelling the word *¡Padriño! ¡Padriño!* Don Martín came out of the hut, put a garland around his neck, and joined in the jig. An Indian then unknown to me, Don Bartolo, who ten years later was municipal president at an auspicious moment for Santa Cruz Etla, had been drinking to himself enthusiastically inside the hut in honor of the *angelito,* whose father was a relative of his. Dragged out of the hut for the dance, he hopped around on one foot singing, to everyone's delight *¡Qué bonito, este angelito!* (How beautiful is this little angel!). The whole dance livened up as the other three tried to keep up with him. When the candy was all gone, each man picked out a woman—not necessarily a young, pretty one; old Doña Estéfana was the best dancer there— and the dance became general, with the barefooted or sandaled couples doing a sort of fox trot on the hard earth. Don Martín asked the teacher to dance and then me; I danced with all the members of the president's council, and even with the happy Don Bartolo.

Unfortunately for this particular *angelito,* a heavy rain came up just as the dancing ended. Rockets were set off as the sun went behind the hills underneath the low clouds across the valley. But the rockets sputtered out, the candles would not stay lighted, and the president and his council went almost unattended down the long, muddy trail to the San Pablo burial ground. This rain was fortunate for us. We were leaving Santa Cruz the next day, and a farewell meeting with speechmaking was to be held for our departure. Because there was no long burial procession, most of the flowers which had been brought to the *angelito* were saved and presented to us. Otherwise, with such an important *angelito* held just the day before, there would have been few flowers left to honor us in all Santa Cruz Etla.

One child I knew died while I was in Santa Cruz on the long visit in 1945. Her family lived on the side of the ravine between the central ridge and the San Lorenzo ridge to the south. Though they had a fine flower garden there in the river bottom, and though the father of that family was to be president in 1954, they had a poor house made of thatch and wattle and no large cleared houseyard. They could not give a party outside, with the San Pablo musicians. Besides, no one ever goes to quite so much trouble for an *angelita,* a girl angel. But Don Martín, then on the town council as a successful former president, was there with the rest of the municipal officials. There were bouquets of roses from the garden for me and for the wives of the councilmen. The little *angelita*, so gaunt and worn with three months of stomach disorder, was there on the altar, like a little bride in veil and lace. Candles all around among the altar flowers were the only light, except when the *petate* serving as a door was pushed aside for someone else to come in. The crowd inside had forced into a corner Santa Cruz's own four musicians, including three friends of mine from the classes we were then conducting for illiterates at the school in the evenings. The bass-viol player broke two strings during the first dance after I came, which put him in the ranks of the dancers for the rest of the afternoon. This situation was fine for me. He had some obligation to dance with me several times, because I was working so hard in the evenings to teach him to read and write. Don Martín himself, though his eldest grandchild was then six years old, was still able to do the sedate fox trot step better than many of the younger men.

At this *angelita* I saw the only sign of of sorrow I ever saw at one of Don Martín's well-managed funerals. This had been the only girl-child born in this family, and the mother had cared for it tenderly through a long illness; she cried silently in the corner throughout the dance, while the godmother officiated. When the altar was cleared and the body put in the little white coffin by Don Martín and the godfather, the mother broke down completely and had to be carried away. But save for the poor mother, I was the only one who felt any sorrow. Doña Pastorcita thought it was "an unusually nice *angelita*," evidently referring to the whole funeral. "How beautiful the dead child looked!" she said.

Thanks to Don Martín, this funeral procession went, not to the San Pablo churchyard, but to the new Santa Cruz Etla cemetery. Don Amado, then the president emeritus of his town, had arranged before his death the legal proceedings to secure community title to the hillside land on which the *Panteón* was to be built. It remained for Don Martín to build it, in his second term as president. Only Don Amado and Don Martín have ever been president more than once, and each of them served four different, intermittent times.

I heard of the acquisition of the land as a great piece of news when I came to Santa Cruz in 1944, but I had only pretended an interest, not understanding then the use of the Spanish word *Panteón*. Besides, it did not seem to me, in my zeal to "improve" Santa Cruz, that having a graveyard was a great improvement.

It was very important to the community leaders in their effort to create a town separate from San Pablo. The dead of Santa Cruz had always been sort of "poor relations" in the San Pablo Etla churchyard. Now they could be decently buried in a graveyard of their own. All processions go to it from the hills and ravines around; no coffin need be carried down through San Pablo Etla. And for a people who go so sincerely on All Saints Day, the first of November, to really converse with their dead relatives in the graveyard, it is surely a comfort not to be crowded into a secondary place during such visits by those pushy San Pablo people!

Hundreds of adobe brick had to be dried in the sun before the *Panteón* wall could be built. First the adobe had to be dug out of the dry ravine; then it had to be mixed with bean straw. The land alloted for it by the public land office of Oaxaca State had to be cleared of brush. Don Martín "drafted" the able-bodied men of the town to do all this in the dry season of the winter months, December, 1944, to March, 1945. The wall was laid three bricks wide and twelve bricks high. Don Martín sent members of the public works committee down into the valley to the clay deposits of Santa María Asumpa to get red clay to put all around the top of the wall, because the adobe mud found in the Santa Cruz ravines was not fine enough for that. Thirty different men worked on and off on the project; then fifty pesos—pesos at twenty cents each by then—were saved from the yearly fiesta fund in May to buy a large iron gate that swung from two iron posts. This gate opens under the shade of the gigantic wild mountain fig tree under which Don Amado was the first to be buried, one of those trees that grow in unexpected places in the hills around Oaxaca. Don Martín had brought the gate up in his own oxcart, he told me in 1954, reminiscing about his public projects. He had not thought his cart good enough in 1934 to bring up his aunt's hundred-peso coffin, but it had been honored by the load of cemetery gates—the same oxcart in which my husband and I had been "honored" to go to market, back and forth twice, in 1934, pleased to be riding behind the municipal president's star-faced ox.

"The *Panteón* is the finest thing we have built; each *pueblo* must have its own holy ground," said Doña Patrocina, the cure woman, my hostess on one long visit. But what's the use of a separate graveyard, if Santa Cruz people must still go down to the church in San Pablo for prayer to the saints or for any kind of religious service? After Don Amado's death, Don Martín persuaded a new, younger president to start the foundation for a chapel right next to the school. It was then too ambitious a project: the church authorities did not help them, the foundation was made too large, and the supply of cement ran out during the restrictions right after World War II. But the idea had been a splendid one, more advanced even than Don Amado's original idea for the school. All rural communities are supposed to have schools; few the size of Santa Cruz Etla have chapels. Most chapels date from the days of the early Spaniards; they are seldom built in modern times by community effort. When Don Martín himself was the "sage emeritus" of the town, and the town's most successful businessman, he counseled a younger president to complete such a chapel. Its building is part of the account of my 1954 visit.

Don Martín's own death came as sad news to me nearly two years after I last saw him in 1954. A group of us had started a project to send his oldest granddaughter on to college, and his sudden death brought the plans to a grinding halt. I was not in Santa Cruz for Don Martín's own funeral and have not been back to visit a Santa Cruz bereft of him. He had become such a leader in his last years that it is difficult to imagine how the community fares without him.

After Don Amado's death, Don Martín had become the most honored man in town; but he never became a "big shot" in spirit, in spite of his gaining the financial success which Don Amado was never able to achieve. He served on the school committee while he hoped for further education for his own grandchildren beyond

35

that afforded in Santa Cruz. His clothing was the same as that worn by all Santa Cruz men—the white pajama outfit, with a pink, orange, or purple shirt for Sunday, sandals on bare feet, straw sombrero on top, and a black, white, and red *sarape,* or Indian blanket from the valley weavers, wrapped around everything, in the rain or on cold mornings, until it wears out from years of use. Miguelito, his son, was seen to wear a store-bought jacket in 1954; and Artemio, his beloved, ten-year-old grandson, put his shirt inside blue jeans when he went to school and even owned a pair of shoes, though he took no pleasure in wearing them.

Don Martín's years of serving the community, building a grave-yard, contacting authorities in Oaxaca after Don Amado's death, gave him ideas of how to improve his own household. His lovely daughter-in-law taught him how to write and to figure accounts; he could receive mail from me in the United States—thanks for his hospitality to me in 1954, copies of all the photos I took then, which he distributed to the townspeople as they came into the store—and he took the initiative in establishing mail service for Santa Cruz, in care of the weekly service up to San Pablo. He told me in 1954 that his father had come as the poorest and last man from Santa Cruz Salinas, that the family had worked the poorest land, that many in his family had died of smallpox when he was ten, that he had herded goats from the time he was eight, without chance for education. He wanted his grandchildren and the other young people of Santa Cruz not to have to work so hard. But in his "prosperity" he gave way gracefully in his last years to presidents poorer, younger, and "dumber" than he; and he still played cards on the school steps or handball on the school playground with the younger men on Sunday afternoons when I last saw him in 1954.

What changes came to Don Martín's family with his death! Miguelito, perhaps after feeling repressed by his father's expansive personality all these years, was suddenly, in 1956, the head of the family. Within months he had moved himself and his wife into Oaxaca City and was attempting to set up a small wheat-bread bakery in the market. He was not going to be dominated by the women of his family either, and he left his mother in the hills with his two youngest girls and the *tonto* hired man to run the Santa Cruz bakery as a minor project. If anyone was to go on for higher education, it was to be his older son and not the daughter in whom I had been so interested. The fact that Miguelito is now head of Don Martín's family is one reason why I have not been back to Santa Cruz.

THE MEN in Santa Cruz Etla could play ball on Sunday afternoons because Don Julio had once been municipal president and at that time had donated land for a town ball-court, but the gift of this playing field was the only magnanimous thing I ever heard of him doing. In the United States or Europe or Asia, surely there is always one hard and selfish person for every two men of public spirit and good will, one Don Julio for every pair like Don Martín and Don Amado. Of course Don Julio, like the other heads of households in Santa Cruz, had to be more public spirited than any city-bred man, and he served on the public works committee and had been often on the school committee—but he seemed so dour, had so little good cheer, and had been so harsh with his first family.

When I had been in Santa Cruz only a week in 1934, I saw Don Julio for the first time. I sat on the school porch at dusk and watched as a stern, forbidding-looking man carried a half-unconscious, four-teen-year-old boy in to the teacher. The child had gone out to cut alfalfa with a sharp sickle, to give the oxen their evening meal; the sickle had slipped and severed an artery in his hand. The father found him nearly fainting in the field and carried him on his own strong shoulders, blood dripping all the way, to get first aid at the school. The teacher and I put on a tourniquet, and I bathed the hand with Lysol from my first-aid kit; but before we stopped the blood, the boy had lost consciousness. I did not fully understand, and certainly did not record then, Don Julio's sharp words – in anger at the carelessness of the unconscious boy, in disgust at the teacher's unsuccessful treatment. His whole attitude was entirely unlike the cheerful and courteous manner of all the other Santa Cruz men.

Though the boy was never taken to a doctor, he grew up, with a slightly scarred hand, to become himself Don Eduardo, operator of the gristmill in 1954. But by that time Don Julio was estranged from the boy and his mother, under criticism from the whole town for the quarrel between them, and had taken on an entire, new family.

In between, he had prospered as a miller. It was he who had watched the *Cooperativa* of Don Amado go to pieces in 1931. Five years later he sold two hectares of land in a good corn year and bought another, smaller gasoline mill. At first he put it right into the one room of his house, while his family lived around it and his wife kept house under the engine belt in the midst of the oil and gasoline. In 1938 we traveled again into southern Mexico on the way to visit Mayan ruins. We took the train into Oaxaca just to see the people of Santa Cruz once more, and we arranged in the city for a truck with skid chains and a powerful low gear (a whole thirty pesos' worth) just to take us into the hills for the one day we had to spare from a busy trip. Having sent up word by the charcoal burners as to our coming for a Sunday, we expected who- ever was president to give us some kind of welcome feast.

We surely did not expect the dour and unkind Don Julio to be president, but there he was. I don't know how he got elected. There is no record of achievement during his term, and he never served as chief again. But we will always remember the smelly mill and its gasoline engine filling all the space of the dark little hut, for we had a "fiesta" company dinner there — chunks of boiled pork, rice, and beans, tequila and strawberry pop — served to the guests at the expense of the municipal president. The food was handed in under the machine belt by his cowed and timid wife, while the boy with the scarred hand and his shy little sister stood in the doorway. All our other, gayer friends waited discreetly outside till the formal dinner should be over. When Eduardo, the boy, was old enough, he himself built a bigger hut for the family and they

Don Amado,
1944
only photo-
h of him in
ence

Doña Rufina, wife of Don Amado, 1945

The grave of Don Amado in the Panteón

Don Martín García,
1944

Miguelito and Chabella in 1944 with th
children Artemio, Margarita, and Adela

Don Féliz Jiménez

Don Martín in the
center of a municipal
committee, 1954, with
the author on his right

moved out of the house up on the main trail which remained in use as the mill, and nothing but the mill.

Women, or mostly the young girls, lined up there early in the morning. The little bride from the house of the cure woman who was my hostess in 1945 always went early to get the corn ground, and once I did this errand myself to help out the family. Sometimes ten or twenty girls waited on the trails, baskets of "hominy-cooked" corn on their heads. Inside the hut Don Julio himself, always on hand to see that no one cheated, would nod a curt greeting, take the corn from the girl's head, and weigh it on a simple hand scale. He charged five centavos for grinding two kilos, about five pounds. Many times the girls would not have the copper five-centavo pieces, and as often as not one would pay with an egg, or two tomatoes, or a few peaches. A girl in front of me that time offered twenty wild pecans. If there was no money to pay or no gift to offer, Don Julio would take out two handfuls of the corn to keep for himself. Then the girl had to put the corn in the hopper and scrape it off the walls of the bin as it sprayed out below, a wet corn-meal dough. Don Julio had responsibility only for the care of the machine, as important as the mighty wheels of a great factory, though it was only a simple gasoline donkey engine connected to the grinder and hopper by the long space-filling belt.

Don Julio devoted all his time to this engine; unlike Don Martín, he felt no great honor and pride in the land. He got more corn than he needed for his own family's tortillas just by collecting tithes from the baskets. He sold all his land except the hard-packed little flat place below the school on which the men played ball; he kept no livestock save the burros that carried the gasoline cans up from market with fuel for the engine. Indeed, he often got milk in exchange for corn grinding, or cuts of meat at butchering time, so why keep livestock at all? Thus was the miller, even before the baker, the first to leave the land, the first Santa Cruz Etla man to launch a private business, city fashion.

Perhaps I should not sound so critical of Don Julio. Just because I did not like his personality is no reason why he and his mill did not help mightily in Don Amado's program to make Santa Cruz into a town. The list of goals for rural improvement set up by the cultural missions includes "mechanical corn grinders"; teachers should establish one in every village. By 1945 the village would have been lost without its own mill. The most upsetting day during my visit that summer was the Sunday the mill broke down. Both Don Julio and his son were such good mechanics that something like that occurred seldom. Surely it couldn't have been that Don Julio, the hardheaded, the practical, actually ran out of gas! I never did find out, and no one would dare ask him, but Eduardo had been sent off immediately to Oaxaca, driving a burro which carried an empty gasoline can. The trip would take all day, everyone knew, and Sunday is a bad day to go to the city.

No one else in Santa Cruz Etla knew anything about machinery, and no one could hope to analyze the trouble. Philosophically, the women where I was staying said: "Don Julio's mill *se rompió,* broke itself." This I could understand, having been on Mexican mixed trains, decrepit, wooden, second-class passenger cars and freight cars combined, when passengers waited in the heat for hours, even all day, and were told merely, *Se rompió la máquina* (the engine broke itself), and no one asked questions, everyone just sat and waited.

But in 1945 Santa Cruz Etla had changed so much in the ten years since I was first there that everyone's family life was upset when the mill broke. That much did they come to depend on the machine age. My hostess said cheerfully, *"Pues,* well, tortillas are always *más dulcitas,* much the sweetest when the corn is hand ground." But we had few tortillas all that day, and no bread from Don Martín's either; other families up the ridge had bought out what bread was left. The little bride spent the whole morning grinding and grinding on the rough stones of the *metate;* she was so young she had seldom made tortillas from hand-ground corn, and she produced only enough tortillas for three apiece for supper. Without Don Julio, the *Cooperativa* having failed, Santa Cruz as a town would still be in the stone-grinding age.

Don Julio sold the last of his corn land while he was municipal president, being too busy with mill and politics to farm again; but he found no buyers for an infertile, hard-packed bit of soil he owned behind the school. Though he gave his son Eduardo little free time and no life of his own — and Eduardo was twenty-five in 1945 — he allowed the boy to indulge his love of handball, and he gave the unsold plot to the young men of the community. Eduardo bought the necessary hard rubber ball, and young men and middle-aged joined to build an adobe wall from which the handball could bounce back, to make the play possible. But that is a story of the young men.

Don Martín and Don Bartolo were still playing handball in 1954, but never Don Julio. He sat on Sunday playing cards with the other less active men on the school steps or in the trail in front of the school, a folded *sarape* in the center of the circle and a jack pot in the middle of the *sarape*. The cards they used were Spanish-type playing cards, with four suits (*palos*), but not the ones to which we are accustomed. There is a suit called *bastos*, which are really pictures of gnarled hickory clubs, and in place of hearts there are *copas*, or cups. A third suit, corresponding to spades, is called *espadas*, swords, and the fourth suit, our diamonds, which has pictures of gold pieces, is called *oros*. There is no queen, but three men instead, a *sota*, or knave, a prince, and a king. The *sota* is ten, so there are only twelve cards in each suit. The game the men played seemed like rummy and was played for five- or ten-centavo stakes.

Once I heard loud argument and wandered up from where I had been gossiping with the women to find Don Julio and Don Bartolo involved in fifty-centavo stakes. The fifty-centavo coin, a silver piece called a *tostón*, is very seldom seen in Mexico any more; ten years ago it was really quite a bit of money to the hill people. Today a game with peso stakes, and all paper pesos at that, would be the equivalent. A peso is now worth only eight cents in United States money; its value in Santa Cruz has lessened by half since 1934 in terms of charcoal, corn, or strawberry pop.

With his own family Don Julio tried to be a tyrant. His oldest girl Juanita, smart and graceful then, had been a pet of the teachers in 1934. When she was fifteen, her father forced her into marriage with a much older man in San Pablo. I was distressed to hear of this; but Juanita, when I visited her in San Pablo in 1954, seemed perfectly happy, boss of her life as she never was at home, and proud of her half-grown children. She had so quarreled and fussed at her father's marriage plans for her at first, however, that he refused in turn to let his youngest child, Susana, marry at all. In 1947 Susana repaid him for his firmness by running off to Oaxaca City where she worked as a chambermaid in a hotel.

I sensed some unhappiness among them in 1945 when Don Julio wanted me to take pictures of himself and the mill house, but refused to have his wife and daughters pose. Doña Fecunda, his quiet, retiring wife, conditioned by twenty-five years of marriage with Don Julio, hesitated to pose for a picture at all. It was only when I spoke of the group pictures I was taking of all the other families in Santa Cruz, and Eduardo summoned his own wife and baby from the inner room, that Don Julio grudgingly stood up with his family. I remember receiving little thanks from the older couple and feeling distinctly embarrassed at having insisted on the pictures.

Thus, I should not have been surprised, though I was, at finding Don Julio with a completely new family in 1954. Going blithely from houseyard to houseyard, I came to a hillside adobe house owned by a pleasant old couple who had only one child, a daughter Refugio, who had been in school in the fourth grade in 1934. The father had even then spoken to me about the lack of sons to help him farm the land, the death of his boys when they were both under ten, the hope that Refugio would marry someone to help him with the corn planting. Refugio had seemed poor marriage material, even at thirteen. Thin, whining-voiced, flat-chested, prone to goiter as are so many Santa Cruz women, narrow between the eyes, she appears often in the school-activity movies we took in 1934. No one spoke for her in marriage through the years. In 1947 both father and mother died, leaving her heiress to the land with no one to work it for her. Now Don Julio lived there as her husband and welcomed me into the house.

It was hard to piece together the story, for family affairs are not discussed by other families in Santa Cruz. Don Martín's lovely daughter-in-law, Chabella, finally told me that Eduardo and his father had quarreled violently about the money from the mill and the use of the house behind the mill. Juanita had dropped them both, her father because her sympathies were with Eduardo, her brother because it was so unseemly for a boy to defy his father. Susana had gone to live in the city. Doña Fecunda, the perhaps never so meek mother, had sided with Eduardo. Don Julio had gone off in a rage, leaving Eduardo to run the mill and in possession of the house. Eduardo is still there, the boss of both, the miller of the town and as such an important person, though it is doubtless hard to live down the scandal of the quarrel and his father's second marriage, and there is probably more of the account of Eduardo I could tell in its own right as a part of the tale of a new generation in Santa Cruz.

Don Julio was most cordial when I visited Refugio's home that day in 1954 and found him ensconced in it, father of a second family. He urged me to take many photos of the son and three little daughters Refugio had borne him rapidly in the eight years since the quarrel. I asked tactlessly about Doña Fecunda — it seems hard even now to write Doña Refugio when speaking of the second wife — and Don Julio launched into a tirade about the "injustice" she had done him, the bad treatment she had always given him. I did not like to ask anyone about "divorce" and "second marriage ceremony." These people are devout in their religion; but it is true that many of the older couples, who in their youth knew neither school nor priest nor civil law authority in the hills, simply lived together as common-law spouses, without the expense of a ceremony and a formal paper. If that had been true with them, then Don Julio could easily have cast Doña Fecunda off in this modern age and have had his first real wedding ceremony with Refugio.

Would Refugio, trained in school, inheriting land, have taken on a grouchy old grass widower, made him master of her land, and borne him children without a legal bond to hold him and to give her status? The whole thing puzzles me still; it is so unlike anything else that ever happened openly in Santa Cruz Etla. And what of Don Julio's economic status now? He is back again at the farming, running Refugio's skimpy acres, living much more poorly than when he ran the mill in such a lordly fashion. Was it perhaps Eduardo who always knew the mechanical side of the mill, Doña Fecunda who always managed with an unseen iron hand behind the mill's affairs, and Don Julio's dour appearance in public really a cover for a hard life at home? I would have thought in earlier visits that it was just the other way around.

I noticed in 1954 that when I offered to take pictures of the public works committee, the officials who repair the trail and keep up the water ditch, Don Julio showed up with four other pillars of society to take his proper place in the photo; and he was on hand as we drove our car down the mountain at the end of our 1954 visit, to see to it that we did not get stuck in the mud and to join the rest of the committee in standing by with ox teams to pull us out if we did. He came up one day to drink with us at Don Martín's and to ask me if I thought the school was well run then and the teacher conscientious, for his six-year-old son by Refugio was to go to school the next year. Of all the well-established, leading families in Santa Cruz Etla, that of Don Julio saw the greatest change in two decades. Successful in "business," he failed in "family life"; perhaps his second try will bring him more personal happiness. And Santa Cruz does not now seem to care. His mill helped make the town independent of San Pablo, and personal family problems can perhaps be soon forgotten among old neighbors.

⚘ 4 ⚘

THAT DON BARTOLO, who drank and danced so ecstatically at the child's funeral in 1934, should ever be elected municipal president was almost as surprising as that Don Julio should acquire a whole new family. True, Don Esteban, a young man hardly old enough to be called a don, had been president in 1944, between the terms of Don Martín and before the death of Don Amado, so that he had good guidance; but even so, Esteban's term was something of a failure and belongs in the story about the school. That after Esteban's youthful bungling the town should turn to such a light-hearted, irresponsible, immature person as Don Bartolo—though he was then more than forty—is still to me one of the puzzles of Santa Cruz Etla politics. Perhaps the shock of Don Amado's death left the town unable to make any wiser choice that year.

In 1945, when I decided to come and spend an entire summer to help teach in the campaign against illiteracy, I was already the guest in Oaxaca City of a former teacher of the Santa Cruz school whom everyone adored and was very anxious to see. She was to accompany me to the hills, make arrangements for my stay, and she had long since contacted the villagers through the young men who came into the city selling charcoal. Hence, I really expected "the works" in the way of welcoming festivals. Arriving in an official school-department station wagon with mountain-climbing attachments, we found most of the townspeople in clean white clothes waiting on the school steps. But no president, no strawberry pop, no speech-making, no rockets!

The people covered up their embarrassment over this lack by crowding around their pretty former teacher and her friend to tell them the news, first of Don Amado's death, and then of all the rest of the town. There were new children and grandchildren to be held up for inspection. There had been a marriage; did we remember hearing about the betrothal party? One lovely girl we knew had died in childbirth. *¡Qué lástima!* It was her first one, and it died, too, the little *angelito*. Don Fausto, of all people, a widower so long, had married a widow from over on the San Sebastián ridge. His mother, left alone and too old to care for herself, had brought her flock of turkeys and come to live with her daughter right below the schoolhouse. The new window frames for the school had come, ordered at a mixed-up meeting held by the young Esteban the year before; they had been brought up from Oaxaca City in an oxcart. Grown people were going to night school to learn to read and write—this was the campaign against illiteracy

I was concerned about. The plot of school land had been planted to corn this year, while the public-land bean crop was being held for a higher price.

One younger man had gone south of Oaxaca City to work on the Pan American Highway into the Isthmus of Tehuantepec, while another had gone on a contract to do farm work in the United States of the north. Spectacular news, these last two items, from a community where no one had ever gone away to work before. The women turned their attention to me, always curious at my hair graying so prematurely, puzzled as always how it could be some years so straight and other years so curly, pleased that I now spoke Spanish so much better than before, instead of that strange *idioma*, English, which I had preferred when my husband was with me. Then they must learn about the teacher's city job, must ask her personal questions why she didn't marry, and must argue among themselves as to whose home I was going to "honor" as a guest this time. All this without any president or speech of welcome.

Then it came out that Don Bartolo was president, and that he had *paludismo*, which is malaria, the "sickness of hots and colds." This news threw the conscientious former teacher into such a dither—"This is a *sano*, a healthy town, there has never been malaria here, something must be done to stop it, the new Department of Health will help, they will be notified tomorrow!"—that neither of us stopped to think that everyone was really covering up for Don Bartolo; he simply had a bad hang-over from drinking and dancing too hard at a wedding in San Pablo the day before. The women decided among themselves where I should stay; the former teacher "called the meeting to order" so that she might make a formal speech and entrust me to everyone's care; and the crowd proceeded to follow us from house to house up and down the ravine while we made calls on old friends, without benefit of presidents, rockets, or pop at all.

I had been in the village three days and was already helping organize an afternoon class for women illiterates when Don Bartolo came down the trail, pleased as punch to see me, the same

46

old gay "wolf," the show-off with the big sense of humor and an eye for anything feminine, young or old, just as though no one had ever reported that he had the malaria at all. The long speech which should have been made on Sunday on the school steps was given to me now, for the benefit of the young women students, but Don Bartolo could only make a pretense of being pompous.

How surprised he was the very next day when a station wagon from the *Departimiento de Salubridad,* one of the new mobile health units operating in Oaxaca Valley, came climbing up our hill, spewing out a doctor and three nurses who proceeded to interview him at length about the malaria and the unusual circumstances about his catching it here in the high hillside community. Unable to locate more malaria cases, they proceeded to vaccinate everyone in town against the smallpox, which effort is really another part of this book. Don Bartolo was pleased with the health campaign, for the nurses were young and pretty. My own heart was sore for him at the way the citified, Spanish-blooded doctor, standing nearly two feet taller than the little Indian in white pajamas and sandals, brushed him off as one of *los pobrecitos,* the poor little ones of the hills, and gave his long speech as welcoming president no attention whatsoever. Don Bartolo was really trying to act too important, anyway, hating to admit that this had all started with his fake story about malaria to cover his hang-over.

His caricature of pomposity, carried out with a wink, was with him as he came to open the classes for the illiterates. He came and unlocked the school every night, lit candles, and stood in the door greeting everyone coming in. He always made a speech to start every Monday night's classes. Here he opened himself wide up for criticism, from the older women especially, who considered him the poorest excuse yet for a president. "Fine president, that Bartolo, why doesn't he learn to read himself?" I heard Doña Estéfana snort to a visitor. "He should be an example to the others."

When I kidded him about it, he always said: "How do I have time in the same year to learn to read and write and to be municipal president?" I remembered from other visits that he was the one who always asked questions about my country. He sat around so much in the market place in Oaxaca City, talking and talking, that he really knew a great deal more about the world in general than many of the more serious hard workers. So I told him, just to spur him on: "You must learn to write if you ever want to come to my country."

"Oh, no, Don Enrique *el Alto*, from San Pablo went there as a field hand, a *bracero*, and he cannot read at all either." Then he showered me with questions about my country. Why did my country need the Mexican field hands? Were there no workers in my country? Were they gone off to a revolution as the men of Santa Cruz had gone in the days of his father in 1910? All the men had gone then; the women had plowed. Did the women in my country plow now? No? Then probably they went off to war, too. If American women could come alone to Oaxaca, they could certainly go to war. American women were brave and bold, *valientes y bravas*. Here he laughed in great glee, kidding me about my "bravery" in riding a borrowed horse up the sierra to visit the woodcutters. And so we got way, way off the subject of how a municipal president should learn to read and write.

We took up the subject again when I went with Doña Estéfana to make a formal call on Doña Sista, his wife. I have never heard the name "Sista" anywhere else in Mexico, and since Sista herself does not know how to write it down, I am just guessing at the spelling. Doña Sista was a very pretty-faced woman with a great sense of humor, developed possibly from seventeen years of married life with Don Bartolo. But when I asked her why Don Bartolo came to the school every night but would not write, she pretended to act out that she and Bartolo were in school. He came into the houseyard from the care of his goats to join in the fun. He would try to write in the sand, hold a stick like a candle to read his letters, call Doña Sista over as teacher to help him, mop his brow with the effort, pretend to sink into a coma because of the difficulty. Doña Estéfana and I laughed till tears ran down our faces; they are great ones to joke and laugh, the people of Santa Cruz Etla.

Don Bartolo laughed often with his *chamaquita*, his little tyke, as he called his six-year-old daughter, Luisa. They were often together that summer around the municipal building. She had started to read in the primer class, and "one literate person in a family is enough." His only son, Timoteo, aged sixteen, had never been to the school and spent his days in the hills herding goats.

Don Bartolo had so much time to talk and laugh and to run politics because he made his living from his goats. He did not have to plow in the rainy season, nor harvest in the dry. He and Doña Sista cared for the thirty or more young kids, while the son pastured the adult goats in the free mountain lands. Don Bartolo drove the goats ready for slaughter into the Oaxaca market for sale for meat, and often he sold a young one in the mountain villages. Whenever there was a butchering at his own houseyard, he sent heart or kidneys down to me wherever I was staying. Perhaps he got elected president because of his friendly custom of caring for other families' goats and setting his son to watch the smaller herds of neighbors, mixed in with his own. Goats from other houseyards stopped off at their own houses as Timoteo drove the large flock home from the hills at night.

I found little change in this whole, happy set-up in 1954. Timoteo, unmarried at twenty-five, was still the shy goatherd who saw few people and talked to fewer, evidently loving the hills more than he was attracted by any hopes for married life or lure of city jobs. Sista looked old and had lost her front teeth in the decade between visits. But she and Don Bartolo still cared for their own and other peoples' young goats, the price of goat meat stayed high, and Don Bartolo looked hardly a day older. The only new thing in his family or change in his way of life that I could notice was a new handguard made of bright red leather so he could "bat" for the winning team at Sunday afternoon *pelota* games. He seemed as lithe as ever, and a third generation of young players accepted him as the leader at the game, though he was already surely in his fifties.

After his presidency, Don Bartolo continued to serve on the public works committee and in 1954 cheerfully helped to repair the road for us so our car could get through. Three different afternoons when I was at Don Martín's house he stopped by to chat, sitting each time

49

on the ground, though Don Martín's house had three rough chairs and a bench for guests, and for courtesy's sake I had to sit on the ground with him, since he was a former president and should not be sitting at my feet. But he had given up the idea of coming to the United States, or of going away to work at all, and was surely glad he had not bothered to learn to read and write. The "educated" member of his family, that "little tyke" Luisa, having three years of schooling in Santa Cruz, had gone off the year before, at fifteen, to work under Don Julio's Susana, and was then kitchenmaid in a home for Jesuit priests. "How will she ever find a husband there, Doña Elena?" he moaned. "Far better that I had never sent her to school but had sent her off like a boy to herd the goats."

Don Bartolo had served the community before he was president, or he could not have remained a respected householder. Every young man begins his public service in Santa Cruz Etla by being a member of *Los Policías*. Of course there is no one to police in Santa Cruz Etla, no infraction of order. *Los Policías* functions more like a young men's club; membership in it initiates the boys at twenty into the responsibilities of the town government. The summer my husband and I lived in the school building, two members of the *Policías* slept outside our room on the porch every night just to give us a feeling of security.

Above the *Policías* are the town committees for school affairs and for public works. Chairmen of these committees, as well as two of the former presidents, serve as *ayudantes* or helpers on the president's council, the *cabildo*. When the election is called every alternate January first, all the grown men, down to the youngest *policía*, go to the town meeting. It is held in the afternoon on the ground outside the municipal building, and undoubtedly the women and children are on the outskirts looking on. No one who talked of these proceeding to me would ever admit that nominations were planned beforehand. Someone would rise and suggest Esteban or Don Martín, or Don Bartolo, or another man. Then all the men would vote by holding up their hands. I don't know whether the candidates "leave the room" or not. "As soon as the president was chosen, they knew whom they needed on the *cabildo*," the men told me concerning Don Bartolo's election. A good council would make up for an irresponsible president like Bartolo or for a too young president like Esteban. By the 1950's there were other elder statesmen besides Don Martín to serve on the council, Don Marciano who had been president in 1947 and 1948 and Don Marcelino, a conscientious farmer who sent his oxcart to San Pablo to get us when we came for a day's visit in 1951 and got stuck with our car in a mudhole near the plaza of that unappreciative town. Both Don Marciano and Don Marcelino had been chairmen of public works or of school affairs during other years when I was there.

They used the Spanish word *alcalde* to describe these committee chairmen. The school committee arranged for work on *la parcela,* the plot of public land belonging to the school, and usually was able to produce a fair-sized crop on it with which to buy school supplies or materials to repair the school building. It depended upon the makeup of the committee how much money was produced on *la parcela;* sometimes the most illiterate committee did the best work for the school fund. The *alcalde* of public works and his four *ayudantes* had to maintain the oxcart trail, to repair the municipal building when the adobe crumbled away, to keep the cemetery free of weeds, and most important, to maintain the ditch system for the drinking-water supply. Whenever any bigger job was called for than the committee members could do, the committee was empowered to "draft" workers. Everyone owed the municipality a week's labor a year, or three days' work with oxen and cart. The man who owned the largest cart could work off his taxes by making three trips to Oaxaca for cement or tile or a new bell. Thus they had built the walls for the *Panteón* and, with a great deal of volunteer labor other than that required, had constructed the two public buildings, the school and the municipal center.

The municipal building was at first one large adobe room facing the school, still incomplete in 1934 when we were first there. A year later the municipal porch was finished in stone; and under Don Esteban in 1943 and 1944, the building was separated into two rooms and the big meeting room was paved with tile and whitewashed. One of the school boys, Perfecto, the son of Don Marcelino, had painted a blue and red border all around inside at eye level. This room is not open often. The current president keeps the key and so often calls a meeting on the spur of the moment, when he has forgotten the key, that most meetings are held outside in the portico or across on the school steps. But Don Bartolo, when he was president, opened the room specially to show me Perfecto's art work. The boy had contributed his labor for the sheer joy of the artistry, even though his father had put in his share of labor on the tiling. Purely incidentally, no doubt, the father was subsequently elected president.

In the municipal meeting room there were a table and two roughly made chairs for the president and his current secretary. Every illiterate president after Don Amado's death had to have a young boy who could read and write to help him keep records of taxes paid and expenses met and labor contributed and votes taken and arrangements made with the city and state authorities. Any others who came to committee meetings sat on the floor. There were steel pens, a bottle of ink, and several copy books full of the records, including those first started by Don Amado.

The other room in the municipal building is the jail, *la cárcel*. The door to the jail room is heavy with hand-carved wooden bars, but the room itself is really a storehouse. In 1945 it was full of chunks of lime to make whitewash for the school room next dry season, and of dry beans from the public land. In 1954, 1953 having been a good corn year, it was full to the rafters with ears of corn being held for a good price before the new harvest came in October, corn which was largely contributed by individual families toward the project of a new chapel. Though the president's room was always locked with a mammoth key, and the key carefully guarded, there had never been a key made for the elaborate lock on the door of the jail. A mere wooden slip bolt was used on the outside. A friend of any unfortunate who was ever inside could easily free him in the night.

Don Martín told me sadly in 1954 that the jail had been put in use during three fiesta seasons "since your last long visit with us, Doña Elena." So now every year, before the town's fiesta time in

May, the beans or tile or building stones stored inside are piled out on the porch. The people of Santa Cruz Etla are never *malo* (bad) but only *borracho* (drunk) during their annual celebration.

Certainly the jail was never built for thieves. Every house in Santa Cruz Etla is open all the time; every family is approximately as well off as every other family. Livestock are tied in every yard; goats, burros, and turkeys run free. Firewood is stacked on the dirt-level porches; corncribs are behind the houses. Even when livestock are lost in the hill pastures, boys from other villages bring them back. "It is not a bad heart, but only a bottle of tequila which ever landed a one of my people in the *cárcel*," said Don Bartolo that day he showed me Perfecto's drawings on the wall.

My first memory of Don Bartolo himself was his dance on one foot, swathed in a huge *sarape*, at the funeral fiesta of Don Martín's godchild in 1934. When I showed the movie I took of that picturesque occasion in front of crowds of Los Angeles city schoolteachers, they would say: "What interesting primitive Indian dances!" They did not know that it was even then a bottle of tequila inside a future municipal president which had produced the dance. I had to laugh eleven years later at Don Bartolo's smug criticism of tequila-filled fiesta dancers.

The contribution of labor or oxcart service does not cover all the taxes which the householders of Santa Cruz Etla have to pay. They must pay in cash a tax to the government of the state of Oaxaca. In 1945 this was three pesos and a half, then seventy cents, for every family who owned two acres of land. The heads of the families go to Oaxaca to pay this tax right after the first of the year. I forgot to ask Don Martín in 1954 how much taxes had gone up with the decrease in value of the peso and the increase in value of his own property.

"What happens if you don't pay the tax?" I once asked Doña Estéfana, who took care of all her family's land so well.

"They have us all on long lists; they know our family names. If we don't pay, they will take away the land after five years," she said. Frankly, I never heard of anyone in Santa Cruz Etla, nor in San Pablo either, who lost his land this way; and there were many hard years in which seventy cents would have seemed like a great deal of cash. In 1945 it was the equivalent of two burro-loads of firewood.

Taxes, if you want to use that unpleasant term for money intended for such a pleasant purpose, are collected to pay for the fiestas. The saint's day of Santa Cruz Etla comes the first of May. Since the town is not named for any special saint, but celebrates the Holy Cross, the celebration just naturally runs on into a famous national holiday. After May 5, the *Cinco de Mayo* when all Mexico celebrates a military victory in 1862 over invading French troops, the people of Santa Cruz Etla finally go back to work. During the five days a hired band from some valley town comes up to play day and night. Chocolate, pulque, turkeys with hot *mole* (a chile sauce), pork, numberless tortillas, beans, squashes, and bottles of strawberry pop must be paid for. All the year's crop from working the public-school land, *la parcela,* would not pay for the strawberry pop alone. If a twenty-piece band comes from a town fifteen miles away, each member of it expects ten pesos and his food and drink for five days. There are two hundred pesos gone already. "Everyone but the poorest, youngest, newly married son pays," said Doña Estéfana.

"And suppose they don't pay that tax?" I asked again.

"Why, they would go to the fiesta, of course, Doña Elena, but everyone always pays."

There is also the custom called the *mayordomía.* This is a sort of personal obligation to entertain in a big way. Often very religious families will promise a saint a festival on the saint's day, if the saint will grant some requested favor. In Santa Cruz Etla such a favor is asked of "all the saints" on the understanding that, if the favor is granted, the family will pay half the expenses of the May fiesta. They may ask the saints for blessings many other times, but once in every man's lifetime he must be *mayordomo* for the fiesta. With thirty families in town, the cost of the fiesta gets spread around over about a third of a century. Then the town tax fund need only pay for the musicians. All food and fireworks are provided by the "honored" family. When there is no *mayordomo,*

Don Marciano
with his wife, his beloved granddaughter,
and two of his younger children, 1945

Don Bartolo

uardo, son of
n Julio, and his
t baby

Don Julio and his two families
1945 — with his daughter-in-law, grandchild, first wife
Doña Fecunda, and his younger daughter Susana
1954 — with his second wife Doña Refugio
and his new family

The school building in 1944.
The man in the store clothes
is Don Solomón, teacher.

The new chapel
as it appeared in
July, 1954

Public works committee
repairing the road in 1944.
Don Féliz insists he is
the one in the background
with the hoe.

the fiesta tax used to be four pesos, raised to ten by 1954; when a family takes the "honor," it was one and a half pesos, raised to five. Don Bartolo himself was "stuck" with the "honor" in 1946, the second year of his presidency.

But he and Doña Sista did not have to provide all the young goats and turkeys and tortillas. Through the years, when any other family head was *mayordomo,* Don Bartolo would send a young kid or sometimes two, as his *gasto.* (Some words are so hard to translate; that one must mean a kind of gift contribution.) Thus, every family who had ever received Don Bartolo's young goats sent him pigs, or turkeys, or chickens, or ground corn, or purchased things like sugar and cocoa. He only had to borrow an oxcart (no use to own such expensive transportation in the goat business) and go down to Oaxaca for pop and beer and rockets. Doña Sista supervised all the cooking and made tortillas by the hundred, but Don Bartolo danced all day and made speeches all night. I know, though I wasn't there!

I have never been in Santa Cruz Etla in September for the great political holiday, the sixteenth, Mexico's Independence Day; but the teachers and my friends among the women have described the local celebration for me many times. All over Mexico on the night of September 15, people ring bells to call whole townships together. Officials make speeches to act out Father Hidalgo's midnight war cry in the town of Dolores in 1810. In Santa Cruz Etla, the *alcalde* of public works rings the school bell. (How do they know it is twelve o'clock? There is no watch or clock of any kind in Santa Cruz Etla.) Everyone rushes to the municipal building as if the news were a great surprise to him. The municipal president, Don Bartolo or Don Martín or Don Marcelino, takes the flag of Mexico from the school, climbs on top of the municipal building where the school bell hangs, and makes a speech in the flare of pine torches. He ends up by crying *¡Viva Libertad, viva Independencia, viva México, viva Santa Cruz Etla!* Surely, there is a great deal of true independence and liberty in Santa Cruz. Then the public works *alcalde,* and the school affairs *alcalde,* and all the president's wise old *ayudantes* on the council make speeches. Towards morning all

55

the torches have burned out, and everyone goes off home in the dark.

When the people are up and around the next day, festivities begin all over again. Already the highest class in school, those few in the fourth grade, have chosen from among the three or four girls the prettiest and most popular to be *La Patria*, the motherland. This custom was started when the school was founded, and the first teacher had made a long pink *China Oaxaqueña* costume with green kerchief that the "spirit of the motherland" still wears. The dress and a paper crown are kept in a chest in the school room, and certainly they look a little shabby now after twenty-five years. But it was so important from the beginning to have a *La Patria* separate from the one chosen in San Pablo Etla and to hold a purely local parade in her honor. *La Patria* rides standing up in an oxcart, Don Féliz Léon's when the municipal president lives below the school, Don Martín's, or recently Don Marcelino's, when he lives above. Roses and hibiscus are wound round the cart; the flag from the school and the portraits of Hidalgo and Benito Juárez are tacked on the cart. They probably look a little tired through the years, too. Bougainvillea is wreathed around the oxen's horns. Behind the cart all the school children march on foot, dressed in their best clean clothes. In front of the cart walk the president and the municipal council.

The procession starts off with the ringing of the school bell. It goes up hill as far as the oxcart can travel on the path, then it turns off and goes over to the San Sebastián *loma*, or northern ridge. Finally, it turns back up to the main trail, past the schoolhouse, and on down to San Pablo Etla. There is, of course, a parade going on there too. Our council sets off many rockets on the edge of San Pablo, and our children keep singing, as loudly as possible, a song aimed at imperial Spain:

> *¡Por tres siglos, O patria querida,*
> *Quisimos libertad, libertad, libertad!*

> (For three centuries, oh beloved nation,
> We desired liberty, liberty, liberty!)

56

Undoubtedly the little children, pattering far in the rear of the procession, are always two or three *libertads* behind on the chorus. I asked one *La Patria,* Chabella, later the daughter-in-law of Don Martín and a good friend of mine who is today a settled matron, what they did in San Pablo Etla. She now has six half-grown children, but she is still very pretty and seems more than ever the "spirit of the motherland." "Our whole council made much better speeches than any San Pablo Etla *político,*" she laughingly remembered. "It was worth staying through the fourth grade just for the sixteenth of September."

Mothers, who do not follow the procession to San Pablo, have a dinner on the school porch ready to honor the city council when it gets back. The portraits of Juárez and Hidalgo are taken off the cart and are banked in flowers on the porch, looking as fine as any *angelito.* The council, the public works committee, and the school affairs committee, which always include half the grown men in town—thirteen out of the thirty households—sit down to dinner at a long banquet table made of the school desks. Until there were chairs at Don Martín's, this would be the one occasion of the year when fathers of the community sat for dinner in chairs at a table; everyone in Santa Cruz Etla has always had to eat sitting on the hard ground in the porticos of the adobe huts or crouched inside in the dark around the charcoal fire. More speeches are made (how they do love long speeches!), more songs are sung. Unfortunately, this festival comes at a very busy season when the early summer beans are ready to harvest, and the festival can last only one day. Everyone has to be back in the fields in the morning. For Don Bartolo September 16 was a big day; he had had ridicule and criticism all year. That day he could hear speeches in his honor, and was able to make at least three long speeches himself—the one in the night, that at San Pablo Etla, and then at the dinner.

This "government" of Santa Cruz Etla — how has it improved in the last two decades? How would it rate on that long list of things the Mexico City authorities wanted the educational missionaries to bring to the villages? I have the printed list before me as I write, and I check it against Don Bartolo's regime, and all those before or since. There is no clinic, though Don Bartolo's "malaria" brought on the vaccination campaign. The school and town authorities have brought no puppet theatre, no traveling library. "Malaria control" is hardly necessary, taxes are "equally laid," there is already an enormous "sense of public responsibility" (in what small Mexican town did that have to be *taught*?), and Santa Cruz has learned how to "vote intelligently for local officials." "Maintenance of a pure water supply" is part of the account of another president, and "provision of well-kept roads," the big problem for us when we arrived in 1954, is in the cards for the near future. Santa Cruz Etla people have been their own cultural missionaries when it comes to problems of local government.

In 1934 I did not know Don Marciano, the 1945 chairman of public works, who was president in 1947 and 1948. He lived on the narrow little trail that went to the San Sebastián, or north ridge. I remembered his face because he brought the only real rifle to the meeting about the *guerrita* with San Felipe de Agua; but I had never visited his house, and he had seldom passed the school because he did not go down to the valley by way of the central ridge. In 1945 he had come to the welcoming meeting from which Don Bartolo had absented himself, and he made an immediate impression on me then by being mounted on a peppy little bay horse with white ankles.

Now, a horse in Oaxaca City is nothing for comment. Mounted horsemen in leather jackets, seated on their silver-studded saddles, are not so common in the south of Mexico as they are in Guadalajara or Querétaro farther north. But they are often seen in Oaxaca on market and fiesta days, and there is a cavalry barracks in the older part of the town with a hundred horses going in and out of the area every day. A horse in the Etla Hills region is rarer. The finest way to see the whole hill country is on horseback; if I were going to spend several months in Santa Cruz Etla, a horse would be a fine companion. The only horses I had ever seen there, however, were those of installment collectors and forestry inspectors and others from the valley who hit the rough trails on business. Now here was Don Marciano on a horse, and he was the chairman of public works, and in the absence of the president, the other officials were offering everything Santa Cruz had for my summer's comfort. No one thought to offer the horse, of course, since no woman ever rode such a thing in the Indian villages, not even down in the valley, and only Don Marciano himself ever rode this one. But afterward, when I was at Don Martín's on Sunday afternoon, Don Marciano came by to pay a respect call on his *compadre*, godfather to one of his children; and I put Don Martín up to asking him if I could use the horse sometimes during the summer.

I think Don Marciano was surprised and delighted. He made a long speech on how dangerous the horse was, how no one could ride it, except himself, without *mucha práctica*. Perhaps the American *señora* could do anything. At any rate, he never rode the horse except to market on Saturdays or to make a *paseo*, a round of visits, on Sundays, or to go hunting in the hills. All week he was busy. Any time the *señora americana* wished to come to his house on a weekday morning, he would be glad to let her borrow the horse for the day. I don't think he really expected me, though. It was a week before I took advantage of his offer, anyway, as I had many friends to visit and much chatting to do the first few days, and then I got the "water sickness," which does not fit in well with horseback rides.

One fine morning, in my second week, I started off with a child from the school to guide me in finding Don Marciano's. My hostess, Doña Patrocina, the cure woman, thought I should not do such a thing. A horse is *muy feroz, muy bravo*. Who could run along all day with me to protect me, when both her sons were busy in the fields? Besides, where could I go? To San Luis Ocotitlán ten miles along the foothills? To Etla back along the railroad? Surely I would not want to go to Oaxaca again so soon, with no market going on till Saturday, and no festival till the third Monday in July.

"I want to go up the trails into the sierra, Doña Patrocina, to watch the woodcutters, to see the high mountains, to get the view, to see the 'divide' of the war with San Felipe—well, just to go, to ride around the hills many different days."

Doña Patrocina shook her head sadly. Probably Doña Elena wasn't happy staying around talking. Well, the saints would protect her. But it was Patrocina who sent over to get a fourth-grade boy from the school to go along with me. I was a little hurt. I considered myself quite a horsewoman and had merely planned to roam around the hills as I pleased. Now I could foresee all the village getting excited about it. I tried to explain to Gerónomo, the fourth-grade "boy guide," as we walked down the hill behind the school and up the other side of the San Sebastián ridge, that in the United States women went riding alone. "We will try to tell that to Don Marciano," said Gerónomo seriously.

I found Don Marciano's houseyard a poor, crowded place. His family had perhaps come late from Santa Cruz Salinas. He had very little land; what he had was far from the ditch on a rocky burro trail which no oxcart could travel. All three of his little shacks were made of straw and bamboo—one for his married daughter, one for sleeping quarters for himself, his wife, and his other children, and one for cooking and eating—with no adobe or tile construction in any of them. His land, most of it on a steep, bare hillside, had been planted to corn late in the season, and none of it was up. One of his daughters had just walked two hundred yards for water, down a steep path to a spring. On the face of it, Don Marciano was poverty-stricken.

But he was really one of the prosperous men of Santa Cruz Etla. To be a town, Don Amado had said, Santa Cruz needed "men with more sons." Don Marciano had eight children, three girls and five boys. His oldest son, Panfilo, whom I remembered from 1934, had been working on the Pan American Highway south of Oaxaca City; he made two and a half pesos a day and sent his mother home a sewing machine. Don Marciano's youngest child was still sucking at the breast. Three in-between boys cared for a large herd of goats; two older girls went to the mill, made tortillas, and cared for the younger children. How so many children happened to survive is a mystery; perhaps it was because Don Marciano's family got water from a spring and not from the main ditch on the central ridge. Don Marciano himself was a strong, tall man, much bigger than Don Martín or Don Bartolo. His wife, Doña Clara, was a gaunt, rawboned woman, one of the homeliest in Santa Cruz Etla; she looked like our United States conception of a middle-aged Indian woman, a Blackfoot, Sioux, or Comanche. All the children looked like her.

His oldest daughter was as homely as her mother, yet surprisingly Don Marciano prospered in her marriage. We had known a pleasant, handsome youngster at the school in 1934, Adolfo Soto. He and his mother lived then with a great-aunt who had sons of her own. When Adolfo's mother died, he was left at nineteen without a family. Don Marciano took him in, married him to the ugly daughter, built them a new bamboo shack, and gave Adolfo the responsibility of the corn land. Thus, Don Marciano had a son who sent home money, a son-in-law who did the plowing, young sons to tend the goats—while he himself became a man of luxury and rode a horse.

He welcomed me enthusiastically as he got up from his breakfast. Had I come to take pictures? He had heard that the American *señora* would take pictures of everyone. Did I know he was a grandfather? His grandchild was ten months old. If I would take one picture of that grandchild, his doll, his *muñeca*, anything he had was mine. The boy Gerónomo shyly interrupted to tell him that Don Martín had made arrangements about the horse. Don Marciano threw back his head and laughed. What an idea! The poor *señora*, she didn't know what she was asking. Why, this ferocious beast was no animal for any woman!

I saw the docile little horse eating his breakfast, tethered in the yard near the goat pen. I went over and patted him. "I'm sure I'll get along with the horse," I told Don Marciano. "Would you like me to take photographs of all your family while the horse eats?"

With such a deal the horse was mine for as many days as I would ever want it. But first I must sit awhile in the "parlor," the shack used as a kitchen, and chat with the family for formality's sake. In a "sociological report" I wrote once about Santa Cruz Etla, I described how little there was, in the way of material things, in the "front room," which is usually the only room in the house. But I would criticize Don Marciano rather for having too much in his front room. There was the sewing machine; there were the bridle and saddle for the horse; there was the ring of stones for the charcoal fire, and all the eating and cooking equipment — everything on the floor since there were no tables. There were two rifles, as Don Marciano had prospered enough to buy a second one for his hunting in the hills. There were dried pelts and half-dried pelts of fox and deer. Between the pelts, hanging on the bamboo walls, were bright calendars of Mexico City girls and aspirin advertisements showing highly colored pictures from the lives of the saints. Over everything was a layer of smoke and dust. I was glad to get out in the sun again, when I was told the grandchild was dressed in her christening robes and ready for the photographs.

This baby girl looked more like her father, Adolfo Soto, and less like the high-cheekboned, eagle-nosed first generation. Perhaps this was why Don Marciano loved her so much. She was much cleaner, and had a fancier christening robe than Don Marciano's own two youngest children. No one else should hold his "doll" while he was around, but I finally persuaded him to let the little girl sit alone on a *petate* in the sun for a picture. But she cried for Don Marciano, and we did not have luck with the photos. Fortunately, I kept at it till she quieted down, for that one good picture is the only thing Don Marciano has now to remind him of his *muñeca*. Adolfo Soto and his wife had no other children who survived a week of life; and the "doll" herself died at three, in 1948, when an epidemic of the measles, the dread *sarampión* so often fatal in the Indian villages, hit the children along the San Sebastián ridge. The poor little photo stands today on the altar in Don Marciano's new adobe house.

Eventually I got photos of most of the family and two of Don Marciano himself on the horse. Then we all went down to the goat pen to watch Don Marciano saddle up. Here the children showed me another pet of theirs, a fawn which Don Marciano had captured alive in the mountains. It had been "adopted" by a mother goat and ran freely with the little kids, sucking on its new mother and coming up to the children when they called. It was already beginning to lose its baby spots. I asked the children what would happen to it when it grew older, and Don Marciano interrupted to say that it would be used for "pelt and meat." The children said not a thing, but merely looked sad and glanced uneasily at each other. "I am hunting in the hills on the horse many times in the month, señora. I have caught the wild fawns before and brought them home on the back of the saddle. This is not the first one we have raised, nor the last. The children will forget sadness," added the matter-of-fact Don Marciano. When I questioned him about the fawn, as I sat in the yard of his new house in 1954 and talked to him and Doña Clara about the days when he was public works chairman and I used to ride his horse, he did not remember any one particular fawn.

In the 1940's Don Marciano was the only hunter in the town. I had seen no pelts, nor guns, nor fawns in any other houseyard. "Don't other Santa Cruz men hunt in the hills?" I asked him.

"How would that be possible, señora? They have no time, no gun, no horse," he answered, smiling at my stupidity as he brought out his saddle and bridle. The saddle had cost Don Marciano one hundred twenty-five pesos in the Oaxaca market. It would be many times that now, as even handmade things have leaped in value in the cities. It was not a fancy saddle, but smoothly made and of a fine piece of leather; it still hangs on the wall of Don Marciano's new house, covered with dust as were all his things in the little old shacks. The horse itself cost him, in 1942 when he had bought it, one hundred seventy-five pesos, or thirty-five dollars. Don Marciano had indulged himself when his daughter married; I am still puzzled how any Santa Cruz Etla man would have three hundred pesos to spend on himself personally, and why he should have chosen to spend it for horse and saddle. He had paid for the town fiesta as *mayordomo* in 1937; perhaps he used to get good money for the pelts. Now, with so much of the sierra cut down for firewood, the wild animals so far away in the hills, bullets and powder (those city-made things) so expensive, the horse dead after twelve years of hunting with Don Marciano and a new horse so hard to buy, with Adolfo Soto and his childless wife gone to work in Oaxaca City, leaving more corn planting for the old man to do—well, times have changed, and Don Marciano is that much older himself. I know that in 1954 I did not myself have the same urge to ride a horse up and down the Etla Hills that I had had a decade before. He said he still hunted occasionally, but I saw no pelts in the house this last visit.

That first morning in the houseyard I asked what the name of the horse was. Don Marciano had not thought a name necessary.

"It is called *el caballo*. Why does it need any other name? It is the only horse in Santa Cruz Etla."

So I got on *el caballo,* and Don Marciano adjusted the stirrups, and Doña Clara pressed my hand, and Adolfo Soto held up the grandchild, and the children held up the fawn. Then I set out, to ride "just anywhere," down the hill to the spring, back on the ox-cart road through to the San Sebastián ridge, and up to the main trail at Don Julio's mill. Gerónomo could not keep up with me, so I waved him back to school. Doña Estéfana and Doña Rufina were in the middle of the trail chatting, as I trotted by and heard their cries of admiration and surprise.

"Where are you going, Doña Elena? How can you manage the horse? Take a boy with you. Do not fall in the mountains"—so everyone warned me as I passed.

Thus began the first of many beautiful rides in the sierra. The people forgot to wonder why Gerónomo or some other youngster never went with me and became accustomed to seeing me gallop by up and down the trails and oxcart roads. When we went to visit Santa Cruz for the day in 1951, one of the first things Doña Rufina told me was that *el caballo* had died of some horse sickness in Don Marciano's houseyard.

Because of the horse, I was able to visit in San Pablo Etla, to see other valley towns, to go twice into Oaxaca—trips I could make in my own car in 1954. But mostly I took the horse into the wooded mountains behind the village, on trails I have never visited since. I would take the central ridge to Don Martín's place, then turn up to the junction where the main trail went downhill to the *Panteón*. It is a steep burro and horse trail from there up to the thick woods, a trail that goes up like stairsteps, rising quickly above the brook and hitting a level along another, higher ridge. The horse knew all the places where it was smooth enough to run. Although never used for such a plebeian, burro-type job as hauling wood, *el caballo* had often taken Don Marciano up this way to hunt. Way below me I could see the brook, clear and sparkling in the sun when it lives in the sierra, though sluggish and muddy when it gets down on the Santa Cruz ridges.

In the floor of the wide canyon far below, where the trees had been cut and the grass was rich and green, two rival herds of goats spent their days. Two of Don Marciano's sons followed one herd around, Don Bartolo's boy the other. In 1954 one of Don Marciano's sons, then probably about seventeen, and Timoteo, Don Bartolo's shy introvert from an extrovert family, were still working the goat herds, though in canyons not so green, showing the influence of ten more years of woodcutting and erosion in the sierra above. On the horse I sometimes took their sidetrail and went up into their little private valley. It winds in two or three miles, hardly a valley at all, narrowing to less than twenty feet at the top. Only the goats can get out of it at that end because the brook makes a series of falls and there is no way for the horse to scramble out and get on the through trail which passes a hundred yards above.

The boys with the goats were very shy. They spent their days talking to no one but the goats, seldom seeing even each other. So they found little to say to the American *señora* who rode the high-stepping horse, sometimes running along the stream and scaring the goats, sometimes climbing the woodcutters' trail high above and hallooing down. They probably thought I was like some crazy, mountain spirit woman. These boys were gone from the village from dawn to dark, and I had no chance to make friends with them otherwise. When in 1954 I tried to visit and talk with every young person I had known well in 1945, to see what Santa Cruz Etla held

for them in the future, I found the goatherds just as hard to reach
and talk to as before.

When I followed the goat trails into the canyon on *el caballo,*
I would have to turn around and backtrack out more than a mile.
I liked better to stay on the upper trail until it crossed the brook
above the series of falls. There it went through thick vegetation for
a hundred yards or so on both sides of the crossing. There was a
pool at the crossing place, a foot deep and perhaps fifteen feet wide,
with big ferns growing on each side. Right below the pool the
stream narrowed and rushed downhill quickly in rapids, until it
hit the falls two hundred yards below and came crashing down into
the goat-pasture canyon. Perhaps the young goatherds were so
silent and morose because they were constantly angry at the goats,
who found all sorts of ways up the canyon walls around the falls
where the poor boys could hardly climb. They probably never
thought about the beauty of the falls, the rapids, the pool, or the
trail crossing among the ferns. Since no one ever sees this beautiful place, except the goat vaqueros and the woodcutters, it seems
all wasted.

I described it enthusiastically to two young men who went up
to cut wood twice a week, Dona Estéfana's grandson Joel and Don
Amado's son Cassiano. They couldn't remember any place like
that. I explained the falls, *la catarata,* the ferns, the pool. I was
afraid I was using the wrong words and was ready to get out the
dictionary, when Joel suddenly said: "Oh, that place? Oh yes, we all
like that place; there is always water there the year round, even in
the driest years." I got the same reaction from Cassiano, who always thought more deeply than the others. He said only: "It is a
hard place to get the burros across, Doña Elena; they don't like
the wide, slippery pool." It took an outsider, riding the trail for
pleasure on a borrowed horse, to tell him how beautiful his own
daily journey was.

But I must have made some impression on him. When I saw
Cassiano in 1954, in Mexico City, he mentioned the former beauty
of the old trail himself, saying: "Heavy rains brought good corn
years, Doña Elena, but many more trees are now cut out, and you

would be sad to see how muddy the falls always are during these years when the rains have been heavy." This depletion of the trees was one of a long series of reasons why Cassiano had to leave Santa Cruz.

Beyond the pool the trail went up sharply again, and soon the brook was left as far below as the goat pasture had been left before. Here the trees grew very thick, like scrub pine woods, mostly second growth from cut-off area during centuries of charcoal burning under both Mixtecs and Spaniards. It was surprising to me in 1945 to see how little of the forest seemed badly cut over as I went on up into the deeper woods, twisting back and forth with the trail and going up stairsteps to climb even higher ridges. In the warmth and rain new growth springs up again, though modern forest authorities are concerned, as well as Cassiano, about the erosion in the whole Oaxaca area. Perhaps just now in this decade the "point of no return" is being reached; the woodcutters have outstripped the rate of regrowth.

In 1945, when I tried to find them with *el caballo*, the woodcutters were scattered all over the highest three ridges where the bigger trees are, so that it was just about impossible to find a particular woodcutter unless you knew exactly where he was going. I seldom saw any friend of mine, probably because I did not go high enough. I would try to describe what I thought was surely the top of the divide made famous in the war with San Felipe, and my listeners would always laugh. I heard Cassiano tell his mother: "Doña Elena has never gone far enough to see any divide." But I did see piles of wood left by the cutters, and charcoal burners' stacks smouldering away. I had had the idea to go in to Oaxaca by way of the divide and really see the town of San Felipe de Agua on the other side; but I gave it up when it took me all day to get into Oaxaca and back by the regular direct road. I didn't want to worry Don Marciano by overworking the little horse.

Coming down from the pool and falls I enjoyed even more than going up. On the ascent, my face was always toward the dark, wooded mountains. Descending, I faced always toward the valley. I never did reach a high enough divide on an open trail to look out and see the city of Oaxaca, as well as our end of the valley; but I could see up to the town of Etla and all the towns between. Santa Cruz Etla is so small and so spread out that all I could see of it from any point on the trail was the school, looking insignificant in its little clearing. But only the church showed even in San Pablo. I suppose the woodcutters never see the beauty of the view of the valley, coming home always loaded and tired and late. At least I could get a permanent memory of it on Kodachrome film, whenever *el caballo* would stand still long enough for me to adjust the camera.

And the valley itself, in spite of many good wet years in between, is much, much drier than it was in 1934. In the long struggle to outstrip San Pablo Etla in being a town, Santa Cruz has the forces of nature on its side. The first things I noticed in driving our own family car up to San Pablo in 1954 were the many abandoned fields, the eroded hillsides, the broad, new gullies. San Pablo, farther than Santa Cruz from the sierra, on a steeper, last incline of the foot-hills leading down to the valley floor, with no trees planted in the houseyards as has always been the custom in the Santa Cruz muni-cipality—San Pablo is surely one of those towns the conservationists are worrying about, a town losing its agricultural fields, a town whose people have to turn to work elsewhere. A few houseyards seemed abandoned, we thought, as we drove up the badly eroded "truck road" which has been "navigable" for years up as far as San Pablo; and I heard in Santa Cruz that the San Pablo school had been reduced to one teacher. Though Cassiano, Adolfo Soto, Don Bartolo's Luisa, Miguelito and his family, and several others have left Santa Cruz, erosion of agricultural land was not the major force which drove them away.

Another thing I had to thank Don Marciano for, and his loan of *el caballo*, was the intimacy with the birds. Few birds came down into the cleared corn land, but up there in the hills I rode with them. There was one like a linnet, with an even brighter red chest and head, another like the big orioles I have seen in Panama, a third black and white like a magpie, a fourth like a sparrow with a peach-colored breast. I asked Don Marciano about the birds, be-cause he, a hunter and not a prosaic woodcutter, might be more apt to know their names. He answered at once. "Don't you know? The large ones are *pájaros* [the common Spanish word for birds], and the small ones are *pajaritos.*"

What I did learn from the horseback rides that everyone in Santa Cruz Etla does know about was the system of water supply for the town, Don Marciano's civic responsibility that year. The supply depends on two streams and two ditches. Above Don Marciano's house a small stream comes out of its own canyon, making the ravine which separates the San Sebastián ridge from the "center of town." This stream is called *el río*, although it is much smaller than my stream of the falls and the pool. It is allowed to meander down its course without ever being tapped, and families in the ravine and on the San Sebastián ridge get their water from it. In the middle of the rainy season it runs about eighteen inches deep and three feet wide; I went to bathe in pools along it in 1934, 1945, and 1954 (and of these only 1954 was a good wet year in the Etla Hills). Don Marciano's spring runs into it above the biggest pool; only near such springs does it have water in the dry season. There is no long trail beside it, though Don Marciano used to take *el caballo* up along it to hunt. (The end leaf map will help.)

My brook from the woodcutters' sierra is called merely *el arroyo*. Before Don Amado's grandfather harnessed and deflected it, it created that ravine between the school and the southern, or San Lorenzo, ridge; and the old arroyo bed is now the dry floor of the ravine. Here are still a few wells, including the one below the old *Cooperativa* from which four children and I all got sick one time in 1945 when the ditch ran dry. Bamboo, the common building material for the house walls, grows all along the dry arroyo bed in the ravine. The water from my pools and falls becomes *la zanja*, the ditch, the giver of life to the main houses of Santa Cruz Etla. Where the central ridge and the San Lorenzo ridge join to become foothills at the opening of the goatherders' canyon, Don Amado's grandfather built a rock obstruction and turned *el arroyo's* water from the ravine to run down the central ridge. In a canalized bed two feet wide and a foot deep, the water rushes down past Don Bartolo's, Don Martín's, Doña Estéfana's, and on to the school. It

69

runs parallel with the oxcart trail, except behind the school building, where it is sidetracked through the school garden. There are
places, of course, where *la zanja* runs through houseyards in which
cattle are tethered, and many places where goats, burros, oxen,
and barefoot people cross it. Santa Cruz Etla does not mind this
and does not connect the recurrent dysentery, the "water sickness,"
with it, but cares only when the stream runs dry.

The six families below the *Panteón*, who are called *la gente del
San Lorenzo lado*, also get their water from *el arroyo*, tapping it to
feed their own little ditch at a place above the dam which makes
our *zanja*. I was sorry for the San Lorenzo people; their hills are
so steep that their land always has been drier and more eroded than
the sloping fields near the main ridge, and their corn crop always
gets in late. Many of their children come to the school; the families
are a part of the community; but scorn is heaped upon them whenever anything goes wrong with the water system. When the main
zanja runs dry, or low, or muddy, it is those *tontos*, those ignorant
San Lorenzo people again. They aren't really ignorant; they just
beat us to the water. But I can see how, if they were to irrigate
just the least bit in the dry season, there would be no water at all in
the main Santa Cruz Etla ditch.

In dry season or wet, and in spite of all the families involved in
the use of the water, Santa Cruz can always feel smugly superior to
San Pablo about the water system. *La zanja* runs on down to make
the water supply there, too, and is piped into the schoolhouse of
San Pablo and into a fountain in the center of the little cobbled
plaza; but in dry years what water there is always reaches Santa
Cruz first. Years ago there were two fine natural springs in the ravines on each side of San Pablo, but they were already dry most of
the year by 1945.

In any year of average rainfall there is water in the mountain
brook the year round; though, as Cassiano says, with more and more
erosion up above, it is increasingly muddy. The flower gardens,
the vegetables in the school garden, and small plots to grow green
corn for *elotes*, corn on the cob, can be irrigated by hand in the
dry season, October through May, if the wet season of the summer

has been good and wet. Irrigation is an important item on the cultural missions list; but even rural schoolteachers and cultural missions can't start dry season irrigation projects when there isn't enough dry season water. There is always drinking water, though, either in the brook or in the springs or in the river wells. Only twice in thirty-five years, Don Marciano told me, has there been no water in the brook at the dividing place. Then the woodcutters brought back skin-bags of water from higher points in the hills and sold the water to other families. "When there are two dry years in succession, then we have suffered, all of us," he said.

Though he lived over on San Sebastián, two ridges away from San Lorenzo and a good half-mile from the central *zanja*, Don Marciano, as chairman of the public works committee, still had responsibility for the whole water system, as well as the road and the *Panteón*. He did a good job, too, though the central ditch was really no personal concern of his. Perhaps he hoped that this service would be a step up toward the presidency; if so, his hopes came true when he was elected for the 1947-1948 term.

Twice when I was present during his term of chairmanship, he was called on to do something about obstructions in the ditch. Raised as I was on irrigated farm land in central California, hearing the ditch committee called out in the night made me feel right at home. The day the ditch ran dry and I got the water sickness from the bad well, Don Marciano had been "called" from his hunting or his goat tending and had spent the day up at the San Lorenzo ditch. It wasn't really the San Lorenzo people's fault, he told me. A large tree limb had dammed up the main mountain stream and sent a torrent down through San Lorenzo, flooding two houseyards.

On a Sunday later in the summer, I was sitting under Doña Patrocina's mango tree watching Don Marciano play cards with the other council members; a dignified man, he never played ball. Suddenly one of the boys in the ball game noticed that the *zanja* was running dry. It was a lark for the young fellows to chase off the mile or so up to the head of the *zanja* to see what had happened. The council went right on playing cards. The boys found that the ditch had broken through its wall in a heavy rain the night before, one

71

of the few good rains in the very dry year of 1945. All the brook water was running down the dry arroyo bed, giving the bamboos a good drenching and flooding out all the wells. The young fellows were willing enough, too, to go back and help fix it afterward. I remember Doña Estéfana's grandson Joel, one of my good friends among the younger generation and an outstanding ballplayer, cheerfully giving up the game to help—experience which served him well, since he has recently been chairman of public works himself. But on that earlier occasion the responsibility and the planning had to be assumed by Don Marciano. In a grave manner he excused himself from the card game and went back up the ridge with the boys. In two hours' time the water was running again down the *zanja* as merrily as ever.

If this occurrence had happened on a day when I had the horse, I could have followed along, watched the "committee" fix things up, and no one would have been the wiser. But on Sunday—every Sunday in Santa Cruz—I did what the women did. I sat on the ground beneath the mango trees chatting in my most formal manner, while Don Marciano rode his own horse to visit his *compadres,* tied it to the school peach tree while he played cards, or took it out patrolling ditches.

Though his horse was dead and he no longer hunted regularly, though he had served as president and felt himself "through with a career of public service," Don Marciano was still a virile, erect, dignified man in 1954. His material condition had even improved by then, good as it had seemed in 1945. Following on foot some of the paths I had known on horseback in 1945, I went down the ravine on my last visit in 1954, across the pools in *el río* and up to Don Marciano's house. I wouldn't have known it, if I hadn't been pretty sure of the trail. Two of the little shacks were gone, and the third, which had been the "front room," was used to house the youngest goats. Surrounded by peach-bearing trees stood one of the largest adobe houses in Santa Cruz Etla. Cut into two rooms, one for living and one for sleeping and storage, it had a tile floor, and while it was not whitewashed, its stone door frame and cement steps were as good as those which Don Martín built before he died.

72

Doña Clara proudly showed me the inscription scratched into the cement step while it was wet, an inscription she knew by heart although she could not read. It said: "The house of Marciano Jiménez, built by his sons Juanito and Panfilo, December, 1952." Juanito still herded the goats in 1954, but Panfilo, who had already left home to work on the highway in 1945, was working for a construction company in Oaxaca City. He had learned to build staunch houses on cement foundations and was something of a hero in Santa Cruz at that time for his expert help on the new chapel.

In front of the well-constructed doorway, Doña Clara had put up a trellis which was covered with red rambler roses. In the confusion and dirt of Don Marciano's houseyard in the days of *el caballo*, I had never noticed the view from there. But that last time, sitting under the rambler roses and discussing old times with my dignified, aging friends, I saw that Don Marciano had really the finest view in Santa Cruz Etla. He saw all the bamboo-filled ravines, the mango trees, and the "public buildings" of Santa Cruz Etla below him, as well as the valley farther below. He could look at almost the whole course of the water supply. Though he said to me: "Thanks to the saints, the *zanja* yonder has long since been the responsibility of younger men," he and all those committee chairmen before and since him have preserved the water for Santa Cruz Etla. Mr. Ximello, that rural school director under whose sponsorship we first came to Santa Cruz in 1934, had told us that he chose that town because of "its fruits and gardens, its fine new school, and its good water supply." As water supplies go in Mexico, Santa Cruz has one of the best, probably more water per capita than has Mexico City.

✺ 6 ✺

I REMEMBER WITH SPECIAL PLEASURE the men who raised gardens," I wrote in the diary notes I kept of a two weeks' visit to Santa Cruz Etla in 1944. "Don Féliz Jiménez is a gardener." This was the Don Féliz who was municipal president in 1954, a decade later, though there were two other older men in the community named Féliz. Don Féliz Léon owned the only oxcart below the school, and he had two sons of his old age who figured in the history of the school. Don Féliz Mendoza from the San Sebastián ridge came to council meetings I attended on school problems; and he always provided a strident note against work on the public land, although *Féliz* actually means "happy." But Don Féliz, the gardener, was happy in his garden and not much in the public eye in earlier decades, although I notice him now in group pictures I took of discussion meetings in both 1944 and 1945.

Perhaps he came into the "public works" picture because of his great interest in irrigation water. In 1944 I jotted down in my notes an account of my visit to his little shack on the dry San Lorenzo hillside. A hard worker, planting corn up and down his steep acres, he had saved enough in the good corn year of 1942 to buy a half-acre of land in that part of the dry arroyo bed near the dry season wells where he could irrigate the year around. He urged me to come and see his garden; one package of the seeds he had used had been accompanied by an English description and his older son, then in the third grade, had told him I could read it. When I went down into the ravine, I saw the "American" plants right away, Kentucky Wonder string beans, not just Mexican frijoles, but green beans whose seeds he had purchased at a real store in Oaxaca. Already the vines were outgrowing him, and I could only look at the Ferry-Morse seed packet he had so carefully saved and translate for him the instructions telling how he could tie the beans up. He also had lettuce and spinach planted, in this community where no one else plants anything but corn, beans, squashes, chiles, onions, and tomatoes.

He was even more interested in the flowers and had purchased lily bulbs in the same Oaxaca store. These store purchases were themselves unusual in Santa Cruz; no one else there buys things in stores, but in the open market, from other Indians if possible. Don Féliz had zinnias, cosmos, and daisies. There were tuberoses in bloom along the arroyo bed. Most of his vocabulary in talking about all this was beyond me; his garden and his scientific attitude toward it seemed so foreign to his house, his cornfield, his illiteracy, and his "barefooted-Indian" appearance. When I asked if he sold the green beans for enough to pay back eventually the cost of the land, he seemed surprised. "How can I pay back the cost of the land?" he asked. "I spent the money when I decided to spend it. It is my pleasure. [Just like *el caballo* to Don Marciano.] Who would buy the green beans? My wife herself does not like to cook these green things. Let me give you a basket of them to take home with you to Doña Estéfana's."

It was the love of experimenting and growing which pleased Don Féliz so much about the whole gardening business. But it did not please his wife. Though I never met her to talk to, I heard undercurrents which made me think she had little sympathy with Don Féliz' ideas. The year 1945 was an especially bad one for water, and Don Féliz had to let a lot of the garden plot go unplanted; that year also his little girl died, she for whom the *angelita* was given at which I danced so often with the bass-viol player. Then his younger son died the year of the measles epidemic; and soon after, his wife. To get a woman in the house, his older son married very early for a hill man and brought a shy sixteen-year-old San Pablo girl into the house to make tortillas for both of them. Then it was that Don Féliz, no longer finding refuge from his wife's nagging tongue by working in his garden, went into politics. For two terms, from 1949 to 1952, he ran the public works committee, supervising all use of water, and in 1953 he was Don Martín's candidate for the presidency, and so naturally the winner.

Thus, it was Don Féliz, already indebted to me because I showed him how to string up Kentucky Wonder beans, who was president in 1954 during our last visit. We had driven up as far as San Pablo during a one-day visit in 1951 and had been picked up there in an oxcart by the artist Perfecto, whose father, Don Marcelino, was then president. But roads throughout Mexico had been improved spectacularly in the intervening three years; surely, we thought, the road up beyond the San Pablo church should be passable in 1954. Of course, the thing to remember is that, while Santa Cruz needed the water supply for its very life and felt civic pride in the public buildings, the people really saw no need for an automobile road at all. Keep the road wide enough for the oxcarts, fill the worst gullies when the storms are heavy so that the ox teams will never sink down or the carts be damaged—and what hill village in southern Mexico needs to do more? "Better wagon roads" is on the cultural missions list, but Santa Cruz Etla did not feel the importance of them. I cannot make a success story of my 1954 visit by saying that Don Féliz' regime improved the main ridge ox trail to such an extent that it was a "better wagon road"; but I do know from bitter personal experience that it was a better trail in August, 1954, than it was in June, 1954.

Station wagons with special low gears bringing school supervisors and health officials, and even a big truck with tractor wheels delivering flour and small merchandise to Don Martín's store, got up to Santa Cruz Etla in the early 1950's. "Why not us?" I assured my skeptical husband. I did not want to bother the people with details of my coming, although their former teacher, then in Mexico City and in constant correspondence with me, had written to Don Martín's literate daughter-in-law that we were on our way. I wanted simply to arrive without bother, on a regular school day and workday, to ask Don Martín or Doña Patrocina if I could stay a while, send my husband back to the nice Oaxaca Courts Hotel for a couple of weeks by the swimming pool, and have him come up to get me when I was ready to leave. I knew the trouble every family would go to, the clean clothes that would have to be ironed, white outfits for the children and pink and orange shirts for the men, if the time of our coming were known. This time we would make no trouble about our arrival in Santa Cruz.

Oh, wouldn't we? A half-mile beyond the San Pablo church we slithered on the edge of a mudhole, tried to find the main wheel ruts, and went down above the hubs on both front and back wheels of the right side, down into the rich adobe mud. There was no backing nor forwarding, no up or down; we were in an inextricable situation; there we sat while my husband strongly wished that there had been a little more progress in my village. Along came the old Don Féliz León, closest Santa Cruz householder to the mudhole.

Immediately he recognized us and went out into his fields to get his sons. They tried an old roof beam, bunches of boughs, big stones under the wheels—all to no avail. Felicito, the oldest son, went up the trail to get Joel, then thirty-two, grandson of Doña Estéfana and public works chairman. On the way he evidently called out at every houseyard that Doña Elena and her husband were trying to drive a car up—no, not a horse, a car!—and the road had not been worked on since the dry season. Now came Don Féliz Jiménez of the Kentucky Wonder beans, introducing himself as president in a much more polished fashion than ever he had used talking about gardens. He sent the León boys for their team of oxen and the yoke. Twenty men were there to hitch the team, *la yunta,* onto our front bumper when finally the oxen arrived. One strong sting at the oxen with an iron goad, and they lunged forward, pulling the car up out of the hole and well on the way toward the Santa Cruz school. Then with Don Féliz riding up front in style, we came to Don Martín's bakery and store.

Having left their work for the day, standing around in their muddy everyday clothes while their outfits for celebrity greeting lay packed in the clothes chests at home, the men of Santa Cruz Etla could at least have the pleasure of speech making. So Don Féliz welcomed me; Don Martín told us how his house was our house; I made a speech; my husband made a speech which I translated. Don Bartolo was on hand this time, quick to leave his houseyard full of young goats when he heard of our coming; and he made a speech, too, as my old friend who was president when I stayed so long before. It made up for his absence that time with "malaria." Never since 1934 had we been so warmly welcomed. Fortunately, we could thank them for their help with the car in a better way than with speeches because of Don Martín's new store full of strawberry pop. We also bought two quarts of tequila, that strong Mexican brandy made of century plants. Since Don Martín had only two small glasses, I went round the circle of men pouring the tequila drinks one by one. It was the first time we had ever been able to buy treats for them as a group, or to provide them with any kind of party.

The car was in Santa Cruz, parked in the school yard; my husband was drinking in the good companionship of his old friends. The hole was still there in the road above San Pablo; the twilight was coming on. With the twilight, in a good corn year, comes a heavy shower that often drops an inch of rain in an evening, and 1954 was a good corn year. My husband's plans certainly did not include staying in Santa Cruz himself until the next dry season. But Don Féliz anticipated all this. Profuse in expressing his *vergüenza,* his shame that the road had not been improved, he sent for another team of oxen. Then with one team hitched in front and another hitched behind to provide moral support and push, the car traveled slowly back downhill after the last speech, made the mudhole before the rain came, and was hauled through it by the oxen without incident, *sin novedades* as they say in Mexico. Don Féliz promised my husband that if Doña Elena would stay in Santa Cruz ten days, the road would be in good enough condition for any car to get through by the following Sunday. Then my husband, Don Enrique, could come to get me, the public works committee would stand by to see him get through the mudhole, and we could all have a real dressed-up, speech-making fiesta.

Four times during the next ten days I walked by the mudhole on my rounds of visits. The first day I circumvented the mud by sticking to the cornfields, for I did not want to take off my shoes and wade. All day the second and third days, the public works committee, led by the tireless, wiry little Don Féliz himself, worked over the mudhole. They took oxcarts as high as they could drive them up the rocky arroyo bed and filled them with large rocks, bringing down five loads of rocks altogether, two days' work for three men. Ten other men worked in shifts putting the rocks deep in the muddy hole and filling sand in around them, until the road at that place was in better condition than it had ever been before. Then they must needs repair it near the school, too, so that the car might turn around. Later in the week two very heavy evening rains fell, so on the last Saturday Don Féliz was himself hard at work again with the oxcarts full of more rocks. July is a busy time for weeding and plowing the young corn, but I don't think one day's work was done in the fields by any full-grown Santa Cruz man the ten days I was there. Never before had there been so much road repair; every bad chuckhole was filled, every rut smoothed out. I understand that Don Martín's delivery-truck driver spoke of the Santa Cruz road with enthusiasm for the first time in his career. Mr. Ximello's driver in 1934 had said: "Christ himself couldn't drive on this road." Inspired by Don Féliz' work, other presidents will keep at the road until anyone can drive into the village. Santa Cruz Etla is only a few miles from the Pan American Highway, the *Carretera Internacional,* down which heavy traffic comes from Mexico City every day of the year. When the Santa Cruz Etla road is really passable, it will be a crossroad on one of the main highways of the world.

Actually, better transportation into Oaxaca City had already come in 1945 by a "backdoor" route. How surprised the central ridge dwellers had been in the spring of that year when a bus company began running one of the converted trucks called *camiones,* which carry passengers and freight all mixed up, every Saturday morning up to the San Lorenzo ridge—of all places! There was no actual road there at all, but the slope was gradual. A lot of the land on the far side of the ridge, belonging to another township nearer the city, was used as community cattle pasture, and the *camión* just slowly crawled up the slope until it cleared the ridge and its driver could look across the ravine below the San Lorenzo houses and honk at the Santa Cruz people. At six o'clock on the Oaxaca City market day, or probably as much later as the driver gets around to it, a rickety Ford truck, with seats running the length of the covered part in back, is up on that ridge honking loudly enough to be heard on the Santa Cruz Etla ridge a half-mile away. If they have not already started from home, families from the central ridge hurry out at the sound of the horn, come panting through the schoolyard and down into the deep ravine, then up the side of the other *loma* through Don Féliz' garden and down the San Lorenzo ridge to the waiting bus. There will be seats on the bus for perhaps twenty, and forty people from all the hills around will get on. Then additional tens will climb on top, five or six will sit on the fenders, and four in with the driver. Everyone has a large pannier in which to carry produce. Any live chickens for the market are carried under the women's *rebozos*. Live turkeys are more of a problem, however, and have to be held upside down, feet tied together, in the laps of the people sitting down.

I never made the trip on that bus. I abhor turkeys anyway (the ones at Doña Patrocina's fought with me all one summer), and there was no point in my getting up before dawn to get a first chance at a seat and then being asked to hold a couple of the hated turkeys on my lap all the way to town. I have ridden on just such buses too often in other parts of Mexico. What with the crowds, the chuckholes in the road, the people on your feet, the babies to hold, the young pigs, legs tied together, on the floor, the difficulty of breathing with everybody packed so closely—well, I had *el caballo* in 1945 and planned to have the family car there with me in 1954, so I was not the one to worry about getting to market. I would have gone to market in Don Martín's oxcart any time before I would take the bus ride.

For Santa Cruz people, however, the bus ride was a new and exhilarating experience, the first ride in an automobile for most of the women and children. The trip costs ten centavos each way. If you miss the bus when it decides to leave the charcoal sellers' street of the Oaxaca market, that congregating point for Santa Cruz people, on its return trip in the late afternoon, you walk the seventeen miles home. But few miss it. The bus just comes squawking down the market street, never coming to a dead stop, and it attracts the hill people like a magnet picking up iron filings. Everyone seems to arrive at the San Lorenzo ridge alive and whole; the driver sorts out the baskets and the produce and the new clay griddles that belong to each family; then the people file back across the ravine through Don Féliz' place and up to the main trail again at the school.

It would surely be an exciting mark of progress and independence for Santa Cruz if such an important development as a weekly bus route could be considered the "Santa Cruz Etla bus" instead of the "Santa María Seminario-San Lorenzo bus." But Don Féliz' regime did not establish such a bus route, and so far as I have heard, no other regime since has done so.

Don Féliz' regime will be remembered for many years in Santa Cruz Etla, however, for the project of the chapel. Though not on the cultural missions list as a needed town improvement, a chapel in Santa Cruz Etla would mean independence forever from any activities in San Pablo. Don Martín had started such a project, had laid a rough foundation near the schoolhouse just before World War II, but had to abandon it when prices went too high. Doña Estéfana, who was quite religious, thought Don Bartolo should have finished the chapel with locally made bricks. "Don Bartolo will never do this," she told me in 1945. "He is just a talker, not a doer. If a chapel were here, the priest would come to Santa Cruz Etla once a month as well as to San Pablo. What a great honor!"

Don Bartolo, who was not at all religious, answered me slyly when I asked him about it. "Oh, we could not finish the chapel with plain adobe bricks; that would be disrespectful to the saints." He would let it wait until the price of cement went down or until he was no longer president. Sometime before 1951 the crude foundation, so much in the way of the school children at play, had been removed chunk by chunk, to reinforce the dam across la zanja and the canalized sides on down the ridge, so they said; and the schoolyard was as hardpacked as ever, the whole chapel project evidently forgotten. I was surely surprised in 1954, then, as our poor old car rolled up behind the ox team, to see a brick church standing in what used to be the school garden, as if a fairy had waved a wand and set it there.

This church had been the joint idea of Don Martín and Don Féliz, on the basis of which Don Féliz got elected president in 1953. I suppose the school was a bigger project, when the people were less experienced; but it had been there before I ever came, and I had accepted it as a natural part of the community. Besides, it was made out of adobe, and it was always sagging at one end or the other, or was in need of new beams or windows or something for which I had myself often been agitating. The chapel, though, was all made out of city-bought bricks and newfangled hollow tile laid in alternate rows to make a pattern. It has an arched roof made of bricks and cement over reinforcing beams. At each side of the big front door—still unfilled by the carved wooden door Don Martín had planned—there is a little cupola for a bell, and on the rear roof there is a dome about four feet across. The whole building measures about twenty-five by thirty feet, larger than Don Marciano's new house, half as big and much better made than the school building. Don Amado had obtained plans for the school from Mexico City; this streamlined little church they had constructed all by themselves, without help or even interest from the bishop or from the Oaxaca State diocese.

The vote to build it had been taken at the election meeting of January, 1953. Every family had pledged one hundred pesos of cash money for the current year alone (what if it hadn't been a good corn year?); ten years earlier a hundred pesos was more cash than many a Santa Cruz family had in its possession in any one whole year. In addition, sixty grown men, grandfathers, fathers, and grown sons, had pledged to work on the church during the entire dry season, a time when they are usually cutting wood for more cash, or preparing the land for planting, or whittling out new farm implements, or repairing plows. They would work on the church until they finished it; they would have a better church than San Pablo; young priests just finishing training in the new seminary on the ridge south of San Lorenzo would come there to say mass every week. And they had finished it!

Don Marcelino's Perfecto, then twenty-three, had drawn a view of how the church should look in front. Don Marciano's Panfilo, home between his construction jobs, had shown the literate younger men, with crude drawings made on wrapping paper, how the foundation should be set, the brick walls laid, the arches set up, the bell cupolas and dome constructed. No homeowner in the United States building a garage for himself would dare start with such crudely drawn, eighth-grade-ish sort of "plans." The Santa Cruz people thought them fine plans. They hired the flour-delivering truck to bring up two loads of the bricks in October, as soon as the crops were in. They constructed the church simply by putting one brick to another, one shovelful of cement on top of another, with a full crew working every day in an old-fashioned barn-raising spirit that lasted for months. The annual fiesta is in May; they must have the church ready by the spring. Running out of funds, they could not put in any kind of flooring; and doors and bells worthy of such a church are expensive, in terms of dollars as well as of pesos. Rough planks used in the cement pouring were cleaned off to make a door that swings open and shut and can be locked with a padlock. The school bell, donated to the school by the Mexican federal government back in 1931 and ensconced all this time on top of the municipal building, serves triple duty now, calling to worship as well as to school and to emergency.

A hillside seminary, a four-mile walk away through the fields, began to take an interest in the earnest little community's brave new church, and it sent a young priest there to say mass for the May fiesta. The last of the funds were used to buy a large crucifix; families donated a Virgin of Guadalupe and various lesser saints; all these were set up inside the nave of the little church, the only part of it then whitewashed inside. Palm leaves from the valley and streamers of white crepe paper decorated the rest of the church. I was deeply touched when Don Féliz took me inside it, although I am a non-Catholic and have no strong religious convictions.

Don Féliz had hoped for my approval, and he hinted that there was something that I, and I alone, could do to help them. Surely he did not mean to give advice about planting vegetables—then what? I had forgotten the enthusiasm of the whole village over sketches I had made in Santa Cruz in other years. In fact, interest in making little water colors of the huts and of the view had been one of the excuses I had given the people for staying and staying on other occasions. I am an artist of the Winston Churchill type, without the Churchill ability, but I loved to sketch the Etla landscapes, and the people loved to watch me do it. On Doña Patrocina's portico in 1945 I had worked up some of the sketches into two oils, twenty by twenty-four inches, in the hope of having something from my Mexican hills to enter in amateur shows back home. Nine years and many amateur sketches later, I had forgotten that one of these was

83

of the church in San Pablo Etla, bright in the sunlight against the dark hills of the sierra and a glowering eastern sky. I remembered that the devout older women had often stopped by to see it, and that the men were only politely interested in a San Pablo picture, preferring an overcolored valley view I had done.

Now Don Féliz was asking me to make a painting of their own church. Though I admired its clean new brick lines, there was really nothing picturesque or charming about the bare little modern building itself. I could paint it only as one would paint a warehouse or a store front to please an advertising company—blue sky, red-brick front, brown-wood doors, white-cement roof. I could not fake in too much of the valley beyond it nor the woods behind it; it was set at an angle where such a view was impossible, and they did not want it faked at all. "*Absolutamente natural,* Doña Elena," said Don Féliz firmly. He knew I had a large paint kit with me, left up at Don Martín's. I could not say no. Two afternoons I spent on the mediocre picture. There is nothing I have done worse than this, with less artistic grace, in ten years; but nothing I have ever done has been more rapturously appreciated.

I spent the rest of the ten days visiting the school, chatting in the houseyards, and hiking over as much of the old trails as my forty-five-year-old bones wanted. On the Sunday my husband and the car came back, Don Féliz and the public works committee got the car easily up the trail. We sat down to dinner with Don Féliz and Don Martín, in Don Martín's houseyard, at a real table on real benches. Already Don Féliz had the painting above his desk in the muncipal building. Now he said he was going to accept it as my gift to Santa Cruz in front of everybody on the school steps after dinner. Everyone in town had already seen it, stopping by on their trips to and fro to watch me paint it. I felt it was so poor, I didn't even want my husband to see it.

Hoping to forestall Don Féliz' ceremony, I quickly suggested a further gift. Don Martín had told me that they could not put any floor in the church because unglazed flooring tile cost a hundred pesos a thousand. It would take two thousand tiles, and there would be no more money in the "building fund" until a crop should come in again. Even when it should, the families had bled themselves white for their contributions in 1953 and 1954. My husband and I have always traveled in Mexico on a very limited budget, forcing ourselves to think and plan purely in terms of pesos, not dollars—and two hundred pesos are two hundred pesos. But actually that was only sixteen dollars. If I had stayed in the nice Oaxaca hotel with my husband for the ten days and had eaten three meals a day there, I would surely have spent sixteen dollars. Life at Don Martín's had cost me nothing but a twenty-by-twenty-four-inch canvas, a little oil paint and turpentine, and a good car-wash job. So when Don Féliz gathered the council in the municipal building portico, preparatory to going out on the steps with the "masterpiece" of the church, I intervened to offer two hundred pesos to put in the tile floor. This unexpected donation made the painting fade into insignificance.

Fortunately my husband had four fifty-peso bills with him. We arranged photographs of the ceremony—Don Féliz taking the money from me, the public works committee posing with me and the money, the crowd in general. This was a larger cash contribution than any other family had made; I hope it has not caused everyone to go to greater effort and sacrifice in later years to outdo me and provide carved doors or an altar, on a two hundred pesos per family contribution!

Then the painting had to be brought out after all, while I apologized, asked what value it had for them anyway, and remarked that what the church would really need was a mural painting inside, not a smallish oil of the outside. Always so inadequate, my Spanish had grown exceedingly rusty, and Don Féliz misunderstood me. He though I was suggesting that I could paint the walls inside with religious murals of some kind. I, the painter of pallid little water-color landscapes! I, the lax in religion, with little knowledge of saints and holy things, much less the ability to paint them! I could only offer a second gift of two hundred pesos, sent them subsequently through the schoolteacher, with which they could paint the walls inside a soft rose color with calcimine, showing them in my paint box the color I would like it to be.

I thought that they were displeased when I said I could not stay to make a mural painting, and that the gift of the rose color seemed a poor substitute. They were all so still. Then I noticed that Don Féliz' eyes were filled with tears, and Don Martín was blowing his nose into a big red handkerchief. To clear the air of emotion, my husband urged us all to get down the trail past the bad place in the road before it should start to rain. So we set off, he driving at snail's pace and I walking with all the people; they bade me long good-byes and seemed undaunted that I had refused to be their Michelangelo.

I have never seen the chapel or the village since that day. Don Féliz would have no place to put me up; the schoolrooms are all in use all the time; and Don Martín is dead, his family in Oaxaca City. The younger generation of Santa Cruz still left in the town are friendly enough to welcome the gray-haired visitor, now nearly fifty, whom they first knew when they were in the first or second grade; but I feel shy about asking them for hospitality. So I don't know if the chapel is rose-colored inside today or not. The school affairs committee used to re-calcimine the school often in a different color. But I do know that the chapel is finished and that it is a great source of pride to those who still write to me.

PART TWO

Women, Also, Make a Town

※ I ※

THE CULTURAL MISSIONS LIST says also that rural improvement programs must "dignify the position of rural women." I don't think Santa Cruz Etla needs help along that line; the women held property, managed fiestas, and ran family affairs long before there was any "rural improvement" program in Mexico. When the school was founded, a mothers' club was organized immediately. Doña Estéfana, its president, had grandchildren, not children, in the school, but she was the only woman who could write, having also been taught by that grandfather she shared with Don Amado. She herself was the most "dignified rural woman" I ever knew—her round, wrinkled little face, thin braids of gray hair wrapped around her head, and her motherly smile only added to her dignity—and she dignified everyone else's position through a lifetime.

Dear Doña Estéfana! I will always be one of her *niñas*, her children. Her house is my house. She told me so everytime I came. *Es tu casa* (it is thy house), even the last time when she was too old and feeble to come out and greet me. She was so little, coming barely to my shoulder, that if I didn't mind being disrespectful, I could have returned her embrace of greeting by picking her right up off the ground.

But that would have hurt her dignity. At eighty, she was still the head of a household; her son, her son-in-law, her grown grand-sons, and her three tiny great-grandchildren respected her every word. She owned eight hectares of land, almost twenty acres, more than any other family in Santa Cruz Etla. Her grandfather had been the first to clear the land and settle in the *pueblo*. Only one of her grandsons had ever gone to cut wood in the mountains; there was always so much work to do on the land. Throughout the last fifty years, it has been Doña Estéfana's land which has provided corn for sale during bad seasons. In the driest year Doña Estéfana had a surplus; she made all the cash she ever needed by selling corn. She could trade it to Don Bartolo for a tender young goat, to an-other neighbor for a side of beef during a butchering. No other family has ever quite as much corn as it needs, for tortillas, for seed, for cash sales, or for the levy for the church building.

By 1950 she was no longer the "wealthiest" person in Santa Cruz Etla. Don Martín made many pesos a month cash on his bread, Don Eduardo on the gasoline mill. These "newfangled" ways of acquiring wealth did not disturb Doña Estéfana's position in the community. She could never serve on the town council, no woman could, but she certainly could influence the choice of candidates for it. Don Bartolo, asking me in 1945 about the abandonment of the old church project, said: "What did Doña Estéfana say to you about my ideas as president?"

Scorn of "newfangled" things kept her very old-fashioned. She wore long, sweeping, full skirts, all hand-sewn—no sewing machine in *her* home. Although her house, one of the largest in town, was always "my house," and I once spent two weeks in it, I preferred in 1954 to live at Don Martín's where there were chairs. I am ashamed of seeking bodily comfort above comfort of the heart, for I have happy memories of Doña Estéfana's house from the first. Here is what I wrote of her in my 1934 notes:

I walked out this morning to visit the home of the president of the Mothers' Club, who lives in a large, two-room adobe house up the hill. We sat down to chat with her and her widowed daughter Doña Sofía, a woman about thirty, who was making tortillas over a wood fire in a little bamboo-and-mud kitchen room off the portico. The glow on the tortillas, the woman's pretty face, and the many colorful clay pots hanging on the mud walls impressed me as a fine subject for an oil. [I considered myself a much better artist in 1934 than I did in 1954.] I asked Doña Sofía if she would pose, and then rushed back to the school for my sketching materials. When I returned, they had cleaned up the houseyard, borrowed a bench across the trail, and were waiting to greet me as company. Doña Sofía had done up her hair and had quit making tortillas. With difficulty, I persuaded her to go back to work. [I had more trouble with Spanish then.] When a preliminary sketch was done, they gave me two fresh eggs as souvenirs.

I finished the picture, as I remember; a large, splashy, chromotype oil with poor perspective on the house beams. The 1954 painting of the new church was surely twenty years better than that. But people have always asked me about this picture, every visit since, and I do not remember where it is. Doña Sofía herself has been very disappointed that I do not carry it around with me.

On one occasion, in that summer of 1934, Doña Estéfana loaned me a burro for a trip to the Oaxaca City market, and she laughed delightedly at my awkwardness in getting on it. A Oaxaca-type market burro always has a large pannier hanging on each side, before any passenger embarks. It is best approached from the top, by climbing on the school porch rail above it, for instance. One of our best movie sequences taken that summer is of Doña Estéfana's face as she watched me do this.

When I came for a two weeks' visit ten years later, Doña Estéfana's house was the logical choice for my stay, since I was not sponsored by the school and there was no longer an empty room in the school building, anyway. "You have such a fine house, with a real bed," I told her in accepting her hospitality, that first time that I actually lived in one of the community's homes. "Everyone will come to see me if I live with you, and will tell me how the ten years have passed."

The first "way the ten years had passed" was news about Doña Sofía, subject of the painting. Tinier even than her mother, Doña Sofía had a pretty little face which made her seem younger than her years. She had married at eighteen, and had borne a son, Joel. Two months after her husband had died of the "water sickness," she had borne her second son, Inocencio. In 1934 Inocencio, then two, had been the pet of Doña Estéfana's household. Our movie shows him pattering along the school trail after his mother or playing with the baby chickens in Doña Estéfana's houseyard. Of course, we asked about Inocencio as soon as we arrived in 1944. Doña Estéfana gravely told us that he was an *angelito*, that he died of the "stomach sickness," *mal de estómago*, and that his godfather had given a wonderful party at his funeral. Happily for Doña Sofía, Doña Estéfana's acreage had attracted a youngish widower, Don Pablo Bautista, who was later to go to work in the United States. Doña Sofía had married him in 1938, at thirty-three, and had borne him a son, Leopoldo, who was five years old in 1944. Don Pablo built a house for her on Doña Estéfana's house lot, so that Doña Estéfana still had a small, spoiled grandson around her doorstep.

Doña Estéfana was not so happy about her only son, Ignacio. He had married a woman from San Pablo Etla, big-mouthed and freckle-faced. Everyone knows how common and homely those San Pablo Etla women are. Don Ignacio, when Doña Sofía's first husband had died and she had come home to live, had removed himself and his wife to the in-laws in San Pablo Etla, taking with him his little son Aurelio, the age of Joel. He had agreed to work his mother's land, a big job then with no grown boys and no strong brother-in-law to help, but his wife refused to be dominated any longer by Doña Estéfana. The old lady cried whenever she spoke about it. The moving of Sofía to Don Pablo's new house had made it possible for Ignacio to live at home again, and they had evidently tried it; but the women couldn't get along. This time they left Aurelio, by then fourteen and in the school's fourth class, to live with his grandmother. Even this did not satisfy Doña Estéfana. Three times in those two weeks I lived with her, she said: "Mothers do all the suffering in the world, and after twenty years have nothing to show for it."

Aurelio, now an important young man of the community, is happily married to a girl of whom Doña Estéfana approved highly, and *his* little son was the pet around the house in 1954. The family had only one favor to ask of me then: Would I take a photo of this two-year-old child in his baptismal dress? They had waited to have him baptised until the young priest came to the new church built in Santa Cruz, on which Ignacio and Aurelio had both worked long hours. This child, as the only son of the only son, will inherit Doña Estéfana's house and yard, and probably a full half of the farm land, since Sofía's half will go to her two sons.

In so doing, Aurelio's baby will inherit the largest house built in Santa Cruz Etla before Don Marciano's Panfilo learned how to build his father such a fine one. Although Doña Estéfana's house was all one room, with the lean-to kitchen, and was old and musty and dark inside, it was honored also as the first house built on the Santa Cruz Etla site. On its adobe altar, built in as a solid "bench" at the end of the room, was a picture of the Virgin of Soledad, patroness of Oaxaca City. Six other saints surrounded her, framed in dusty lace. Wreaths of paper and bouquets of faded paper flowers dating from Doña Sofía's second wedding were still on the altar in 1944. At the other end of the room was the "real bed" I had spoken of so hopefully. It was made of three boards nailed to a head and a foot. The head was carved in a Spanish colonial style, and it had been brought by Doña Estéfana's grandfather to the house when it was built. On top of the boards was the usual straw mat. The carved head was the only thing which made the bed any different from any other "bed" in Santa Cruz Etla. Since the three boards had been slept on so long, and had helped wear out so many straw mats, they were the home of various insects by the hundreds.

Once when Doña Estéfana came to visit me at Doña Patrocina's in 1945, she asked: "Are those bites on your legs chinches [bedbugs]? You did not get bedbugs at my house. Do they have bedbugs in the United States? There are very few here because bedbugs do not like a *petate*, but only a mattress. When a *petate* gets full of bedbugs, it can be used for burro-pack pads, or charcoal brazier fans, and you can buy a new *petate*. You can never get the bedbugs out of a mattress, and people can afford only one mattress in a lifetime."

By a mattress, Doña Estéfana meant a pad as thin as a sleeping bag; I had no such pad on Doña Estéfana's ancestral bed. So it was probably not bedbugs I had there, but fleas, those elusive disturbers of the night which can never be found in the morning. The bed, fleas or no, gave a distinction to Doña Estéfana's house. She had also an unusually fine carved chest, perhaps older than she was. It always held her clothes, her neatly ironed pink and yellow Oaxaqueña-style skirts, two yards around the bottom and gored at the top, her white blouses with lace yokes, her petticoats edged in lace, as were no others in Santa Cruz Etla. Behind the chest, when I lived there, were strange things to be side by side: one a bright 1944 calendar showing luscious young Mexico City girls in the red, white, and green *China Poblana* costume practically unknown in Santa Cruz Etla; the other, a dusty dancer's mask of the ancient Indian dances. Sometimes there is dancing in costume at the May fiesta, but such a crude animal's face mask has not been used in Santa Cruz Etla since Doña Sofía was a little girl.

One night, when we lighted two candles for me to eat my *cena* (which is what they call supper) sitting on an upturned log at the adobe altar shelf, the flickering light lit up the tiger mask and reflected back from many glazed Oaxaca-ware pots hung on pegs among the cobwebs against the bare adobe. Doña Estéfana's house was not whitewashed inside and would never be in her lifetime. It was inconvenient to live there, but I loved it anyway. The carved bed and the chest represented the integrity and the changelessness of Santa Cruz Etla. And I had a white drawn-work altar cloth made by Doña Estéfana's mother, as finely worked as lace made by a Spanish grandame, to serve as a tablecoth at the altar. It was here, after these suppers, that Don Amado came to his cousin's house to

93

tell me all the history of the Santa Cruz community, and to inspire me to try sometime to write about it.

I had no complaint about the food at Doña Estéfana's that year. She had half a small goat from Don Bartolo's and served it three days with rice, like mutton stew. Full of tomatoes, chiles, and onions, it was very tasty and fairly fresh, since the goat had just been butchered. Fresh rice was cooked every day. The fourth day we went back to beans; but Doña Estéfana had many chickens, and we always had eggs. Two that I ate were laid right up on my bed, for the chickens came in the house as soon as we got out in the morning.

After the egg breakfast, I would watch women who came to buy corn, as it was just before the harvest when the last year's corn was gone. If Doña Estéfana did not have it shucked, the women would stop to husk the dry ears and to shell off the kernels. Doña Estéfana, as a matter of family pride, kept the pure white ears and sold the ears mottled with black. Thus, her tortillas would always be pure white, while those of the families who had to buy her corn would be streaked blue-gray. No one seemed to resent this, and Doña Estéfana always did it. The women chatted with me about my previous visit, about the days when the school was first founded, about its years of success under its first teacher. "They were good years for corn, too," said Sofía.

The last morning of the 1944 visit, I sat in the middle of the ox-cart trail and made a water-color sketch of Doña Estéfana's house, much better work than my ambitious attempt at the interior ten years earlier. Her porch, with its red-brick columns against the dark of the doorway, made a contrast of light and shadow. (Where did her grandfather get the red brick? it occurs to me to wonder as I write this. There was no other red brick in Santa Cruz Etla until Don Féliz built the church.)

Soon a crowd had gathered as I painted. Don Pablo, Doña Estéfana's son-in-law, talked to the crowd for me, as he had seen me sketch before. The *señora* used only brook water to mix the paint; the little tubes and cakes were full of color; those dark green splotches were supposed to be the trees. With all this help, my drawing prospered. Doña Estéfana was delighted with it because it showed her, a vague figure in the doorway. Her spirit must have cast a charm on it, because it is one of the few water colors I have ever successfully entered in a competition. When I tried to tell the people about it during the next visit, bragging of the success I achieved with the painting of Doña Estéfana's house, I could not explain to them what a water-color competition was.

When I left Santa Etla after that 1944 visit in Doña Estéfana's house, the director of rural education in Oaxaca sent his young man secretary in a station wagon to get me. It was a Saturday market day, and everyone was going on foot or on burro to the Oaxaca market, this being before the dramatic coming of the San Lorenzo bus. I was loaded with the usual presents of fruit and eggs which the people always gave me at parting. My husband, who had been staying in Oaxaca, came along with the secretary to see his old friends, as he has done since in our own car. I had bidden a lingering good-bye to Doña Estéfana and Doña Sofía and the rest of the family when the *camioneta* called for me, far up the ridge. Then we stopped below the school to say many more good-byes, and the *camioneta* bumped slowly down the trail, while I leaned out to shake hands and to receive more presents. Still, a station wagon is pretty big, and there was room for one more. Then down below on the trail we espied Doña Estéfana; she had evidently left for market right after my departure and was walking briskly along carrying a huge donkey pannier.

"Pick up my friend and hostess, will you please, señor?" I asked the secretary. Undoubtedly he was surprised. Although the director was in charge of rural schools in Indian villages and was a fine man who had done a great deal for the people, they were *los pobrecitos,* the poor little ones, to him, and doubtlessly to his secretary also. *Los pobrecitos* did not ride in official station wagons; they walked. They had always done so, and undoubtedly always would. Still, to honor the request of the visitor from the United States, the secretary stopped and Doña Estéfana got in.

It was her first ride in a private car. If she was thrilled, she did not show it. She knew the secretary considered her a *pobrecita.* Perhaps she almost considered herself one, as we reached the better-traveled road and sped on into the modernized city. She had nothing to say, while I chattered to my husband in the back seat, relieved to let out a torrent of English for the first time in many days. I did not mean to neglect her, but I stopped first to thank the driver when he let us off at the inn door. When I turned to embrace Doña Estéfana once more and to tell her my good-bye and heart-felt thanks all over again, she was gone. She had vanished into the crowds of the Oaxaca market, just another poor old Indian woman in from the hills on market day.

The next year, at the age of seventy, she was still able to walk with me halfway to the bus road when I left, tears running down her face. "When you come again, Doña Elena, perhaps I, like Don Amado, will no longer be here," she said. In 1954 this was so nearly true that I have tears running down *my* face now writing about her. Helpless with arthritis, her mind wandering from her eighty-year-old body, she lay in the dark in Dona Sofía's house. Her "bed" had been brought over there, because Aurelio's busy young wife could not give her the constant care she needed. Surely Sofía would never admit that she was waiting for the old woman to die; but it is true that the rest of Sofía's family, Don Pablo her second husband and Leopoldo her youngest son, were both in Mexico City, and they told me later in the same summer that they could not send for Sofía because she had to stay with the old lady.

Doña Estéfana called me by name, even there in the dim adobe room, and embraced me, and held my hand all the time I stayed. But I am sure she did not know what I was saying. I came in three other times during my ten-day visit at Don Martín's; every time she greeted me afresh as if I had just come to Santa Cruz after long absence. Don Ignacio, coming up from San Pablo to see me the day of Don Féliz' little ceremony, had wondered why I did not go to visit his mother. She had begun to whimper when he mentioned the fiesta dinner for me and had said: "How long has Doña Elena been in Santa Cruz? She has never been to see me one time. How could she have neglected me so?"

So I went again just an hour before I left, and she was surprised all over again, saying, "I must tell Ignacio you are here; he will be

96

so pleased when he comes up from San Pablo." I hoped then that Doña Estéfana, she who had done so much to "dignify the position of rural women," would not have to linger long in such indignity. Only a few months later the son of Sofía and Don Pablo, the boy Leopoldo who now works in Mexico City, wrote me of her quiet death and of the fine funeral Don Martín, himself still alive and in fine fettle, arranged in order to honor her in the eyes of all Santa Cruz Etla.

I REALLY LEARNED the ways of life in Santa Cruz by living for a summer in Doña Patrocina's house. In 1945 when I knew I would be making a longer visit and there was still no room for me in the school building, I decided to live with Doña Patrocina, midwife and cure woman for simple little ills in the town. There were two rooms at her house. I could have a little privacy there, or so I thought. Doña Patrocina's son went back and forth oftener to market; they all lived a little more "modern" life there than at Doña Estéfana's. I gave Dona Estéfana the excuse that I wanted to "visit around," that Patrocina's was closer to the school where I hoped to help in the campaign against illiteracy. Doña Estéfana was satisfied, if I would visit her often. So I took all the things I had brought with me and moved into Patrocina's house for a long stay.

I had purchased staple foods in Oaxaca City—sugar and cocoa, rice and macaroni, onions and cheese, tomatoes, and many candles. I knew the people of Santa Cruz could not afford to buy these staples in any quantity, and I did not want to be a burden. I took no bedding (we had taken blankets and mattresses to the school in 1934) since I was to be a house guest this year and did not want to offend my hostess. I was sorry for this many chill nights at that altitude, when I was wrapped only in one old flea-infested *sarape,* lying on a hard *petate,* night after night; but Patrocina's family made sacrifices to give me that one blanket. As for clothes, I had three khaki shirts, a divided riding skirt (the good ladies of Santa Cruz Etla would be offended at a woman in pants), and one change of underclothes. I had also some simple first-aid supplies, water-color and oil sketching equipment, a Spanish dictionary and grammar, a camera and films. All but the sketching things were fitted into one suitcase. In 1954 I wore dark, little, crinkled nylon dresses, so easy to wash in the brook below Don Martín's, but they were not yet for sale in 1945. The suitcase, the first-aid container, the oil paint box, all have now been to Santa Cruz Etla four times.

Doña Patrocina, my hostess, was more than a friend; she was practically my foster mother. Busy as she was with her routine of daily tasks the year round, she concentrated on my comfort and happiness all summer.

There is a "Song of the Mixtecs" which is sung everwhere in the Oaxaca Valley. *Qué lejos estoy, del cielo donde he nacido* (How far I am from the skies under which I was born). It has a very sad tune and ends tragically—"I long to cry, I wish I might die, from sentimental feeling." I had heard this song when visiting schools in Oaxaca City just the week before, and it was still running in my head. The first days at Doña Patrocina's I sang it over and over under my breath. On the third day I came into her little kitchen portico to find her standing looking at me with tears in her eyes. She opened her arms and took me in a great *abrazo*, or embrace.

"Poor Doña Elena, we have not made her happy. She is longing for her own country. She is so far away and alone. Don Enrique is at the ocean; she is worrying about him," she said, speaking of me in the third person, as she patted my shoulder.

"Whatever makes you think that, Doña Patrocina? I have never been among better friends in my life," I retorted.

"But you are singing the 'Song of the Mixtecs'! You keep singing it every day. The little grandmother here in the house heard you yesterday singing 'I wish I might die.'"

It was very hard to convince her that I merely liked the tune and couldn't get it out of my head. Since so many Spanish or Mexican folk tunes are concerned with the same general theme—the sadness of parting, the longing for home and sweetheart, the tragedy of being exiled—I had to be careful what I was singing the rest of the summer. It was best to hum American tunes so Doña Patrocina would not worry about my homesickness.

Doña Patrocina herself had had a life of tragedy. She was married at eighteen into the house of Don Pedro López. It was a fine house on the central ridge, and her husband was in possession of five acres of land. Soon her husband's parents died, and he was in possession of the house also. They seemed destined for a happy life together. Chico, who was really named Francisco, was born to them. Then followed tragedy. Three children in succession were born dead, or died before their first birthdays. Nico (Nicolás, twenty-three in 1945) was the only other child who had lived. When he was eight years old, and two other children had been born and had died, the father himself died in an accident. I never quite understood about it, some sort of mishap while cutting timber. All such accidents, falls, or axe blows are described by the single word *golpe; un golpe en la sierra* is never explained further.

This *golpe* left Doña Patrocina desperate. Chico was fourteen, a young vaquero for his mother's goats before any school came to Santa Cruz Etla. Doña Patrocina sold her few goats and her cow to pay for her husband's funeral fiesta. Chico drove the oxen to plow, while Doña Patrocina herself went on foot to town in the valley, every day for months, to visit with an old medicine woman. There she learned to be herself a *curandera*, a healer. She could prescribe herbs or hot packs for small ills, and serve as midwife at births. For this she would get a few eggs, or in the case of births, a chicken or even a young pig.

So they managed to live. Nico was the best boy student in school when we lived in the school building in 1934; Chico, working in fields in the daytime, learned to read and write in evening classes that were held the first few years after the school was founded. At one time he wrote the best hand in Santa Cruz Etla, after Don Amado died and before Cassiano and Perfecto grew up. From his mother's brother, Don Fausto, one of the town's musicians, he learned to play the violin. When Nico was old enough to plow and care for the stock, Chico became a *leñador*, a woodcutter. By 1944

99

he could make three pesos a day, any day he went to the sierra, and so he had recently married and brought his bride home. Doña Patrocina's household was again one of the important families of Santa Cruz Etla.

Doña Patrocina held her own mother and brother together as well as her sons. When her widowed mother could no longer live alone, she too came to Doña Patrocina's. Don Fausto, the musician, Doña Patrocina's only brother, took as second wife a widow with land, and she would not care for the little grandmother who had been keeping Don Fausto's house for him. So she came to Patrocina's and brought her flock of turkeys with her; Fausto told me he had "all respect and gratitude to Patrocina for taking the little grandmother." By 1954 the little grandmother was dead, and Don Fausto's new wife, on some kind of an arrangement like Don Julio's and Doña Fecunda's, had left him. So the kindhearted Doña Patrocina, her house now overflowing with daughters-in-law and grandchildren, had taken Fausto in also, and thus he was able to play the fiddle with Chico every night.

Doña Patrocina was lean and lithe, though she must have been sixty, as light on her feet as her young daughter-in-law. She wore long full dresses, originally like those worn by Doña Estéfana, but the few she owned were ragged and patched and faded out to a dull grayish-white. She had never worn shoes; she had few pretty things in her house; but she was always very clean and was a very good cook.

You have to be busy all day to be a good cook in any Mexican Indian family. The mainstay, the "staff of life" is the humble corn tortilla, that flat cake made of ground corn and water and patted out by hand. Doña Patrocina's family, small in 1945, ate sixty or seventy a day. In that year Esperanza, the new little bride, made them, as befits any young daughter-in-law. But think of the years Doña Patrocina did it, probably thirty-one years at least when she was the only one to make them for growing boys, fifty tortillas a day, three hundred sixty-five days a year, for thirty-one years, and most of those years before any gasoline mill in the village did half the corn grinding.

To make her tortillas, she put a large cooking jar, an *olla,* on the charcoal fire burning in a little pit hole in the floor of the earth-packed portico, and filled the *olla* with whole kernels of corn mixed with salt and a pinch of lye. She let the corn cook soft like hominy. Next morning Esperanza took the cooked corn to Don Julio's mill when she first got up, and it came back a moist mass like cooked corn meal. Even then it was not ground fine enough for any Santa Cruz Etla housewife. Everyone of them felt that she must always grind it again to a paste, working it back and forth under the "rolling-pin stone," up and down the *metate,* which is the three-legged stone grinder that they use. Then with a quick movement, Doña Patrocina, who after those thirty years was much better at it than Esperanza, picked up a little pat of corn paste. In a twinkling it was patted out expertly between her hands into a broad thin flat pancake.

This is not as easy as it looks. My husband took a movie of me trying it myself, that summer at the school in 1934, and a sorry mess I made of it, ending up with a great hole in the center where most of the tortilla should be. Tortillas in Santa Cruz Etla are very large, anyway, probably eight or ten inches in diameter; anyone could make the four-inch tortillas of the Mexican west coast. When I asked Doña Patrocina about the size, she was surprised that I thought her tortillas were large. "You should see the large ones made by the *primitivos* [the non-Spanish-speaking Indians from the high sierra]. They are big enough to use as a *petate,*" she exaggerated.

Tortillas are cooked on the greaseless, flat, clay griddle, two at a time. Most women use kindling wood instead of charcoal to make the griddle really hot. At just the right moment, Doña Patrocina would flip the tortillas over. Sometime I would like to try one hot from Doña Patrocina's griddle, filled with melted butter—a thought I also had in connection with Don Martín's bread hot from the oven—but it would be impossible in a town where all milk is either drunk fresh, boiled for "coffee with milk," or curdled for cheese, and never allowed to set for cream to be churned for butter.

When twenty or so tortillas were made and packed under an

101

embroidered tortilla cloth in the bottom of a basket to keep warm, then we all knew it was time for breakfast. There is no "time" in all Santa Cruz, not clock time. The women get up and take the corn to mill; the men care for the stock; the women make twenty tortillas, and it is breakfast time. Nico and Chico came in from the house-yard; they sat with Doña Patrocina and the little grandmother on the floor of the "kitchen," the outside portico. Esperanza served them hot tortillas, beans warmed from the day before, and black coffee without sugar, made from home-ground coffee berries.

Unfortunately, I was seldom allowed to eat with them this way. Knowing that I ate at the "altar" at Doña Estéfana's, and at a school desk when staying in the school building, Doña Patrocina was deter-mined to have me eating at a table. Her only table, which usually held *ollas* for cooking and baskets of onions and Chico's fiddle and some candles and the curing herbs, was taken from the dark, inside room and set out on the porch. The articles from it were piled on the floor next to my *petate*. Three tortilla-warming cloths served in turn as tablecloth. I sat in stiff formality on a homemade chair to eat my breakfast and my dinner.

It was the preparation of my dinner which made the most trouble for Doña Patrocina. She had asked me what I would eat, there all summer so alone, so far "from the skies under which I was born."

"Oh, eggs, tomatoes, avocados, and cheese," I told her, showing her also the rice and macaroni I had brought. "Don't worry about me."

The tomatoes and cheese I brought myself were gone the first night; I had asked so many people in for supper. Chico brought more cheese when he went to market. A family in San Pablo sent up tomatoes, which were cut up with onions like a salad. Doña Patrocina boiled the macaroni in plain water; I eased it down with bites of avocados and white goat's-milk cheese spread on tortillas. This lasted five days. I got sick from the water. I got better. I looked with longing at the beans and the little green-corn tamales the family had for dinner the sixth day.

Would Doña Elena just try the green-corn tamales; a special

ía Estéfana in 1951. The baby is her great grandchild,
of Aurelio.

Doña Estéfana's beloved
great-grandchild in 1954.
Taking this photo of the
child was the last favor
I could do for her.

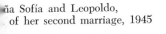

ña Sofía and Leopoldo,
of her second marriage, 1945

On the porch at Doña Estéfana's, 1944
left to right – Doña Rufina, wife of
Amado, Doña Estéfana, Leopoldo then
four years old, his mother Doña Sofia

La Abuelita feeding the terrible turkeys in the cold gray dawn, 1945

La Abuelita in 1945. this photo of her which Pat had enlarged in color in O

Doña Patrocina making tortillas in 1945

Doña Patrocina with her two daughters-in-law and the author in 1954

treat, from irrigated land planted to corn in the dry season, and ripe early?

Surely Doña Elena would—almost anything. Then I found out about the misunderstanding. I had meant only that I *could* get along on that simple list of things, but I would joyfully eat anything else.

So I had other things. Little beefsteaks pounded tender on the *metate* with a pestle and fried in lard in the bottom of a green-glazed pottery dish. Whole roasting ears of green corn. Ribs and kidneys of freshly butchered young kids, and sometimes tough pieces of salted, fried old goat. Once tripe, and another time liver, and a third time heart, from butcherings on the San Lorenzo ridge. Chicken twice, too, boiled with onions in my rice or macaroni. But never pork or turkey; they are for fiestas. With the meat I often had *garbanzos* (the Mexican chick-peas), green bean pods, and always *salsa*.

Salsa is what makes Mexican cooking be Mexican cooking. Doña Patrocina made two kinds, red chile sauce and green chile sauce. She would take two or three little red tomatoes, pound them up in the stone mortar with a pestle and add a diced-up onion. Then she took a dried red chile pepper and ground it up on the *metate*. This added to the tomatoes and onion makes a sauce strong enough to take the skin off the roof of your mouth. If the chiles Doña Patrocina had were green and fresh, she would use the *tomatillos*, small green tomatoes. Either one or the other was served me in a little clay dish at every meal. The family would also have such a dish on the center of the floor, and would dip each bit of tortilla into it. Most Mexican food—beans, squashes, boiled meat, rice—is tasteless of itself. You need only to add as much *salsa* as you want.

Doña Patrocina cooked some things with the chile right in the cooking, so hot I couldn't eat them. Chicken was often covered with a sauce called *mole*, made of special dark-red chiles. Eggs were fried in a sort of omelette with onions and green chiles cut up in them. Cheese was stuffed into green chiles, rolled in egg, and fried. These green chiles would almost cause a blister in my mouth anywhere they touched the membrane.

The green chiles, or the cheese, or anything else on hand for cooking, were kept in baskets on pegs around the walls of the main room. Doña Patrocina would take a big, flat basket and collect the few things she needed to cook for the midday meal, then sit or kneel down on the floor of the open kitchen portico before the charcoal fire. The fire itself was made by burning chunks of charcoal in a ring of stones. The charcoal was lighted by blowing on the still-live embers of yesterday's charcoal. I saw Doña Patrocina use a match only twice all summer.

The list of goals for cultural missionaries to the hill villages mentions many things housewives and mothers should be taught. After the use of pure water and green vegetables, the third item of importance is: "Teach them to construct elevated cooking places." Even the families of the teachers who lived at the school cooked on a floor-level charcoal fire in a bamboo lean-to at the back. Doña Patrocina couldn't have cooked efficiently on a waist-level stove, for she had everything she used around her on the floor—a jar of water from the brook, six glazed clay bowls for individual family servings, the three metal spoons and the one sharp knife she owned, the two china cups, the clay dishes for frying and boiling. Hunched there on her knees, she would work all morning getting me the midday meal. Each little clay pot would boil away on a separate little charcoal pile, propped up by stones. She often had to stop her preparations to fan the charcoal vigorously so the pots would go on boiling.

The last pot she boiled for me every meal was a little *olla* of hot water and orange leaves. This orange-leaf tea is very tasty and fragrant, and I pretended to like it even more than I did. At least it was always boiled; that was one way of drinking lots of water without getting the dysentery. I did not care for the scorched, black coffee served in Santa Cruz Etla morning and night. Only Doña Estéfana, who owned a milking cow, or those families who used goat milk, made the common Mexican breakfast coffee with boiled milk.

All these elaborate preparations were for the *comida*, the midday meal, which was their big meal of the day. It was served about

104

an hour after noon, a time everyone kept track of because the school
bell rang every day when the children went home for dinner. In
many parts of Mexico the people take a nap after this heavy dinner,
returning to their work about three-thirty. I never saw anyone in
Santa Cruz Etla take this siesta. Spoiled by a lazy life for several
days in Oaxaca City, I took siestas myself at first. I only made Doña
Patrocina worry about me all the more. She feared I was sick. There
are so many jobs in a hill village for everyone to do, that only the
teachers take an hour or two off after dinner.

Supper comes just before dark, a very light meal called *cena*,
usually warmed over from dinner. It was at a *cena* that I myself
first became one of the family. I had had a good new dish for
dinner, *papitos,* potato cakes made with egg and onion and fried
in lard. When Dona Patrocina asked me what I wanted for supper,
I said: "Are there any more *papitos?*" not realizing what a favor I
was asking.

Assured that there were more, I wandered off down the brook
in the twilight. When I returned fifteen minutes later, she had
just finished peeling fresh potatoes and was blowing up the fire to
get them boiling. I took over the blowing job when she went to
get more water. Then we sat in the now darkened portico and chatted while the potatoes boiled. Soon Nico brought the oxen up from
the fields, Chico came down from cutting wood in the mountains,
and Esperanza came back from a visit home. We all sat around the
charcoal fire teasing Esperanza about going back to her mother.
Doña Patrocina took the potatoes off the fire, mashed them up,
steaming, on the stone grinder, and added eggs to make the patties.

When the *papitos* were finally done, an hour after I had asked
for them, I passed them around to everyone, one apiece. We all had
the common Mexican brown beans, left over from dinner. I drank
my orange-leaf tea, they their coffee. That was the first time I had
ever been asked to eat with the family; and I wasn't really *asked*
that time; I just "horned in" during the long wait. But I had *cena*
with them always after that, sitting cross-legged on the dirt floor,
eating my beans by the light of a wood torch and dipping my
tortillas in the *salsa* bowl on the ground in the center. It broke the

lonesomeness of my dignified noonday dinners at the table with the tablecoth. We often sang at the *cena,* and Chico would play his fiddle in the dark. No one had that much time at dinner; someone had to keep watching all the *ollas,* and someone else must keep making fresh tortillas for the hungry men.

There were two *metates* for making tortillas at Doña Patrocina's. One of them Doña Patrocina herself brought as a bride, the traditional gift of the bride's family. The other was in the house when the house was built up around it by the first bride and groom, fifty years before Doña Patrocina became the third bride. She did not know where the second, in-between *metate* had gone. Neither Esperanza, nor later Nico's wife, the most recent bride, brought a *metate* with her, so perhaps this custom as a gift for brides is going out; not the use of a *metate,* however, which will last as long as Mexican villagers eat tortillas, mechanical corn grinders or no. An individual *metate* lasts forever. In the most ancient ruins of the earliest Indians in Mexico, stone grinders have been found on which any Santa Cruz Etla housewife could make tortillas today.

Doña Patrocina's house is a good house; there are two rooms (my reason for choosing it above Doña Estéfana's) and in one of them is a window with wooden shutters. The bride and groom used this room, sleeping in the part of it which was not used for storing corn or fodder. But they closed the window very tightly at night, and the wooden door as well, to keep out the "bad night air." I slept in the "big" room, as they called it. Doña Patrocina and the little grandmother slept there too, as well as the dog, the two cats, and the four chickens. My presence put Nico out in the cold on the open portico, but he bundled himself into his large *sarape* and did not seem to mind. I preferred myself to sleep indoors, even in the stuffy, airless adobe house, because at that altitude it was cold at night.

In the big room, after the table and the "chair" were put outdoors for me to eat my dinner, nothing was left but the altar and the *petates* and the two bridal chests. A bride's godmother gives her a carved wooden chest which she uses as a dresser and closet all her married life. All the clothing of the family was kept in Doña

Patrocina's old chest or in Esperanza's new one. So also were painted gourd dishes for fiestas, and extra candles for the saints, and the music for Chico's fiddle, and other such special things. On the altar in the center was a picture of the Virgin of Guadalupe, the patron saint of Mexico. This was the only picture of this Virgin in Santa Cruz Etla, a fact which worked hardship on Doña Patrocina during her years of widowhood, since she was obligated to give a sort of "open house" celebration for all the village on December 12, the saint's name day.

As soon as Don Féliz opened the new church to let me see the inside of it in 1954, I noticed a painting of the Virgin of Guadalupe at the improvised altar he had set up. I never liked to ask, but I am sure it was Doña Patrocina's; that year there was no Virgin of Guadalupe in her house, but only a chromo of the Sacred Heart of Jesus. A water-color sketch, eight by ten inches, that I made of the San Pablo church preparatory to painting a larger oil, was still on her altar in 1954, by the way, very faded and warped after nine years in the dust, but perhaps seen constantly by enough people to remind them that I must eventually make a better picture of the new Santa Cruz church.

In my 1934 diary, when I described a visit I made to Doña Patrocina's, I made a notation about a sign stuck on the door. It was during the difficulties between the church and the government in Mexico, and I was quick to pick up "sociological data." "Protect our church from the president," it said. "Our schools should belong to the church!" In 1945 the sign was still there, dusty and yellowed, but well pasted on; in 1954 a large fly-specked corner still stuck tenaciously through the two decades. Since there has never been but the one school in Santa Cruz Etla, and Doña Patrocina has never voted for a president in her life, and cannot read the sign anyway, I do not think the sign really ever was a point of "sociological data" at all. I never asked her how it happened to be there.

Doña Patrocina had been able to raise a little livestock. Chico had three burros, a brown one and two gray ones; there were a team of black and white oxen and two hogs. The little grandmother had brought turkeys with her when she came to live at Doña

Patrocina's, and they had the run of the house and yard all day, making life noisy and unpleasant, unless by chance you like turkeys "in the raw." The chickens, cats, and dogs lived in the house, really, not in the yard where the oxen were tethered. Of all these *animalitos* only the two cats had names; Doña Patrocina called them Sentinela and Golondrina and was very fond of them. When I asked her in 1954 about Golondrina, she knew right away what I meant; and tears filled her eyes as she described how the poor tabby, grown old and feeble, had been crushed under the plodding hoofs of the yoked oxen.

The pride of Doña Patrocina's house is the three great mango trees. I have never seen bigger ones. They shade all the place where the animals are tethered and cast a shadow over the portico most of the day. Mangoes are thick in them all summer long. Doña Patrocina had not time through the years to grow a flower garden; she could only keep the little orange and lemon trees for the leaves of her poultices and the little square of herb garden behind the house.

I had the idea of making a list of the things inside such a house as Doña Patrocina's, the things she and the boys really needed to carry on their life. There were those dishes they ate out of, the eight clay pots or pitchers of various sizes she cooked with, the ten-gallon clay water jars. Five market baskets hung on the walls; two woven corncribs held shelled corn and beans in the bridal room; two round baskets were used to take corn to the mill and to keep the tortillas warm when they were made. In the corner behind the two *metates,* were six little sadirons to be heated over charcoal. In the bridal room also were kept the plow, the pack harnesses for the burros, and a few simple tools for woodworking.

Four *petates,* woven of river reeds in the valley towns, were kept for the family (and the guest) to use as beds. They could be rolled up in the corner in the daytime. There was a clay tub as big as an old-fashioned washtub on the edge of the portico where Esperanza did the washing. Behind the altar was a lantern of the American barnyard type, which Chico used when he had kerosene. There was another lantern, a *farol* or candle-holding, tin and paper lantern on a long pole, used in funeral or fiesta processions, which

I saw again in 1954 in the corner of the new church on a pile of
bricks. My list of things in Doña Patrocina's house ends with the
farol, and I don't remember another single thing.

Many times I watched Doña Patrocina or Esperanza washing.
All Santa Cruz women wash in the large clay tubs in their own
houses; only I, the outsider, washed my clothes over in *el río,* having
more time to go there to bathe myself than they did. I am ashamed to think how in 1954 I surreptitiously washed out my little nylon
dresses every night in the brook above Don Martín's; the women
themselves never wash in the brook where they get their drinking
water, even though it runs through everyone's houseyard. Washing
in the clay tub means a great deal more carrying and rinsing and
scrubbing than would be necessary on river stones in a running
stream. The soap is not made in Santa Cruz Etla; it is bought for
cash or corn or charcoal or mangoes in the Oaxaca market. Doña
Patrocina would spread the clothes out to dry on the little orange
and lemon trees or down on the alfalfa patch that Nico kept for
cattle feed. She would always finish the washing in the middle of
the morning, so the regular late-afternoon rain would not spoil it.
The tropical sun of noon dried the clothes in an hour.

Sometimes she put starch in the boys' best pink or orange shirts
so that they would look nice going to market or to a fiesta or to a
council meeting. For the ironing the six little sadirons were piled
up in a crown around the burning charcoal and changed in rotation
every five or ten minutes. She ironed squatting over a cloth doubled
up on the ground. I always marveled at how fast Doña Patrocina
did everything up. Her family had very few clothes, all covered
with patches, but they were always clean.

Doña Patrocina's family changed most in the nine years between
1945 and 1954, changed towards more happiness, that is. Though
Esperanza bore three children and lost two, she had a fine little
boy in school in 1954. She and Chico took over a small, ruined
storage house, left abandoned on the house lot by an earlier generation of Lópezes, and built it into a nice, little, two-room adobe
house with a thatch roof. It had no cooking portico, but Esperanza
cooked in the "front room," which could be turned into a porch

merely by taking down the *petate* which formed its third wall. The interior bedroom had four solid walls, and a shuttered window for light. In all it was as nice a new little house as any young couple ever had in the hills. Nico, as the most recently married son, was living in the old bridal and corn-storage room with his wife and two little children; and Patrocina was in my room, with her brother Don Fausto when he was at home. Devoted to her grandchildren, Patrocina, more than any other of the older people in Santa Cruz, had greater happiness in her house in 1954 than in 1934.

She still had time above the neat housekeeping to practice as a medicine woman. I have heard of Mexican villages in which the medicine women opposed the teaching of sanitation, turned the people against the schools, and held up progress in every way. Not so Doña Patrocina, although she was a respected member of the community and her advice was asked on all occasions of sickness. She did not try to cope with cases like malaria or a broken leg. She just tried to give simple cures for simple ills. I surely could not see any "witch doctor" mysteries surrounding her practice in Santa Cruz Etla.

My husband and I have been sick with a mild form of dysentery every time we have come to Santa Cruz Etla. (Oh, Santa Cruz, you do this to me when I love you so!) Armed with a new-type preventative, I approached Santa Cruz Etla unafraid in 1954. Then I came down, but not all the way down, with the old trouble on the third day at Don Martín's, having trusted the "preventative" and eaten or drunk everything offered. Back in 1945, I was determined to avoid trouble by using the orange-leaf tea. Careful as I was, though, mangoes, unwashed tomatoes, or homemade goat's-milk cheese gave it to me twice. The first time Doña Patrocina insisted it was my overemphasis on cocoa. The second time I was more seriously ill and spent four days in bed. Three little children in houses below us on the hill were sick at the same time. It was the time when the brook broke loose down into its old ravine and ran dry on the ridge, and we were all using an old well below the *Cooperativa* for water. Doña Patrocina went to the houses of all three of the children, giving them herbs for purging, and hot packs

110

of tortillas and leaves on the stomach to ease the cramping. She herself said we all had the "water sickness." That is the same word they use for the much more serious typhoid, against which I have always taken shots.

Doña Patrocina was very worried about me, unnecessarily, for we had been just as sick at the schoolhouse in 1934. Since she had to be gone half the night to see the sick children, she sent for Doña Estéfana and Doña Sofía to care for me. The two had long discussions about my "taking a purge," about the coldness of my feet. They wanted to massage my poor, sore stomach. I was embarrassed by so much attention and asked only to be left alone in the dark room.

Doña Sofía was a little scornful. "Doña Elena has been eating such strange things, salad all the time, not enough beans."

But Doña Estéfana came to my defense. "We would probably be sick in her country, if we ate her strange food," she said, holding a candle to my face, so I wouldn't be "lonely in the dark."

Then Doña Patrocina came home. She put hot coals from the *cena* fire into a small clay pitcher, wrapped it in rags, and set it on the middle of my stomach. It felt warm and I was comforted. Doña Sofía and Doña Estéfana went home, and I found some peace in the dark with my warm *olla*. Next day, I "took a purge" from my own first-aid kit, and in two days I was up and around, sketching, chatting, and taking pictures. The three "water sickness" children got better, too, so Doña Patrocina could claim a successful cure.

That same week she "cured" two children of toothaches by pressing hot leaves into the aching teeth. She massaged an old woman from up the sierra for rheumatism pains three different days, rubbing hot lard up and down her legs. Undoubtedly the patient felt better; Doña Patrocina's strong, quick hands would massage pain from almost any aching joints and muscles. A boy in the fourth-grade class whose sore eyes ran with pus came to Doña Patrocina's every week; she washed his eyes with hot water and a clean rag, laid herbs on them, and washed them again. I tried to get this boy's family to send him to the Department of Health in Oaxaca City, but they said, "No, he is getting better." I was glad he was being treated be-

111

cause he always paid with a pitcher of milk, and we would have hot chocolate that night for supper. It is true that this boy, Isaías Pérez, did get better in the weeks I was there; and in 1954, then twenty-two, he was a leader in *Los Policías* and on the ball field, with eyes as clear and sharp as any in Santa Cruz.

She even cured her old black and white ox when it was sick in the night. Chico got the lantern, which was used only in such emergencies as that. There was much hustle and bustle; everyone was up except me. I never did know what she did to cure him, as I was too sleepy to ask. In the morning she was off early to cure someone else, but the old ox was already yoked to the plow when I got up.

She talked to me once about doctors and medicine in my country. She knew that things were easier and safer there when babies were born. "In your country the fine doctors could have saved Esteban's María," she told me, referring to the girl who had died in childbirth the year before. It was a matter of deep concern for her, since she had been present in Esteban's hut and helpless in the face of the hemorrhage that had brought death. Though she went to help at two births during my summer with her, and I went afterward to see the babies, I was never present to see her deliver a child. Deaths of babies in Santa Cruz were caused much more often by lack of proper diet and by bad water than by Doña Patrocina's gentle handling at birth.

That list of things for the cultural missions to do in Mexican villages spoke of "scientific training for midwives" and "maintenance of first-aid stations." With a little more room, a little more help, a little more chance for complete cleanliness, and a little more knowledge, Doña Patrocina could have taken care of these two items herself. She also rates as the head of a happy family group still, for both her sons are content to stay in Santa Cruz Etla. She seems today to love her daughters-in-law, Nico's wife now as well as Chico's, and surely dotes on her grandchildren. Probably both her sons will have served as presidents by 1964, and perhaps her grandsons by 1974. If I go back to check on Santa Cruz again at the end of the third decade in 1964, her home would be one place where I would surely feel welcome.

112

❧ 3 ❧

AFTER DON AMADO'S GRANDFATHER moved Santa Cruz Salinas to the Etla ridge, Doña Patrocina's mother, Doña Nícola, was one of the first babies born on the new site. No one really knew how old she was in my day; but if the village was moved right after the defeat of Maximilian, she must have been nearly eighty in 1945. She was famous then as the oldest inhabitant of Santa Cruz Etla; in fact, the oldest of the whole hill region. There had been a man in San Pablo in 1944 who, Don Amado told me, had been brought as a young child to the new San Pablo village; and of course, this would have made him four or five years older than Doña Nícola. But he walked with a stick, had no teeth, and was very deaf. During the winter of 1944, he died, leaving Doña Nícola, hale and hearty, in undisputed possession of the "oldest resident" title. She was surely the "voice of the past," product of an era before anyone had any idea of rural schools at all. It would have taken much more than the Mexican government's cultural missions program to make her change in any way at all.

I never heard her called Doña Nícola and had to ask her name myself. All the village called her "La Abuelita," the little grandmother. She heard everything that was said; she could see to sew; she walked with a lithe step around the yard, caring for the turkeys. She spent the afternoon dozing on the hard-earth floor of the "kitchen," in the corner beyond the charcoal fire; but when she wanted to get up, she merely pushed herself erect with her hand, turning it over and putting her weight on the knuckles. She never needed any help. In fact she was a great help to Doña Patrocina, shelling corn, cleaning beans, grinding coffee. All the family were very proud of her, as they might be of a smart baby boy.

I do not know how long it had been since her husband had died. Her daughter, Doña Patrocina, had married and left her house; Don Fausto, her only son, had married and brought his first wife home. After Fausto was widowed he lived happily alone with his mother in her house near the San Sebastián ridge. But when he took on a second wife, he moved into the new wife's house, and left La

Abuelita alone with her turkeys. Soon her two children decided for her that she should no longer live alone; then she and her turkeys went to Doña Patrocina's, leaving Don Fausto to till her four acres of corn land.

Twice in the summer of 1945 she herself went to bathe with Esperanza and me in a pool in *el río* near her old home. She "had not bathed for fifteen years," she said, because of "the chills," though I know she took sponge baths at Doña Patrocina's house. But she took us by to see her old house, a wattle and thatch house with a tile roof and a heavy wooden door, shut against intruders but not locked. There was a smaller building for grain storage, both buildings about as old as the old lady herself. La Abuelita stood unhappily under her one great tree and looked at the house, while Esperanza and I waited for her at a respectful distance.

I only wish that she could have left the turkeys at her own house. She had a flock of twenty, including five loud and unpleasant gobblers. At Doña Patrocina's they had been accustomed to sleeping in one corner of the front portico. When I moved into the main room, Nico had moved out and set up a *petate* on boards across sawhorses in the turkeys' corner. I used the portico all day to write and paint and entertain company. The turkeys surely acted as if they knew their being shooed away was all my fault. They "ganged up" on me at every possible opportunity, pecking at me viciously, gobbling and running at me as I walked around the yard, often following me when I went visiting, stealing up behind me to leap up and tear at my clothes. I grew to hate them; they are my only unhappy recollection of Doña Patrocina's. In the long run, they won out, because their descendants still "rule the roost" there; and I saw them terrorizing Nico's two-year-old boy during my 1954 visit.

I had the advantage over the baby in fighting them, because I could try to beat them off by throwing rocks. Once in 1945 I was sitting sketching by the ditch, *la zanja*, with my water-color box filled with thirty different tubes of color lying on a dead stump by the running stream. I had successfully stoned the turkeys away and had settled down for a peaceful afternoon. Then the most vicious gobbler, leader of the flock, sneaked up to the stream from the other side, and leaped with both feet on to the paint box. All the tubes of color went down the ditch, while the turkey laughed sneeringly and strutted away. I was almost in tears with rage and frustration before I found all my sad little tubes again, full of mud, with the labels all washed off. But I could do nothing in revenge against the turkeys at home, for fear of hurting La Abuelita's feelings.

She was so fond of me personally. She had been delighted that my name was Helen, the Spanish Elena. "With us, all Elenas are good and beautiful," she said. She told the story of Santa Elena Emperatriz, Saint Helen the Empress, mother of Constantine, who had helped to legalize the Christian faith in the Roman Empire. Surely La Abuelita knew nothing of early Christian history, nor of any country where there was an empress; but she connected me with the story and often murmured, "Santa Elena Emperatriz," as she looked at me. Like Doña Patrocina, she was concerned at my being so far from home and would hold my hands, saying *pobrecita, solita,* over and over, "poor little thing, all alone little thing"—this to me who towered head and shoulders above her.

She was concerned about my country. How could it be so far away, have a different government, speak a different language? Was that because it had changed? La Abuelita did not want anything to change. She hated to see the truck come up to Don Martín's. She did not like the gasoline mill and spoke strongly against the San Lorenzo bus. She would no longer go to visit some old friends in San Pablo because some of the girls in that family wore modern-style dress, and even shoes. In her childhood there had been spinning and weaving in everyone's house; goat's hair had been used for sashes and *sarapes*. "Better *sarapes* were made here than ever were made in Teotitlán del Valle where those gaudy things are woven today," she said. She did not know that I was worrying whether rural schools would bring changes *enough*, that I had a list of suggested changes rural-improvement programs ought to be making. Had she known, perhaps she would not have thought all Elenas so good.

Mostly she was concerned with the lack of interest in religion.

115

She was by far the most religious person I knew in Santa Cruz Etla. The night before I left in 1945, she lit a candle for me on the family altar above my *petate*, praying to the Virgin of Guadalupe that I would have a safe journey home. She used religious words with every other breath. She got us all up in the night to "thank the dear Father" for a drought-breaking rain in that dry year. This rain, the season's first real downfall which was more than a fifteen-minute afternoon shower, lasted for two or three days, to the un-happiness of me and the turkeys, as well as of the boys who cut wood. But she kept calling it *¡Chulíssima, dulcíssima!* (dearest, sweetest little rain!) and burning candles in thanks for it. These were not really tall white candles, which few of the people ever had, but wicks set in oil in cups.

The finest thing I could possibly have done in her eyes was to paint the church in San Pablo Etla—that project of mine which start-ed all the elaborate ideas about painting murals. The church is a small stone building with two towers, hardly bigger than the new chapel in Santa Cruz. Perhaps it is the second chapel built on the San Pablo site. There are ruins of other stonewalls near it, and no one knows how long it was on the hill before the people built a town around it. Burros graze among the crumbled walls and the marked graves of the churchyard. But the church is situated dramat-ically between valley and hills and made a good composition (which the new Santa Cruz church does not), so I went down three afternoons to make water-color sketches in preparation for the oil. The whole project brought great honor to Doña Patrocina's house in the eyes of Santa Cruz Etla, but in the eyes of La Abuelita it brought great honor to me—me the irreligious, the skeptical, with only a "sociological" interest in La Abuelita's faith. She was so breathlessly delighted at the first little water color that she could hardly speak; she let her hands flutter from her heart to my face and back again. "How could you possibly be so sanctified as to be able to draw the House of God?" she cried. "How could we be so holy and so blessed that someone who can draw a picture of the House of God actually lives here in our house?" I had little use for the water-color sketch, and when I had finished the oil copy, I gave the small one to La

Abuelita to keep always as a *recuerdo,* a remembrance of me. For her this was almost too good to be true. She herself is now in her own "House of God," but that is how the faded little picture happens still to be on Doña Patrocina's altar today.

I was seldom inside the San Pablo church. It had not occurred to us to go in 1934, and as I grew older through the years, I preferred not to get up at four-thirty in the morning for anything, especially not for a walk to San Pablo, no matter how "sociologically interesting" it would be to go down to mass with all the Santa Cruz families. The priest comes to San Pablo Etla every month, supposedly; but if he misses a couple of times, there is no mass for eight or ten weeks. No one certain priest comes to serve these mountain villages; the people do not get to know well, or to confess to, any one *padre.* The church in San Pablo is open all the time, anyway, as is the Santa Cruz church now that it is finished, so that people can go any time to pray. The religious devotion of the people seems to be a direct one—appeals from them personally to the statues and pictures on their own home altars and in their own little chapels —and has little need of a priest, except for weddings and baptisms. I never saw a priest at a funeral. Anxious as Santa Cruz Etla is to have a regular priest come to say mass in their finished church, they will be happy for years without one.

But we received word in July of 1945 that the priest would come on horseback to San Pablo for an early mass on the day of the Virgin of Carmen. Since all of Doña Patrocina's family, myself included, had been invited to a private fiesta in San Pablo on the day of the Virgin of Carmen, I went down with Nico, Chico, and Esperanza to the mass at 5:00 A.M. We were awakened, way up in Santa Cruz, by the rockets being set off and the bells ringing.

The fiesta, or *mayordomía* as it was called, the most elaborate private party I ever went to in the Etla Hills, was given at the expense of Don Bernabé, whose grandfather had been a cousin of La Abuelita's people in Santa Cruz Salinas. Along with many other Santa Cruz people allied to Don Bernabé by bloodlines or by "godfather, godchild" connections, La Abuelita's family was obligated to go. This was that San Pablo family in which the daughters wore

117

those tight-fitting, short, rayon dresses, and La Abuelita herself would not go. Chico was a godchild of Don Bernabé, however, and I went as his guest.

On the way down in the dawn, he told me how Don Bernabé happened to be giving the party. "The family owed that Virgin a fiesta, a *mayordomía;* it was a promise they made her."

"What virgin, what promise?" I asked stupidly.

"Oh, you must know the Virgin of Carmen, Doña Elena, *pues* she is the Virgin who lives at Carmen. We have a statue of her in the San Pablo church. Last year the mother of this family, Doña Socorro, my little godmother, was very sick. All of us prayed. Don Bernabé promised that he would give the *mayordomía* to the Virgin on her day, July 15, if Doña Socorro got better. Certainly she got better."

Hence, the unusually loud rockets were paid for by this family, as well as the mass itself and the decorations in the church. When we got inside, the church was lighted with many expensive candles and strung with pink and white crepe paper. There were flowers in all seven saints' niches, and many lilies in front of the blue and white Virgin. There are no seats or benches in the San Pablo church; everyone kneels on the tile floor. There were about sixty people kneeling there that day, including twenty-five from Santa Cruz. In front of the church, special holy musicians, a piper and a drummer, the most primitive, pre-conquest musicians I ever heard in the Etla region, were playing an endless, plaintive tune. Every five or ten minutes the "rocket-setter-offer" who was with them would put some black powder in a small clay dish, light it with a charcoal ember at the end of long wooden tongs, and turn to run quickly as it exploded.

When we came out of mass, we followed the "holy" musicians up the hill to the house of Don Bernabé. Here we found that Doña Sista, wife of the then president of the Santa Cruz municipality, and as such obligated to help in San Pablo, had already been there two days grinding chile into *mole* and making tortillas, while Don Bartolo, the Santa Cruz president, having contributed young goats, was helping in the butchering of a hog. Now at 6:00 A.M. they

The León Boys in 1934, with
Crescencio — Francisco is
on the left

Francisco León with his
mother Doña Angélica
in 1954

The fine big church
of San Pablo Etla

View of Doña Patrocina's house in 1954. The addition built by Chico for Esperanza is on the left.

The primitive piper, angry at the rival musicians, sitting up behind the house at the *mayordomía*

Don Fausto, musician and brother of Doña Patrocina

Grandsons of Doña Estéfana, 1945
Joel   Aurelio

were both helping Don Bernabé serve chocolate out in the house-yard for all the visitors from the mass.

As a special guest of Santa Cruz Etla, I was ushered inside the one-room adobe house. Here two long tables from the San Pablo school had been set up and covered with embroidered altar cloths. Two tortillas apiece were given to each guest with the chocolate, which was served in *jícaras,* small painted gourds. No one washed out the gourds; they were just drained of chocolate and passed on to someone else. The chocolate was made with cocoa, crude brown sugar (*panela*), and wheat flour gruel (*atole*), all boiled up together. Really it didn't taste very good.

I was seated, unexpectedly, at the table with the San Pablo Etla lady schoolteacher, the members of the Santa Cruz town council and the San Pablo town council. We sat and sat and sat. The "musicians" piped and banged outside in the growing sunshine; the co-godmothers, and the poor Doña Socorro, the mother whom the Virgin of Carmen had saved for this occasion, made tortillas and watched chunks of pork boil. Above my head dangled two more fresh sides of pork, hung inside the house for convenience away from the sun, but certainly inconvenient at my corner of the table. At my right, tied together, hung the eight raw pigs' feet from both butcherings.

It was eight o'clock; it was eight-thirty. Other friends came and breakfasted and went. The solemn town councils showed respect to the Virgin of Carmen by staying silently on. I tried to catch Don Bartolo's eye to see if I could leave the stuffy little house. Finally the San Pablo teacher excused herself and went home. Boldly I said *Con permiso,* and just walked out.

It was three o'clock when I went back with Esperanza, Joel, and Sofía. Doña Patrocina, out all night on a sickness case, had gone as soon as she got in to help her *comadre* Doña Socorro; but Esperanza and I did not have that much vitality and rested during the middle of the day. By the time we arrived, all the pork, *mole* sauce, and beans were gone, fed to the hundred or more people who had come from both towns. Now they were serving pulque, that sour beer made from the century plant. They had mixed it with the *panela.*

Esperanza thought it was the finest *dulce,* or sweetmeat, she had ever tasted, so I was glad to give her my full *jícara.* I was more than contented with three bottles of the strawberry pop which had been the *gasto,* or contribution, of Don Martín's family. (The cultural missions list does not include "the use of strawberry pop" as an improvement for rural Mexico; but the quantities of it consumed are surely an indication of the modernization and prosperity of any community, although it was being edged out in popularity by Pepsi-Cola at Don Martín's store in 1954.)

The women were still working in the bamboo kitchen outside, washing up the ten-gallon water jars in which they had cooked the pork. The babies were parked in a corner, asleep on a *petate.* Esperanza sat with the young women outside in the houseyard on other *petates,* and I joined them, even though the only place left to sit was right under the noses of Don Bernabé's oxen, which had been yoked together and tethered close for the day in order to keep them quiet while the rockets went off. Inside the dark little house, among the pigs' feet, the San Pablo Etla band, two clarinets, a bass viol, and our Don Fausto at the guitar, kept playing all day, dance music mostly, while occasionally people danced between the *petates* spread outside. Up on the hill behind the house, from sunrise to sunset, the "holy" musicians continued also to play, the piper with his shrill little four-note pipe, such as one associates with Inca llama herders, and the drummer with two Indian-type skin drums, as well as the famous "rocket-setter-offer," all well paid by Don Bernabé to provide the music that the Virgin of Carmen particularly liked for the entire day. They took up their stand on the hillside trail and kept up their mournful little refrain hour after hour, eight notes up and down the pipe, then four hard beats on each drum. The rocket-setter-offer had to retire when he ran out of powder, but the piper and drummer never gave up.

The dance band inside the house, close to the pulque, stopped to rest and drink and chat quite often. Whenever the dance music stopped, the piper and the drummer would come down from the trail into the houseyard and play more and more loudly nearer and nearer the door of the hut. When the dancers would start again, the primitive piper would wrap himself in his *sarape* up to his eyes, and stalk off up the trail to take up a position behind the house until the dance band stopped to drink once more. I saw this happen, like a repeated movie, at least six times during the afternoon. When it became too dark for Don Fausto's friends to play inside the house, they moved outdoors onto the ground in the late afternoon light. Set face to face like this with "modern" music, the piper and the drummer gave up and went home.

It is just such changes as this in the old ways, such clashes between old things and new things, that La Abuelita never wanted to see. Her son Don Fausto felt just the opposite; he was one of the best "modern" musicians in the whole region. He said to me as we sipped tequila at the *mayordomía:* "I hoped we had outgrown such *tonto* music, such primitive, ignorant things." It was only to please the Virgin that Don Bernabé had hired the drummer and piper, anyway.

So we danced till sunset in Don Bernabé's houseyard, waltzing in honor of the Virgin of Carmen, while she sat, a blue and white statue in the flower-filled San Pablo church, and La Abuelita who loved her sat at home and fretted about change.

San Pablo himself (Saint Paul), the patron saint of both church and town, was not inside the San Pablo church at all, but in a niche on the outside between the two towers. He was a dumpy little man in a blue cloak, with his plaster nose nicked off, and he did not look at all important to me, so I had just left him out of my first sketch of the church. La Abuelita did not mention or notice this absence, but most other people who saw the picture asked where he was, and I finally painted San Pablo in the larger oil copy to please everybody. When San Pablo Etla people heard of it, two families who had been at the *mayordomía* at Don Bernabé's, but whose names I did not get, walked all the way up to Santa Cruz to see the painting. It was the first time the mother of one of the families, a native of San Pablo Etla, had ever been up the trail into the "sticks" of those "poor relations," the people of Santa Cruz Etla.

For seventy years the "poor relations" of Santa Cruz Etla were buried in the San Pablo churchyard; now they are in the new

Panteón. At my first sight of the new Santa Cruz church, I thought how pleased La Abuelita would have been if she had just lived to see Santa Cruz have its own chapel. Then as I sat in the school-yard making the flashy oil painting of the new chapel and thinking about her pleasure in my other church painting, I remembered that she had been deeply distressed at the new *Panteón*. Too much change. Sprightly as she was in 1945, she was old and it was impossible for her to visit both burial grounds and to see all her friends and relations in each on All Saints' Day. With all her contemporaries dead before her, these visits were a heavy responsibility for her.

The first two days of November, the feast of *Todos los Santos,* or All Saints, is a very important time in Mexico. In the two weeks before November first, when the harvest is in, all the able-bodied young men go to the sierra to cut a great deal of wood and make cash money. This money is all spent in the market the Saturday before Halloween, spent on fruit and hard candies, sugar and chocolate, and special frosted cookies with skulls on them. Each family fills at least two burro panniers with these riches, depending on how many dead people they have in their families. I use that expression "have" on purpose, because the dead children are always counted among the living children when families are listed. "I have twelve children" may mean five living and seven dead.

On the night of October 31, all the families kill chickens, turkeys, or hogs, and the women work hard grinding chiles for *mole*. That night they set up tables, or *petates* if they have no tables, on the floor below the family altars. A place is set on the table or *petate* with a dish of food, a lighted candle, and a bouquet of flowers for each person who has died out of that household. In Doña Patrocina's house they had to do this for her husband, his parents, her own dead children, and all the relatives and lost children of La Abuelita (and now, of course, for La Abuelita herself and for Esperanza's dead children). The little dead children will come and eat in the night, and the grown-up dead the next day. Throughout the first day of November families visit each other to see the familiar dead friends and to pay their respect, though food and refreshments are served for the dead only. I have never been in Santa Cruz at any such festival; and I have only the vivid description of my friend, the first teacher in Santa Cruz, to go by. Twice during the six years she taught there, she saw the people of Santa Cruz dress up a bride and a groom, a father and a mother, a boy child and a girl child, and have them visit in a group at each household to represent all the dead people of all ages.

Supposedly the food is eaten, or at least the essence of it is consumed, by the spirits before dark on November first. Then all the ghosts go back to the burial grounds, and the living members of the family eat the delicacies. On the morning of November 2, more *mole* is made and a tortilla full of chicken *mole* is taken to each grave of a person dead in the last year or so. Flowers and hard candy and the special frosted cookies are left on every grave connected with the family. This is the day when La Abuelita went to visit her beloved dead. Weeds are pulled, the graves cleared of the faded paper flowers from the year before, and shrubs and flower cuttings planted.

All this takes time. La Abuelita had a hard enough task doing it for her people in one cemetery in one day. It was mostly worry on her part, however, as there were only three people she had to care for in the new *Panteón.* Chico knew them by heart without her listing them, and he would gladly have cared for them if she would just have shifted the worry and responsibility to him. Really Doña Rufina had much more worry of this sort, and she was also quite religious. Her own parents, her two first-born, and her godmother were in the San Pablo churchyard, but Don Amado and their daughter Juana were both in the *Panteón.* La Abuelita was afraid the younger generation "will neglect all the older ones buried in San Pablo as soon as the *Panteón* has many graves."

She said this in conversation with the family at *cena.* I asked them all, then, what they did at Christmas. I knew the Christmas customs of many Mexican people, the *piñata,* a clay figure full of candy that is broken in games of blind-man's buff, the *nacimiento* or crèche with its clay or porcelain models of the Holy Family and the manger. These seemed expensive things for the people of

Santa Cruz. They had no clay figures for their altars, but they often had homemade *piñatas* in their houses or at the school during the last days before their annual vacation, which begins at Christmas. Also they play the "game" called *las posadas*. Just as on All Saints' Day, they send a group of townspeople from house to house. This time the members of the group represent Joseph and Mary looking for an inn in Bethlehem. The Holy Couple go to every household on the main ridge asking for shelter, but they are told everywhere that there is no room, that the guests must sleep with the cattle. Doña Patrocina and Chico, who told me about this, said that "naturally everyone comes into the house to drink chocolate or pulque," and that then "we join them also and go over to Don Féliz León's," next down the ridge. Before the celebration is over, of course, all the families have joined onto the tail of the procession.

They asked me if I had ever been the Virgin in a *posada* procession, and if I gave gifts to my family on the Day of the Three Kings, January 6. It seemed so difficult to explain that we did something entirely different, that our Saint Nicholas seemingly has no connection with the San Nicolás after whom towns and boys (including Nico) are named in Mexico, and that our Saint Nicholas brings gifts on December 25 in a wealth of pageantry as pleasant as *las posadas*. To them who had no chimneys nor fireplaces, no stockings, no fir trees, who had never seen even pictures of sleds or reindeer or snow, our Christmas customs seemed incomprehensible. The only thing they understood was the description of the Christmas turkey dinner. For them also a turkey is killed only for a great fiesta.

Holy Week is for them a much more important celebration than Christmas. There is no work for four days. In the back alcove of the church at San Pablo there is a glass-covered coffin with a plaster model of the corpse of Jesus inside. He lies asleep, a crown of thorns on His head, blood staining His bare trunk. He seems pitiful, but the people love Him. On Good Friday, the people of both towns used to carry Him in a long parade with candles, up from the church to the Santa Cruz *municipio* and back; the bells of both schools were kept ringing for thirty-six hours, little boys tugging in shifts at the bell ropes. I am prone to wonder what has happened to this joint effort, with the one Holy Coffin, now that Santa Cruz Etla has its own church. A statue like that in a coffin must be very expensive, and Santa Cruz, taxed so hard for the completion of the church, could not hope to buy one for years. But its church is actually dedicated to the Holy Cross (the Santa Cruz) and not to a mere saint like San Pablo, and by rights the Easter parade should center in the Santa Cruz church. On Holy Saturday, the men play cards and *pelota* all day, but the women grind *mole* and chocolate, make tortillas, butcher hogs, and cook turkeys. A priest always comes to San Pablo for the five o'clock mass on Easter morning, and the rest of the day, Doña Patrocina said, is spent in eating all the good things prepared.

In some Mexican villages there is continuous dancing, in masks and costumes, for Easter Week. One of my few disappointments in Santa Cruz Etla was that there is no longer such dancing held there for any fiesta. As late as 1942, when Nico was nineteen, he, Joel, Adolfo Soto, and the León boys, all dressed in green and red spangles, did a Maypole type of dance called *los jardineros,* the gardeners, at the May third town fiesta of the Holy Cross. I have never seen this done, and I asked the boys to describe it to me; but they always said, "Oh, it is just an ordinary *jardineros* dance, you know." Nico still had the suit and kept promising to show it to me, to get the other boys to pose with him doing the steps, or to act it out in some way. But I could see he didn't want to do it; he kept putting it off till I was ready to go. He would never do it again for the town fiesta. As for dancing with animal-face masks, only the *tontos* in the high sierra did that any more. On the cultural missions list the admonition "save the regional dances" ranks high on the programs for the rural schools; but I am afraid the school came too late to do this in Santa Cruz Etla. No one there is interested any more. La Abuelita hated this attitude, just as she hated all the changes that came to Santa Cruz Etla. "They will be sorry in twenty years," she said. "Then the way of dancing, the tunes, and the costumes will all be forgotten."

Even Oaxaca City does its native dances now mostly for tourists, at the big *Lunes del Cerro*, the Monday on the Hill festival which occurs the third Monday in July. Valley and hill towns send their finest dancers, the "plumed warriors" come from Benito Juárez' country, and gorgeous girls in lace and embroidery from the Isthmus of Tehuantepec. Santa Cruz Etla would have nothing that could compete with such as these.

In 1954 the San Lorenzo bus came on the morning of that Monday, and Don Martín's whole family went into the city to see the festival. His grandchildren, as well as most of the children who come from rural villages in the state of Oaxaca, now see religious dancing in costume only on such tourist-attracting occasions. I have seen the *Lunes del Cerro* myself four times in two decades. It is beautiful, a "perfect" for every user of Kodachrome film, but it gets more commercialized every time. La Abuelita had never been to see it, and I am certain that she would not have approved it if she had.

She went in to the Saint's Day of Oaxaca City in 1940 for a last visit, so Doña Patrocina told me. This is the day of the Virgin of Soledad, who is a very different saint from the Virgin of Carmen in the San Pablo Etla church, and from the Virgin of Guadalupe, the patron saint of all Mexico, whose picture has been transferred from Patrocina's to the new chapel. The real statue of the Virgin of Soledad is right there in Oaxaca, in a special church just for her. A colored postcard of the Virgin is on Doña Patrocina's altar, and La Abuelita showed it to me when she told me about it. That last time she went to this Oaxaca fiesta, she rode Chico's brown burro, although she was only an occasional guest at Doña Patrocina's then. She took hibiscus flowers from Don Féliz' garden in a basket. A sort of state-wide fair is still held in Oaxaca on that day; all the handicraft villages from miles around bring in their finest wares. The *sarape* under which I slept was bought that last time La Abuelita went, and the black *rebozo* she wore on Sundays. She kept the *rebozo* at the bottom of Doña Patrocina's chest; she was afraid perhaps that even it might change too much if she had it out in the light too long.

After I was with her in 1945, Doña Nícola, La Abuelita, lived through two more Holy Cross festivals in Santa Cruz Etla, the local fiesta for which the householders pay their cash taxes in to the town fund. I ought surely to have gone to Santa Cruz Etla some year in May, just to see the whole town dancing the *jarabe Oaxaqueña* and to eat all the good things provided by the *mayordomo* for three days straight. I have heard enough about this fiesta to know that the Santa Cruz band, along with imported musicians, plays till it is ready to drop. No woodcutters go to the sierra for a week afterwards, to rest up from the dancing, the pork, the *mole,* and the tequila. I do not know how La Abuelita felt about the town fiesta, whether she considered it religious enough, or whether she was concerned with too much change in the customs connected with its celebration.

Three weeks after the fiesta in 1947, the first week in June, she simply did not get up in the morning; and when Esperanza went to help her, she was dead. In 1954 Doña Estéfana was the oldest person in Santa Cruz Etla, lying so pitifully on her hard bed and not remembering who came to see her. I am glad that La Abuelita went quickly, without worry or pain or querulousness, without herself changing into a helpless person.

I had taken several snaps of her, and a print of one of those, the one shown in this book, was carried by Doña Patrocina and Don Fausto to a "trick" photographer in Oaxaca City. La Abuelita had always said how much Don Fausto looked like her long dead husband. The photographer took a photo of Fausto and Patrocina in their best clothes, then took the smiling face and head of the old lady from my little snap, enlarged it to fit exactly over Doña Patrocina's face, and made a composite photo.

Doña Patrocina has this enlargement, garishly tinted, on the wall next to the altar and the water color of the San Pablo church, and she likes to pretend that it is *both* her parents standing side by side. When I thanked her for a pleasant *comida* in 1954, and repeated my thanks for her hospitality through the years, she said that nothing she could do would repay me for the possibility of having a "portrait" of the beloved Abuelita, a *recuerdo,* a remembrance forever.

127

❧ 4 ❧

THERE ARE SO MANY of my other friends in Santa Cruz Etla who are
worth writing about, who help make up a town! I think of Doña
Beatriz, sedate and fat, and of her husband, Don Casimiro, in a
large house on the main ridge; they had one son, the Gerónomo
who helped me start my horseback rides in 1945 and who was an
important member of *Los Policías* in 1954. Don Casimiro had more
pigs than anyone else, and he butchered hogs any time the fancy
struck him, without waiting for a fiesta, sending us cracklings
whenever he tried out lard. Then there was also the religious, grave
Doña Margarita, who lived as the matriarch of a group of grandchildren in a ravine behind Don Martín's. She was stern but
kindhearted, and she made a home for Adolfo Soto, an orphaned
grandnephew, until he was old enough to marry into Don Marciano's
family. She was active in the Mothers' Club in 1934 and signed an
autograph for me, being then the only woman besides Doña
Estéfana who could sign her name. She had learned how from the
schoolteacher. In 1945 she would come to visit La Abuelita early on
Sunday mornings when there was no mass, and I would stop by to
see her when I took the horse back to Don Marciano's. In 1954, on
my second day of visiting, I ran into her on a trail, and found her
as hale and hearty as ever, showing little sign of the twenty years.
She recognized and remembered me instantly, embraced me, asked
for a photograph, and told me news of all her family. Then, straight
as an arrow, she walked off down the trail as if only a week had
passed since 1934.

Doña Angélica León, wife of the Don Féliz León who had been
so active in politics before I ever came to Santa Cruz, lived just
down the oxcart trail and across *la zanja* from Doña Patrocina's. She
was small and wispy and seldom stood around chatting and gossiping as did Doña Patrocina, Doña Estéfana, or Doña Rufina. She
would speak in friendly fashion as we passed, but always she seemed
very busy. I went with Patrocina to her house at the beginning of
the summer in 1945, and we spent the time talking about how to
grow wheat and how much of it her family had been able to grow

128

on a half-acre. She had the wheat there and ran it through her hands to show how easily it had been thrashed with a flail, so much easier than shelling corn off the cob.

Weeks afterward I went across *la zanja* to the field beyond Doña Angélica's and sat on the steep slope looking toward the San Sebastián ridge at a beautiful red and gold sunset. As it grew darker, Doña Angélica suddenly slipped out of the shadows and came to sit down beside me. We said *buenos noches* and sat silent as the colors faded. Suddenly she said: "Do you live in a land beyond there, señora?" and pointed at the sunset.

"To the north, yes," I answered, "beyond the mountains, many ranges of mountains, but not beyond the sunset."

"Are there beautiful sunsets in your *tierra*?"

"Not so beautiful as in Santa Cruz Etla," I could say truthfully.

She was silent a long time. Then she said: "My daughter is beyond the sunset."

I did not say anything more, and then I noticed she was crying. Finally she began to talk again, and spoke at length about her daughter, who (she said) had remembered me well at the school in 1934, though I cannot place her face. This daughter, María, evidently the great joy of Doña Angélica's life, had married the young Don Esteban two years before he served as president. In the winter of 1944, María had died in childbirth, that "case" that Doña Patrocina had lost and felt so bad about. "I lost the baby also," said Doña Angélica. The daughter must have been an unusually lovely personality. Not only did her death bring such sorrow to Doña Angélica, but it warped and changed Don Esteban's whole life and caused him to leave the community.

She had had two other girls and a boy die in infancy, but she had raised two boys, Francisco pudgy and shy, and Féliz who, though tall and handsome, was always called Felicito to differentiate him from his father. These boys were in the elementary class in 1934, and must have been eighteen or twenty years old in 1945. They were then great chums of Nico and played around Doña Patrocina's houseyard in the early evening, or sat chatting over our *cena* fire. Now they are young men about thirty. Felicito was married in the dry season of 1955 to a grandchild of Doña Margarita; but Francisco, as shy as his mother, had no eye for the girls. He had joined his father in helping us get our car out of the mudhole in 1954, so I went by the house a few days later to thank him.

Doña Angélica just seemed wispier than ever; she had even lost a few teeth. She and Don Féliz had given up raising wheat, she said, since Santa Cruz had been having such good corn years. Yes, Felicito was to be married; had it been Don Martín who told me? The bride was a godchild of Don Martín. Well, she, Doña Angélica, had waited a long, long time for a grandchild she could hold in her arms. As for Francisco, he seemed afraid of girls, no woman save his mother "had a warm heart for him."

I took a special picture of Francisco and his mother, for I have a warm spot in my own heart for Francisco León. There is a sequence in our old movie, taken in 1934, showing him leading a pig up the trail past the school. He was then not much bigger than the pig, and every time he got started up the hill, the pig would pull him back down again. Finally the pig won, and the long, comic shot shows Francisco at the end of the rope being pulled out of the picture back home to the León houseyard. This series of pictures delighted school audiences in the United States more than all the rest of the film. It won attention for lectures on several occasions, and it is one reason that I remember Francisco with such pleasure. But even then it showed that the forces of life were unfriendly to Francisco León, that he would not win out against fate, and that he had better not venture out far from his mother.

On a hillside above our bathing pool lived the old Doña Carmen. She had a lovely site for a house, with six orange trees and a view from her portico across the San Sebastián ridge and down the valley. She was a cousin to La Abuelita, not a first cousin, *hermana prima*, but close enough to be called *prima*. Because she was a relative, Esperanza and I often stopped at her house to eat oranges and to sit and rest and look at the view, an "opposite direction" view from the one at Patrocina's. But we did not chat at Doña Carmen's very much, for she had great difficulty hearing. She would often start a new conversation while Esperanza and I were right in the middle of the old one. Her conversations were all about one thing, how her daughter Carmita had left her.

She had only the one surviving child, not an attractive one at that, for we remember Carmita as the homeliest girl in school in 1934. I would have thought that deaf old Carmen, widowed as she was, was fortunate to have married Carmita off to anyone. But Carmita, once married into a family beyond San Sebastián, never came back to see her mother at all. When the old lady walked the three miles over to see her daughter, Carmita and the in-laws treated her coolly. They did not ask her to sit down in the portico, when she was there, they kept right on with their work, making tortillas or washing clothes; and they never gave her presents of corn or eggs or milk, although she always brought them oranges. And this when she went to Carmita, whereas Carmita should by rights have come home to her every few days with some little gift.

So old Carmen quit going and stayed home, bitter, among her orange trees, living alone, *solita,* and renting out her land on shares to Pedro Rivera, one of the sons of Doña Margarita below *el río.* But the longer she stayed away from Carmita, the more she brooded about her. She came to Doña Margarita's house one day while I visited there in 1945; and, holding tight to Doña Margarita's shoulders, she told the whole story over again, while the tears streamed down her face, and other interrupted conversations came to a standstill. Esperanza made fun of her, I am sorry to say, the second or third time we went bathing, and acted it all out, the way she thought Doña Carmen would tell us the whole story if we went to see her. Esperanza decided the oranges were worth the story, so we went; and sure enough, Doña Carmen told it all again, almost exactly as Esperanza had pantomimed. But the old lady was so touching that I think even Esperanza was ashamed.

In 1951, though I stayed only for a day's visit and had time for little gossip, I heard that Carmita had had a bad miscarriage and had been very sick. She and the in-laws sent for her old mother soon enough when she was needed in a case of illness. Carmita recovered under her mother's devoted care, but the strain of the nursing or the joy of being wanted was too much for the old lady, and her heart just stopped beating soon afterwards. In 1957 I heard that Carmita and her unpleasant husband have inherited the house and the land and the orange trees, where, because of them, the deaf old lady ate her heart out so long.

Doña Paula, mother of the unhappy and unsuccessful Don Esteban, and of two very ragged little boys just younger who were students in school in 1934, owned the largest flower garden in Santa Cruz Etla and neglected her house, her children, and herself for the flowers. She never combed her hair in neat braids as the other women did. In fact, it was short and frowzy and looked as if it had never been combed or washed in her whole life. She was wearing still, in 1954, the same kind of dirty rags that her children had worn to school twenty years earlier. She scrubbed around in the dirt among her yellow roses and brought each one to a perfect bloom. But even the garden was messy and disorganized, not well arranged like the one which used to occupy Don Féliz Jiménez. Geraniums, roses, hibiscus, jasmines, and cannas grew in such profusion, in such a mat of mango, avocado, and peach trees, that you could not see anything but the tangle as you went along the ox-cart road. Doña Paula made some money by selling flowers for *angelitos,* saints' days, and family altars. More often she just gave the flowers away; she sent a yellow rose over to me by her only daughter, Alicia, every morning that I lived at Doña Patrocina's. Though my visit nine years later found me with headquarters at Don Martín's, a half-mile up the central ridge, she heard I was there and sent up yellow roses three mornings in succession. But I could never get her to talk very much.

Fortunately for her family, her second son Máximo married in 1936 a freckled little Elodia from the San Lorenzo ridge who proceeded to take over the household, do the washing for the younger children, keep cooked food in the house, and encourage the older brother Esteban to try and do something with himself. Elodia also kept the little Alicia clean and neat, sent her to school in pink, starched dresses, and kept her there till she finished the four grades offered, which few girls do. Alicia was even *La Patria* in the patriotic parade; in 1952 she married into Santa María Asumpa down in the valley, and she brought me up the yellow roses to Don Martín's one time when she was visiting her mother two years later. Soon Elodia had her own young children to keep clean and to send to school, and evidently she never made any attempt to tidy up her mother-in-law. Each of them just followed the policy of live and let live, the one in the house with the babies, the other in the yard with the yellow roses.

There was another Santa Cruz woman connected with gardens, a stately, white-haired Doña María Teresa, who lived on the hill above Doña Estéfana's. The ancestors of her husband, Don Florenzio, came early with the "founding fathers" to the ridges and chose a good site, setting out not only avocado and mango trees as did everyone else, but putting in peach and plum trees, oranges and lemons, apples and guavas. By 1954 Don Florenzio and Doña María Teresa had four banana plants in bearing. The peaches, called *duraznos*, were very hard and small, but at that they were better than the apples, better than any apples I ever ate in southern Mexico for that matter, where temperate-climate fruits do not do too well. The plums, when Doña María Teresa let them ripen on the tree, were worthy of California, although they were not an even trade for Doña Patrocina's mangoes. I liked to go to Don Florenzio's and eat his bananas and guavas, as there were no others in Santa Cruz Etla. I liked also to chat with Doña María Teresa; she and her husband were important members of the community, Don Florenzio having been one of the men who helped Don Amado organize the township and served on his early councils. They had no children, all three babies having died in infancy; and they lived a rather sad life, with no children to inherit their orchard and no grandchildren to eat their bananas.

Doña Enriqueta, about whom I can think of no interesting different thing to write, deserves to be listed as one of the best friends of mine through the years in Santa Cruz Etla. She was a sister of the Doña Pastorcita who was married to Don Martín, and I found her always less stuffy than her sister, more jolly and gay. She would call outside Doña Patrocina's with a whistled call for me, like a schoolgirl friend, though she must then have been forty. She was

133

still very light on her feet and tripped along like a girl, her long braids of heavy hair flying behind. Her husband, the Don Pedro Rivera from Doña Margarita's family who farmed the deaf old Doña Carmen's acres, was stodgy and plodding and serious; and their only surviving child, Ordón, a boy in school in 1934 and now a young "pillar of the community," seldom smiled at all. Doña Enriqueta always did the smiling for the family. In 1945 when I was trying to get away secretly without the community knowing I was leaving and making a great "to-do," she found out my plans and came running up with two fresh eggs after I had already started down the road with everything packed on Chico's burros.

In 1945 I had no plan or idea of ever coming back, having worked in the campaign against illiteracy all summer, finished my "stint," and being full of ideas for other projects. But I was not happy about leaving, and Doña Enriqueta's gift of eggs, the finest gift a Santa Cruz family can give a parting guest, symbolic of the white, round wholeness of friendship, almost made me break down. And so it was that I left Santa Cruz Etla that year, tears in my eyes and a fresh egg in each hand.

Nineteen fifty-four saw Doña Enriqueta, if not myself, still "bouncing" with her same old unchanged vigor. Since she was often with her sister Pastorcita, with all of both families grown and most of the grandchildren out from under foot, I saw her every day of my visit; and we laughed over many events in the two decades.

PART THREE

Rosita's Children

1. Rosita: *The first teacher of Santa Cruz Etla still is the town's guardian angel.*
2. School days in 1934: *The generation which runs Santa Cruz today went to school then.*
3. Augustina: *The delight of two years at school changed her life little in the long run.*
4. Crescencio: *This naughtiest boy did learn to count and to sing.*
5. A decade in between: *In these days the school was sad and neglected.*
6. The problems of 1944: *Were they ever really solved?*
7. Doña Ofelia and Doña Ester: *Neither of these teachers really loved Santa Cruz Etla.*
8. Don Alfredo: *Here was a teacher twenty years afterward who worked hard for the school.*
9. Los analfabetos: *The unlettered ones became the lettered ones.*

How HAVE I WRITTEN this far into the story without naming María Rosa Arrieta?—the "Rosita" of Santa Cruz Etla, the first teacher in Don Amado's new school, Rosita who still loves the people of Santa Cruz as they love her, even though the two decades carried her far beyond Santa Cruz in her profession. Half of what I know about customs and traditions and history in Santa Cruz Etla I learned from her; I was first welcome there as her guest, and I am still most welcome when she or her family comes with me.

I went to Santa Cruz Etla in 1934 because I was interested, as a very young and idealistic sociologist, in studying the splendid rural school movement of Mexico, which started in the 1930's and has served since as an example for all Latin America. Peasants the length and breadth of Mexico had fought in a bitter, ten-year civil war from 1910 to 1920, under Zapata and Villa and Obregón; first they wanted land, and second they wanted schools, free public elementary education for every village. When peace of a sort came to Mexico in the 1920's, the new presidents, first Obregón and then Calles, set about starting the schools wherever they could. The people in the villages had to build the schools themselves, from plans sent out from Mexico City; then they had to wait their turn for a teacher, since so few young Mexicans had been trained in such work.

Naturally, in Santa Cruz Etla Don Amado had heard all about this. Until I knew at first hand about the construction of the chapel, the school building had always seemed a miracle to me. It consisted of three rooms, two for classes and one for living quarters for the teacher, the whole more than seventy feet long. The rooms opened on a covered porch, or arcade, which ran the length of the building. The whole school was floored with unglazed terra-cotta tile, the type we paid for to put in the new chapel, and roofed with tile over great rafters cut in the high sierra. The building was made of adobe, the arches of the porch of cobblestones, and the whole building was not merely whitewashed, but heavily plastered, and repainted, every dry season, white, green, pink, or orange at the whim of the school committee. It was a stupendous building to have been constructed in 1929 and 1930 by a green, "new" town in which only one man, and he an impractical dreamer, could even read the blueprint directions.

Santa Cruz finished its school in 1930, and Don Amado applied for a teacher. It hurt his pride to realize that San Pablo had started and finished a school eighteen months earlier and already had a *matrimonio* (which is a married couple, or *two* teachers) teaching sixty children in two rooms with glass windows and real doors. But since Santa Cruz children *could* walk down to school in San Pablo, if they were ambitious, and San Pablo had already received two teachers, the harassed new office for rural education in the state of Oaxaca pigeonholed Santa Cruz's request for a teacher. The new training school in Oaxaca City could not turn out teachers fast enough. Young people graduating from the six years of public school offered by the Oaxaca authorities were being urged to take up rural teaching and to go into the mountain villages. The training course took three years, however, and even though girls and youths were sent out on the program at sixteen or seventeen, there was no backlog of them to be sent. Santa Cruz Etla must wait.

At last in 1931, though, a teacher was to come to Santa Cruz. The people lined up on the wide school steps leading to the porch; this was the first of countless receptions and celebrations that were to take place there. Rockets were ready to be set off, many bottles of strawberry pop (no doubt) to be consumed, and small, green-corn tamales to be passed around for everybody, once the speech-making and the welcoming were over. Don Amado was then president, and he stood in front with the council to greet the teacher. A caravan of burros bearing the teacher, her family, and her possessions approached up the trail. Don Amado stepped forward to greet "the honored ones."

A frail, sweet-faced, middle-aged lady got off the second burro. She courteously shook hands with the councilmen, listened to Don Amado's long-winded welcome, quickly turned to greet the older women who stood in the background. She asked about the living quarters which were built into the school, about arrangements for cooking. The women touched her store clothes, her hand bag, inspected the suitcases on the third burro, complimented her on her "pretty young daughter," a girl of sixteen or seventeen who still sat astride burro number one.

Then Don Amado asked the lady to make a speech, to tell her plans for organizing the classes, her program for the first week, the costs of the necessary materials. There followed a long hushed silence. Don Amado looked hopefully at the lady; she looked at him in bewilderment. All the members of the council, and the families behind them, stood waiting eagerly, for the whole community loves long, formal speeches. Now it was the teacher's turn.

Suddenly the guest herself sensed the mistake. She left the group, walked over to the first burro, helped its rider down, and led her by the hand to greet Don Amado. The pretty daughter Rosita, the sixteen-year-old girl and not the middle-aged lady, was the teacher. Rosita's mother, Doña Rafaela, her advisor, companion, and dependent, had come along merely to keep house for her and to watch over her. If Rosita had a long speech ready to make that day, I never heard about it.

What a shock this all must have been for the municipal council! A girl of sixteen in Santa Cruz Etla is of no importance at all, unless she has just been betrothed or married. Don Amado told me ten years afterwards how he had felt. "She was just a *chamaca*," he said, using the Spanish word as we would use the word "kid." "But we remained solemn," he added, "we said no word. We could not show our disappointment." They could not foresee that day how important Rosita was to become to them. "How much she has learned since!" said Don Amado in 1944, one of those evenings at Doña Estéfana's. Santa Cruz Etla, too, has learned much since.

I met Rosita myself for the first time in Mr. Ximello's office in Oaxaca City in 1934, when she had already been in Santa Cruz three years. I wrote of her in my diary notes that year: "She seemed a starry-eyed little high-school girl to me." How much younger she must have seemed on the Santa Cruz steps in 1931.

Rosita, the only child of a frail, widowed mother, was herself of mixed Spanish and Mixtecan Indian ancestry, that lower middle class in Oaxaca City called *mestizos*, whose members try to get some education and carry on trades or run small shops. Her mother was one of a large family, and her brothers and sisters helped support Doña Rafaela and Rosita until the girl was twelve or fourteen.Then had come the nation-wide need for rural teachers in the new program of education under Calles. Older cousins had advised Rosita to take the normal-school course for rural teachers being offered in Oaxaca as a new thing in the late 1920's. Her married cousins kept her mother and Rosita herself for the two years of this course, on the understanding that she would then be self-supporting and would take on the support, not only of herself and her mother, but of her mother's spinster sister and semi-invalid unmarried brother as well. Thus, before she was seventeen Rosita was a full-fledged, certificated teacher, ready to handle any rural education situation, and had already assumed the support of three middle-aged people whom she "carries on her back" to this day.

None of this burden ever weighed heavy on her. Tall and lithe, with a mop of brown curly hair, a bubbling laugh, and an exuberant enthusiasm for everything she undertook, Rosita has been the "good fairy" for the children of Santa Cruz Etla, her own younger relatives, and many kindergarten children in other places. I could not call her a "fairy godmother," as that phrase implies a kind of dignity and stuffiness which she never had. Her success as teacher has been the result of her ability to be "one" with the children, to play with them as a kindred spirit, though the grown people of Santa Cruz Etla loved her none the less for that.

Although the normal-school training course was hurried to meet the nation-wide need for emergency teachers, it was practical to a remarkable degree. So in 1931 Rosita came to Santa Cruz Etla, full of ideas to teach little Indians music, drawing, basketmaking, reading and writing of Spanish, first aid, vegetable gardening. In other words, a major part of the cultural missions program for rural schools was in her mind already when she came. When we were there three years later, she was the "director" of a two-teacher school, which had expanded enough to have a sixteen-year-old boy assistant from the Oaxaca normal school. Rosita was the town medical adviser and sanitary expert, the authority on scientific agriculture, the court to settle domestic-relations disputes, the teacher of a night school for adults. The whole community revolved around her. It is hard even to think of the group of hillside houses as a "community" before she came.

She stayed there six years. In her third year she received some recognition from the rural-school authorities in Oaxaca, since we, the visitors from the United States, were to spend the summer in her school. We were full of the idea of bringing her to visit the United States; she had never seen any city other than Oaxaca. Three years later, in 1937, a teachers' group in Los Angeles was anxious to finance a project in Latin American friendship. Rosita's vacation from Santa Cruz Etla came in the dry season, January and February. Mr. Ximello and the Mexico City rural-school office procured a free pass for her on the railroad as far as the Arizona border. The Latin American project funds brought her on from there, bewildered and alone. Young Americans of Mexican ancestry helped her while she was on the train, bought her meals, got in touch with us on her arrival.

In Los Angeles Rosita won a happy triumph. Eyes dancing, she posed for photographs in the *Los Angeles Times*. In the costumes of Oaxaca and Tehuantepec she appeared at school assemblies and Chamber of Commerce meetings. She danced, she sang, she played the guitar. The movies of life in a rural school, which my husband and I had taken in Santa Cruz Etla in 1934, were shown as a part of the program wherever she spoke. Not one word of English would she learn, sensing how much more effective she was with her liquid flow of Spanish, pirouetting and flashing her eyes, while I, or a young Mexican-American, laboriously translated after her. She spent many hours also among the underprivileged Mexican people of the Los Angeles area, talking in Spanish to mothers' clubs and visiting kindergartens for children who spoke no English. She made long trips with interpreters to visit rural schools in southern California.

The older teachers in the group which financed her treated her like a doll. They bought her new clothes, entertained her in apartments where the beds came out of the wall, and where the elevators ran to the tenth or twelfth floor. They took her to a cafeteria, gave her rides on double-decker buses, showed her the Pacific Ocean. In 1954, in her nice apartment in Mexico City, she beguiled me still with pantomimes that mimicked the way the ladies had babied her and tried clothes on her, and my silly looks when I had interpreted what she said in some dignified meeting and had tried to cover up how poorly I knew Spanish. Life has always been a very gay event for Rosita, and the trip to Los Angeles was a high point.

When the school year opened for her in the spring of 1937, she returned to Oaxaca, loaded down with presents. The teachers' club even bought her a pullman berth as far as Guadalajara, a thing most Mexican teachers never even see. She took back a suitcase full of picture books and primary-school equipment. But she did not go back to the school in Santa Cruz Etla. She was met at the train by Oaxaca school dignitaries and escorted to meetings where she made speeches. Mr. Ximello arranged programs at which rural teachers for thirty miles around could hear her tell about the kindergartens and primary schools in Los Angeles. Then Mr. Ximello offered her the best kindergarten job the rural authorities had available in the Oaxaca Valley.

Santa Cruz Etla had given her one assistant in her last three years there and had paid her fifty-four pesos a month, at that time about eleven dollars. The town of Mitla, thirty miles down the valley, had a "rural school" of two hundred students with six teachers. There she could teach the kindergarten only, the little ones she loved the most! She would be paid one hundred eight pesos; she could live in the nice inn where Mexican archeologists stayed when they came to study the ancient ruins of Mitla. A regular bus ran back to Oaxaca every day. Her mother could be happy among the ladies of the two educated families who ran Mitla's affairs. It was like coming to teach in Main Street after six years at the Bear River school.

But she left Santa Cruz with regret, and no community she has known since has loved her so much. Two years in the Mitla school, combined with her speeches at teachers' meetings, brought her to the attention of Oaxaca *city* school authorities at the time they first began to found kindergartens in the poorer sections of the city. She was willing to start in the city as a beginning assistant because her mother could be with her relatives there. When I came again in 1944, she was directing a city kindergarten for sixty children, with five assistants to help her.

She had refused four different offers of marriage, probably in the same gay, bantering tone of voice in which she told me about them. No marriage in the Latin American provincial style, wherein the woman loses independence, would have satisfied her, she repeated scornfully. She loved the work with the *probrecitos*, the poor little ones of the kindergarten, too much. Besides, there was her mother, Doña Rafaela, her much older aunt, Doña Mercedes, and her oldest-of-all uncle, Don Octaviano—all these people now lived on her salary in the three rooms she rented off a nice old colonial patio near the Benito Juárez Park. What man would support all these people? and, she asked, what man would all these dear old relatives like well enough to approve as her husband?

Then in 1948 she was promoted suddenly to an office for kindergarten directors in Mexico City. Soon she was writing me about a wonderful doctor she had met in her work there, a doctor sent to the slum kindergartens to check on X-rays and eye tests of children. When I wrote her that I was driving through Mexico to Central America in 1951, she urged me to come in the spring so that I might attend her wedding to this "wonder man." Then thirty-seven, she was still a pretty and charming bride.

During my 1944 visit at Doña Estéfana's and my 1945 visit at Doña Patrocina's, she came up from Oaxaca City in the school authorities' station wagon, or on the San Lorenzo bus, to spend occasional week ends with me. In 1951, being a new bride in Mexico City, she did not want to leave her husband, busy with his health department work, and we did not have her with us on that year's one-day visit. The people were so disappointed not to see her that I chided her about it on my return through Mexico City. Perhaps this scolding, perhaps her boredom with the inactive life of a well-to-do doctor's wife, perhaps the urgency to contribute something herself to her husband's generous support of all her relations, led her to go back into teaching again the next spring. Mostly, I think, it was her love of the little children; she never has had any of her own. Her husband discovered, in his medical work, a newly built shanty-town slum area without any kindergarten. Rosita went to the authorities for whom she had been working two years previously and got their consent to open a kindergarten in an empty house. She organized a mothers' club, raised money for equipment among the doctor's friends, and soon had a hundred twenty children in an authorized public kindergarten, with herself and five young assistants on the pay roll. She found time to teach in the same area in the program against illiteracy among adults. She kept her now invalid mother in Mexico City with her, and she continued to maintain the three-room "flat" in Oaxaca for Aunt Mercedes and Uncle Octaviano.

Busy with all this new activity and interest, she still had time to love Santa Cruz Etla. Young people who came from the Etla Hills to work in Mexico City, men who came from any part of that region to work as field hands in the United States, Don Martín who came to Mexico City for a trip in 1954, all these people "cleared" through Rosita. She found them places to stay, helped them find their way around the city, sometimes bought them tickets back home. She could not leave the city kindergarten to drive down with us in 1954, but she knew more about the families and the present problems of everyone in Santa Cruz at that time than I did after having just spent ten days at Don Martin's. She has maintained the liaison between those of the younger generation who have moved to Mexico City and the old people in the home town, and she has been the source of much of my information on the villagers while the years since 1954 passed so swiftly.

Though I have not meant to judge other teachers harshly, no teacher at Santa Cruz Etla since Rosita has approached her in interest, enthusiasm, and long-term success. Considered a model school while she was there, Santa Cruz was able to get a good teacher as her successor, a fine young married man whose wife worked with him as primary teacher. We watched them teaching during that day's visit to Don Julio in 1938, and we never doubted that the school's fine service and reputation would go right on. But they were too good to stay long in the poorly-paid mountain position. Then the fame which had accrued to the school because of our visit there and Rosita's subsequent visit to the United States faded as the teachers changed; and soon the job was no more desirable for ambitious young teachers than any other mountain village far from good transportation and comfortable living. When I write about the classes I have visited there over the two decades, it is impossible not to compare everything I saw after 1934 with Rosita's methods and successes.

❧ 2 ❧

MY FIRST FRIENDS in Santa Cruz Etla were the children, those who were in school in 1934—Nico, and Joel, and Don Martín's future daughter-in-law, Chabella, who were in the upper classes; Espe-

144

ranza and Don Amado's Cassiano just entering the first grade. I told Rosita in a letter in the spring of 1944 that I was coming back for a couple of weeks that summer to see how much the school had accomplished in the ten years since my first visit. Had a rural school raised the village's standard of living? Would the children who went to the school raise more corn per acre when they were grown than their fathers did before them? Would they practice the rules of sanitation, and thus lower the death rate? Can a school over a ten-year period bring about all this progress in a primitive community where there has been no school before? These were the learned sociological questions I intended to answer in a formal university paper by going to Santa Cruz and living two weeks with Doña Estéfana in 1944.

But when I came that year, I was immediately so absorbed in the families of all my old friends and in their fortunes and adventures during the ten years that I almost forgot about that last abstract question. Even now, after more than two decades, not just one, I don't want it answered about the actual school itself, for the classes and the spirit are not the same as they were in 1934. The school is no longer a splendid new victory in the battle to make Santa Cruz a separate town. Don Amado, its idealistic founder, is long since dead, and his fresh enthusiasm for the school as a wonderful new idea died with him. All the towns between the sierra and the city have schools now; and present-day Santa Cruz, most of whose young fathers and mothers went to school themselves, takes the school very much for granted. Teachers come and go; the school committee plants a crop on *la parcela*, in a good corn year, about one in two or three years, to raise money to paint and repair the building. The little equipment the teachers have wears out, and sometimes is replaced and sometimes isn't. Santa Cruz Etla has just the ordinary rural school today. "Remember the days of Rosita in the school, Doña Elena?" Nico and Chabella have often said to me. They were good days.

Of course, even in the days of Rosita it did not seem like a modern American school. Nothing was done "efficiently" or on time. Attendance was not compulsory; few children went regularly every day. Rosita would get up and ring the bell about eight. But no one came to school until the stock was watered, the alfalfa cut, the goats sent off to pasture, the corn ground, the tortillas made, and the babies tended. Every child had a job to do in his own home. The children would begin to straggle into school at nine or nine-thirty. Of the fifty or more children that Rosita had on the registration lists, perhaps thirty-five would show up any one day.

They worked hard at reading and writing and arithmetic all morning. I was particularly interested in the textbooks they had then. The primer started with a simple story about Firmín, an Indian boy in a small town where a school had just been started. Firmín wanted to go to school; all his village felt it was a wonderful opportunity. In the morning Firmín cared for the burro, ate his tortillas, put on his sombrero, and went happily to school.

The second grade continued the story of Firmín in another reader. These little books were printed on newsprint paper and contained only black and white line drawings, but they were about something Santa Cruz Etla children could understand. The third- and fourth-grade readers carried a "special message" about Firmín. He was able to go to school because the peasants had won the revolution of 1910 and 1920. His father would vote for the first time and would own his land. The Mexican federal government, under a wise president, sent money for the new rural school. Firmín was proud to be an Indian, because Mexico was the real Indian country. The wicked, Spanish-blooded landlords had lost their land and their power. Firmín would learn to do the handicraft work of the Indian people; he would dance the old folk dances and sing the regional songs. He would join the revolutionary political party and go to the finest fiestas on the birthdays of the revolutionary leaders, Zapata, Carranza, Obregón, and Calles. Especially he would revere Benito Juárez, who was the first Indian reform leader.

Firmín also grew a scientific garden, in the fourth-grade book, and helped his father plant diversified crops as well as corn and beans. He encouraged his family to use clean spring water for drinking. He was a "cultural mission" for his own family. His young sister helped his mother keep the baby clean and fed it warm cow's milk. In short, to the children who went through four grades in the days of Rosita, Firmín was a model for peon behavior and village improvement. Certainly Firmín's school in Firmín's village raised the standard of living in less than a decade.

But the Firmín readers did not last. Only one set of twenty books for each grade was ever sent to Santa Cruz Etla, and the cheap little books were nearly worn out when I was there. In Rosita's last year of teaching they were replaced with prosy citified little stories without the "political propaganda." Chabella and Joel both referred to the Firmín books in 1954, though, and they thought of Firmín almost as if he were a boy who had gone to school with them.

"Progressive" as the readers were, Rosita and "El Maestro," as the young man teacher was called, taught them by the old-fashioned method of having everyone read aloud at once, not in unison, but each at his own speed. Soon some were on page ten, while others were still on page two. If the students hurried with the reading, they could get to the written lesson sooner. When they finished all the written lessons in the third Firmín book, they "took a test" and passed the third grade. All this reading and writing took place between the time the children got to school and about the middle of the morning. Then they did arithmetic till midday, when the sun was highest overhead. There were no arithmetic books in any grade. El Maestro taught the younger children problems on a large abacus or counting frame; Rosita wrote out sums on paper for the older ones. At noon Rosita rang the bell, and everyone went home.

The afternoon at school was the most fun. Rosita would eat her dinner, chat with us, or visit families where children had troubles. Sometimes she took a siesta. She would ring the bell about three, and the children came trooping back by three-thirty or four. Then the little girls would embroider, while the boys worked in the garden with El Maestro. The boys raised flowers and spinach, squashes and beans, corn and chile. They learned to put manure on the land, to save the best seed, to thin the young plants. They had already learned in their school garden half the things about agriculture which the cultural missions were supposed to try to teach.

The young man teacher was an enthusiast for a better garden. He himself was a Yalalteca Indian from the far sierra, where the women still wear long, nightgown-type dresses of hand-spun white cotton and wrap their heads in heavy turbans of black wool. In his mountain home he knew no Spanish, but he came as a scholarship student to Oaxaca to learn the language and the methods of rural teaching. There was then no school building in his own region, so he served an apprenticeship at the Santa Cruz school for two years. When we came back in 1938, he had gone home to his own sierra. The Yalalteca country seems as far away as the United States to the people of Santa Cruz Etla, and they have asked me about him every time I have come since. I have never seen him again, but Rosita used to see him at yearly school conventions. She has kept up with him ever since and tells me that he is now a director over several schools in his own hills.

In the late afternoon he would teach the children to drill, to march in a column behind the flag, to turn and salute. They had just learned to do this when I took a movie of them which shows the younger ones all right-facing when El Maestro called left-face, and saluting with the wrong hand. On the days of the births of Hidalgo and Juárez, they marched behind the flag up and down the central ridge.

In the afternoon the children sometimes had art lessons. Under Rosita's guidance they had stenciled a geometric design in red, blue, and green calcimine all around the school porch. I took over from there and earned the hospitality extended me by helping the two higher grades make drawings and designs with crayons. I soon ran out of what paper and crayons I had with me, but I was able to buy more when I went in to the Oaxaca market in Don Martín's oxcart.

Yes, the school was a gay place when Rosita was there. Everyone stopped to chat when passing the school porch. The children sang and danced to Rosita's guitar. They kept chickens and rabbits in the school garden, and they had two dogs, a baby goat, and a baby burro as pets. All these *animalitos* had names and were considered the children's friends. A year-old baby named Aurelia, a child of a young Don Lalo who lived in the ravine just below the school, came by with her father every day to see us and to play with the rabbits. She learned to walk that summer on the school steps.

The children of the "days of Rosita" I remember so well because they are in the movie we took, preserved forever in celluloid, frozen at six, at eight, or at ten, working in the garden, dancing on the school steps, drinking at the brook, or even, like Francisco León, trying to lead a recalcitrant pig. Though I know many of them well as grown people, I still think of them as they were in those happy days of 1934. Two of them in particular, Augustina and Crescencio, in the movie so often, are connected with special recollections of that first decade.

◈ 3 ◈

Augustina, I suppose, would be chalked up as a failure for a cultural missions program, a failure even for Rosita, though they loved each other so much. She was *tonta* when she came to the school, and all the Santa Cruz people consider her yet "one of those *tonto* people from up the sierra." In fact, she does not live as well now as she did when I first saw her, although maybe she is just as happy. She was only eight years old then, a tiny scrap of a ragged little Indian. It is the custom in many Oaxaca City families to provide board and room for a small girl, or more often for a small boy, in return for dishwashing, table waiting, errand running, and charcoal fanning. When Rosita and her mother came to Santa Cruz Etla, they took a different child each year to live with them in the schoolhouse. Augustina was the third such child Rosita had helped that way to stay in school, so she told me.

And it is not incorrect to use the word "helped." Augustina was poor and ragged and dirty. She slept on a *petate* in the shack which served as Rosita's kitchen. She often looked as if she slept right among the ashes, for she came up all dusty in the mornings, and

Rosita seldom had time to comb her long braids of hair. Augustina was the second girl in a family of woodcutters up at the head of *el río*, people whom I never heard called by name. Her father was spoken of only as the woodcutter, *el leñador, padre de la Augustina de Rosita.* Dirty and overworked as she was, Augustina was better off under Rosita's kindly eye than at home; and she got two years of schooling, which none of the rest of her family ever had.

While we lived at the school, she went every morning at dawn to Doña Estéfana's to get a pitcher of milk for us. She would relight the charcoal fire from last night's embers by vigorous fanning, and put on the milk to boil so that it would keep all day. Then she would be off with the corn to the mill down in San Pablo Etla, for Rosita's mother wanted the corn ground early in the day and there was no mill nearer than San Pablo then. It would be two hours before she would be back, and we would barely have got up.

The rest of her day was just as busy. She never was able to go to school on the days when Doña Rafaela washed. She had to stand by every minute to run to the brook for more water, and she always helped to wring out the clothes, tiny as her hands were. On other days Doña Rafaela or Rosita or I would comb out her hair, and she would sit with El Maestro's primary class, chanting the numbers to fifty and learning to write her name.

But she had to leave class early to help Rosita's mother get our dinner. She spent an hour fanning the charcoal, bringing more water for the cooking, setting up a school table for us at the end of the school porch, and making the *salsa*. I have movies of her grinding tomatoes for *salsa*, turning tortillas on the griddle, and washing off the *metate* after the tortillas were finished. She seems so busy and efficient that it is hard to realize that she is now a grown person working with giant tortillas, and no longer an eight-year-old.

After each meal she washed the dishes. As we had had the dysentery quite badly, we had all sorts of ideas about boiling all the water, since no one had suggested orange-leaf tea to us then. The ideas seemed hopeless when we watched Augustina washing our dishes in the stream, sitting on the little stone bridge that crossed the brook and tilting herself upside down to wash each

Rosita with Nico
and Doña Estéfana, 1944

sita
mmercial photo taken of her in
s Angeles in 1937

Two happy couples in Mexico City, 1951
left to right: Rosita's doctor husband, Rosita, the author,
and Mr. Henry Morle Bailey, the author's husband

The meeting about problems in 1944

Left to right: Don Luis Varela, the director; Chico López; Rosita; the young man secretary; the inspector; Don Féliz Jiménez, president in 1954; Esteban, president in 1944; Don Féliz León; Máximo, brother of Esteban

The famous photograph of the little girls and the costume dolls taken in 1934, and shown afterwards to so many school children in Los Angeles. From left: Rosario now dead; Augustina; Don Julio's Juanita in front; the Eleanora who now has eight children, in rear; Domitila, married in San Pablo; at rear the Carmita who mistreated her mother; a María from San Sebastián; Chabella who became the daughter-in-law of Don Martín

individual object back and forth in the water. Her afternoons were freer than those of the children who lived at home, because Rosita took two hours off after dinner before she rang the midafternoon school bell. Often she had time then to play with, and talk to, Augustina, sewing up rents in her clothes or making her new ones. Sometimes she would take the girl alone into the primary room and have her count or write on the piece of oilcloth used as a blackboard, for Augustina was so shy she would never recite when the other children were there. She would do it for Rosita only because she loved Rosita so much. She was like some wild little mountain spirit who had never before been caged. Until her seventh year she had doubtless never gone beyond the head of the ravine where she lived and had seen no other children except her own brothers and sisters. The school at Santa Cruz Etla must have seemed the whole outside world to her. She was still afraid even to talk out loud.

Without talking at all, she was able to help me a great deal when I first came in 1934. I had come to Santa Cruz Etla determined that my husband and I would not be any bother to the teacher or her family. We had told Mr. Ximello that we would care for and cook for ourselves. We had brought dishes and cooking pots and staple things with us, a long list of things purchased in Oaxaca. Rosita fell in with our plan right away and "assigned" Augustina to help us. When I think of those hectic first days during which I tried to do the cooking, my later visits at Doña Patrocina's or at Don Martín's seem restful periods of bliss. "The tiny little Indian who lives with the teacher was sent in all directions to buy eggs, milk, white cheese, onions, peppers, and squash for me," I wrote in my diary of that first day. As I remember, we did not have many five- or ten-centavo pieces, and we sent Augustina out with silver pesos and five-peso bills, which she had never seen before. I marvel now at how she bought things, but then I was impatient at my difficulty with the small amounts of things and the limited variety. When Augustina was not running around trying to buy me things, she crouched on the floor and fanned the charcoal.

Whatever made me think I was less bother to them when I did

151

the cooking, I don't know. Doña Rafaela not only had to loan me Augustina all the time, but she had to "translate" for me when I made purchases from visitors, repeating slowly to me how much the squash cost, or how soon I would be able to buy a chicken. Augustina went down the ridge to buy more charcoal for me when I ran out, and we delayed dinner endlessly, taking up Doña Rafaela's kitchen and cooking space all the while. Augustina would patter back, her bare feet hitting the road in a sort of dogtrot; we would get more charcoal on the fire, fan it into a blaze, and start the squash cooking again. Surely Doña Rafaela and Rosita were laughing at me all the while. But not Augustina. She would look wistfully at me as we crouched together on the dirt floor trying to get the charcoal lighted. When it finally glowed she would flash me a shy smile of triumph. And she so loved the glazed ware, the knives, the forks, and the glasses which we had brought with us that she washed them over and over for fun. We were kindred spirits, two strangers in Doña Rafaela's kitchen in Santa Cruz Etla; I because I had never cooked under such difficulties and the things seemed so primitive, Augustina because she had never cooked in such splendor and the things seemed so sophisticated.

After a week of this I went to Saturday market along with Rosita and Doña Estéfana in a burro caravan. Doña Rafaela and Augustina were to take care of my husband's midday meal while I was gone. When I came back in the evening, he was enthusiastic about the dinner and had even saved some of it to be warmed over for supper. He wondered why what Doña Rafaela fixed was so much better than anything I had been able to cook, when I seemed to work so hard at it. I apologized for the "bother" it had been to Doña Rafaela to cook for him. She hastened to assure me it had been less "bother" than usual. Only she and Augustina had been in the kitchen! After that we gave her one peso fifty a day, and she purchased and prepared everything for us. Augustina ran the errands, made the purchases, and served the meal.

Augustina remained our good friend after I was thus "eased out" of the kitchen. My husband won her, and several other children who hung around the school all day, by making them pinwheels. She would have time to watch him make only one, and then she would dart off like a wood sprite for more water or milk or corn for Doña Rafaela. Sometimes she would be watching me sketching or writing. I would feel her presence and look up. She would whisper, *Con permiso,* and slip quietly away.

Augustina began afterwards to call me the lady of the dolls, *la señora de las muñecas.* I wanted to take something back to the Los Angeles schools as an international friendship exchange, and I had been disappointed when I first came to my *pueblecito* because no *sarapes* were woven there and no pottery was made. Rosita helped me by suggesting that I buy dolls, and she and the children would dress them in costumes of the Oaxaca region. She told the little girls of the sewing class about the project, and they were enthusiastic. Augustina, who seldom had time to sew, listened from her hiding place behind Rosita's chair.

That first trip I made to the market on burros (the time Doña Estéfana laughed as I climbed onto the burro between the baskets, and the time my husband got his first good Santa Cruz dinner), Rosita and I went to buy dolls to dress. It was not as easy as it sounds. No dolls were for sale in Oaxaca in 1934, at least not what we would call modern dolls. Today, since the Pan American Highway has been opened, there are many shops around the plaza which sell all kinds of factory-made articles, including toys. But twenty-five years ago we looked in vain. A peddler in the open market, wandering without a stall, displaying wooden monkeys on sticks, found eight little doll bodies for us in his big sack—doll bodies made of cloth, with painted tin heads, the type of doll the little girls of 1849 brought to California with them in covered wagons. Rosita was very pleased with these dolls, and I thought them so quaint and old fashioned that the project took on renewed interest.

Then the big problem was to buy cloth for the dresses, a quarter of a yard of this, a half-yard of that. We had to buy much more goods than we needed. We bought so many pieces of things that I really could not visualize how Rosita thought the costumes were going to look. We were nearly all day doing the buying. At three-thirty we wearily loaded dolls and finery into the burro panniers, piled ourselves on top, and started the long trek back uphill. Doña Estéfana had gone on long before us, and we did not pull in till after sunset.

The little girls came on Sunday to ask if we had been able to purchase dolls. Most of them, like Augustina, had never seen any dolls before, and these primitive ones delighted them. The bright silk and wool, the six colors of embroidery thread, the bands of lace were theirs to look at, to feast their eyes on, but not to touch until Rosita made the plans on Monday afternoon. There was a record attendance of little girls at school on Monday.

Only eight girls actually sewed; Don Julio's pretty little daughter Juanita whom he married off so early into San Pablo, Chabella who married Don Martín's only son Miguelito, Carmita who was afterwards so unkind to her old deaf mother, a Domitila from the San Sebastián ridge who has died since, the Rafaela who is married to Don Julio's Eduardo, the Refugio who is married to Don Julio himself, and two others of the older girls whose names I don't remember. Augustina counted as a ninth. Although she took no permanent stitches, she did the basting, picked up all the scraps, and held the dolls while Rosita tried the clothes on them. She made friends with the other girls and quite blossomed out during the sewing of the doll costumes.

The women of the Isthmus of Tehuantepec, who are sometimes seen in full regalia at Oaxaca markets and fiestas, wear the most beautiful costumes in Mexico. A full, bright skirt of silk, red or green or blue, is covered with heavy floral embroidery in all colors; around the bottom is pleated a white lace flounce ten or twelve inches deep. A square, straight blouse, or *huipil,* hangs sleeveless from the shoulders and is even more elaborately embroidered than the skirt. On the head is worn a sort of wide halo cap made of many yards of pleated white lace. Our two dolls dressed as Tehuanas were the most beautiful ones. Chabella did all the embroidery on these Tehuana dresses, making half-inch flowers of blue and yellow on the red silk of the dresses. Lace intended to decorate the white panties of rich little city girls had been purchased for the flounce and the headdress. Chabella was chosen not only because she was one of the best seamstresses, but also because she had actually seen a Tehuana once in the market at Oaxaca. Domitila, as I remember, had been to the great Oaxaca July fiesta, the *Lunes del Cerro,* and had seen resplendent Tehuanas there, but she could not sew as well as Chabella.

The traditional Mexican fiesta dress, called a *China Poblana,* which appears on all the gaudy, pretty-girl calendars, is seen in Oaxaca occasionally, but only on that July fiesta day; it is not considered the custom in Oaxaca. But I knew Los Angeles students would expect such dresses, and I insisted on having two dolls in the *Poblana* dress. I had to help with the sewing of them myself, as Rosita had seldom seen such a costume. It has the heavy, red-wool skirt covered with spangles, the green, pointed insets of silk in the top of the skirt, the wide sash made from a *rebozo,* and the embroidered, white-silk blouse with a Mexican eagle in front and flowers on the sleeves.

Two dolls were to be Indians from the sierra, Yalaltecs from the country of El Maestro. He superintended their preparation himself. They were dressed in long loose sacks of unbleached muslin, hung at the shoulders with black cord (we used shoestrings on the dolls), and embroidered with lines of blue and red around the bottom and around the neck. We wrapped black shoestrings around their heads to satisfy El Maestro's demand for the heavy wool turbans of his mother's people. The three older girls who had been in the market had often seen these Yalalteca people there. They come on foot and on burro-back from fifty and sixty miles away. Though Oaxaca City is now very sophisticated and fewer and fewer Indian types are seen there today, I saw a whole family of Yalaltecs, still in the costumes of the dolls, walk nonchalantly across the plaza on a market day in 1954.

Everyone knew the *China Oaxaqueña* costume. Rosita had made one for *La Patria* to wear on September 16. Most Santa Cruz mothers had that style of dress, a full-gored skirt set into a white, lace-trimmed blouse, with a *rebozo* crossed on the chest. Rosita had one made of silk which she later brought with her to Los Angeles, knotting her *rebozo* on her head in true Oaxaca Indian fashion whenever she wore it. Our doll dresses were made of pink and lavender silk. I think all the little girls loved those two dolls the most; their dresses were easy to sew, and the dolls looked like Rosita when the dresses were finished.

We had taken many movies of the preparation of the costumes. Then, to accompany the dolls to the Los Angeles schools, we took a posed shot of the dolls and the girls who had worked on them, though I had only a Brownie camera and one roll of film for it. We let Augustina be in the picture and hold a Yalalteca doll, since she had been so enthusiastic and had worked so hard. Even in the picture she seems so shy; she would not look up into the camera.

To conclude the saga of the dolls, they were brought to Los Angeles and packed in a fancy chest, with the story of their preparation and this picture of the girls pasted in the lid. Thousands of Los Angeles school children, both of Anglo-Saxon and of Mexican ancestry, saw and touched them and looked at the picture of the Indian girls who had sewed the dresses, with Augustina standing with downcast eyes in the front row. The dolls went on tour with Rosita to schools in California in 1937. A home-economics class in Los Angeles dressed eight beautiful little china dolls in American clothes, play clothes and school clothes, packed them in another chest, and sent them back to Mr. Ximello for the children of Santa Cruz Etla. But a year and a half passed before they arrived. Mr. Ximello was no longer director; Rosita did not know of their whereabouts when we were with her at Don Julio's in 1938. I hope only that some little Indian girls in some Oaxaca village had a chance to love them.

At least Augustina got a doll. I was determined to buy her one and dress it for her myself, after all the costume dolls were finished. I intended to make the purchase on our last trip that summer to the Oaxaca market, the time we went in Don Martín's oxcart. My husband and I, Rosita, Doña Rafaela, all went. There was room to squeeze in Augustina, too—Augustina who had never seen a paved street, nor a glass window, nor a two-story house. She sat crouched at Doña Rafaela's feet without saying a word all through the trip, even though the oxen ran the cart into a ditch near the city when the train went by. She pattered along behind us at the market and sat swinging her legs from a high bench in the big Oaxaca plaza. She was most fascinated with the automobiles. Even then there were ten or twelve taxis in Oaxaca, and a bus which ran all around the residential district on the outskirts of town.

My husband, sitting in the park with Augustina while Rosita and I finished shopping, had the great idea for the climax to Augustina's day. When the bus came next to the plaza, he paid four fares and took her on the three-mile trip all round the town, twice. Still she had nothing to say. Words were inadequate for the woodland sprite. The only doll I could find her, since we had already bought up the town supply, was a ten-inch celluloid kewpie doll, with a turnip-top knot and little blue wings at the shoulders. It was very fat and was, of course, completely naked. I was embarrassed for it in Santa Cruz Etla. I wrote in the diary about it the next day: "It is a wiser purchase than I thought, for everyone is so delighted with it. I promised to make some clothes for it, as its nakedness shocks even its most enthusiastic admirers. I explained that it is neither a boy nor a girl, and is supposed to be a sort of an angel. I spent all morning making it two little dresses out of the rest of the scraps and helping Augustina put them on and off."

A week later I wrote: "Doña Enriqueta wanted to know in what part of the United States the babies looked like Augustina's kewpie, and I have to explain again that it is an *angelito*." Perhaps Santa Cruz Etla people still think today that when babies die they go happily to a heaven full of kewpies.

But the Augustina story does not end happily. We asked for her in 1938, that day at Don Julio's, when Rosita had already been gone from the school a year; and we were told that she had been living with her father for the past two years, and that no one ever saw her pass on the trails. She had vanished from sight. I inquired in vain about her many times during the days I spent at Doña Estéfana's in 1944. When Rosita was with me for a week end the following year at Doña Patrocina's, a shy young Indian mother slipped from behind the mango trees. Rosita recognized her immediately. "It is Augustina," she called out.

Augustina had been married at fifteen to a Juan López, a third son in a crowded family on the San Sebastián ridge, near Don Marciano's. It would have been following the custom for Augustina to bring a bridal chest and a *metate* and to move into the one-room López shack. But she and Juan López had decided otherwise. They had gone above the highest woodcutter's hut on the trail up to the sierra, where they had built a thatch and bamboo shack. When we saw her at Doña Patrocina's she had a sickly son about two years old who was still sucking at the breast. She was willing to pose for a Kodachrome picture with the baby, but she had very little to say to Rosita, and nothing but shy smiles for me. Afterwards I tried to find her little house up the sierra when I was out on *el caballo*, but I could not locate it.

In 1951 Doña Patrocina, who knew I had always been interested in Augustina, volunteered for me the information that the baby had died. Augustina had brought it to Doña Patrocina for treatment; the cure woman had told her to bring lard and alcohol, and to come back the next day. These things were luxuries to Augustina, no doubt, and she had never come back. Members of the López family, always unfriendly to people on the central ridge, told Doña Patrocina that the baby had died "doubtless because that foreign woman had taken its picture," a very distressing comment for Doña Patrocina, who hesitated to pass it along to me. In 1952, however, the cure woman went up the sierra on burro-back to deliver another, healthier child, a girl this time; and as far as she or anyone knew, this child thrived. I asked all the people, especially the woodcutters, to get word up to Augustina in 1954 that I was there at Don Martín's and wanted to see her for more photos, a mistake perhaps, for she did not come near and never exposed this new baby to "the evil eye."

Neither Doña Patrocina nor I ever saw her husband. Since they own no corn land and must depend on the woodcutting, he is always gone from dawn to dark, even depending on others in his family to market his wood for him in the city. How lonesome Augustina must be up there, four miles above the school and the mill. On the face of it, she seems the only pitiful one, now, of all the children whom I knew in 1934. She has probably forgotten how to read; she has never again had a glimpse of that outside world she saw when she washed our dishes, dressed the dolls, rode the bus in Oaxaca City, and owned a kewpie. In comparison to Chabella, she is no credit to Rosita's program.

But she is independent. She runs no errands for a mother-in-law. Her house is her own house; no one tells her anything. She has lost a baby, but she has another, and she is barely thirty. Who knows but that she is happier than Esperanza or Juanita? At any rate, she is a mountain sprite who still lives on the mountain.

✦ 4 ✦

WE WERE GIVEN a big send-off fiesta when we left the happy life of the school in 1934, that fiesta at which we were donated all the flowers left over from the baby's funeral the day before. In connection with that celebration we always will remember one child, Crescencio, the youngest of Doña Paula's three very ragged and neglected sons, and the "bad-boy" comic character around the school porch all that summer, twenty-five years ago. The internal conflict between his shyness and refusal to speak on the one hand, and his large bump of curiosity on the other, was always getting him into difficulties. He was one of the first children whom we had known by name during our stay at the school. I wrote in the third day's entry of my 1934 diary: "There is a child named Crescencio, the neighborhood comedian, who climbs mango trees when he has only a rag or two on, and who simply lives off mangoes." He looked like the poorest city beggar, his hair an uncombed shock, his face always dirty, his shirt and pants blackened and tattered shreds.

When we woke up in the morning, his seven-year-old face would be peering around the school door. He was five or ten feet behind us everywhere we went. When Rosita spoke to him, he would dart away like a frightened animal; but he always came back. My husband won his confidence by making him paper pinwheels, and since

159

he could not understand Crescencio's words anyway, they got along splendidly without talking. He is in every movie shot we took at the school in 1934, his mouth full of mangoes, his stomach protruding. Show a picture of an oxcart loaded with firewood for the market, Crescencio is seen hanging on behind as the the cart passes the camera. Show a sequence of school classes, children busily taking drawing lessons from me on the school porch, Crescencio is seen eating mangoes under the table. In a sequence in which Rosita is directing work in the garden, Crescencio is climbing up a tree in the background. In such a purely feminine activity as the sewing for the dolls, Crescencio peers between two girls' heads as they work. But actually studying in classes, never!

He was supposed to have been registered in the primary class, and he listened outside on the porch while the children learned to count out loud up to fifty. This was done in a singsong way, in unison, and seemed to Crescencio like a tune. Through this song he found his voice and went around singing "thirty-one, thirty-two, thirty-three, forty-one, forty-two, forty-eight, forty-nine, fifty," which really sounds much more musical in Spanish than in English. He had a nice voice for a little boy, and his song pleased Rosita. Soon we were all singing *cuarenta y ocho, cuarenta y nueve, cincuenta.* He never learned to write down the figures, though.

He had every excuse to be around the school. Doña Paula's old mother lived with her then, though she died in the early winter of 1934. That summer she was helping augment the little money the widowed Doña Paula could get from selling flowers by making the tortillas for the teacher's family—for Rosita herself, Uncle Octaviano who spent months at a time up in Santa Cruz, Doña Rafaela, and then for us. Crescencio was expected to carry the water, collect the wood, and make the fire for old Doña Nobarra's work. It was Doña Nobarra who tried to teach me to make tortillas, a thing I have not mastered to this day. Doña Nobarra hardly figures in this book, for she never exchanged conversation with anyone, not even during a lesson in tortilla making; she was as shy as Crescencio and as much a recluse as Doña Paula. But she did provide the excuse for Crescencio's being always around the school.

Rosita decided that the whole school and grounds should be cleaned for our farewell fiesta. She set the children to pulling the weeds out of the brook, sandpapering off the tops of the desks, sweeping dead weeds off the open place between the school and the *municipio*. Crescencio was everywhere very much in evidence, changing jobs very two or three minutes. I was working on the porch with the members of *Los Policías*, helping make wreaths of the greens which had been cut down at *el río* in the morning. Rosita and the children were pruning the rosebushes, throwing away wilted flowers, and even some good ones. It was Crescencio who thought of sticking the flowers around in the wreaths. He kept at one job after that, running back and forth from the porch to the garden. The wreaths were tacked up all round the arcade, and the silent Crescencio himself was moved to exclaim over the beautiful effect.

I was greatly flattered then, and I still am to this day, when I thought of Rosita's fancy preparation and decoration for our fiesta of that year. I understand that the school porch has been decorated with rose wreaths on only that one occasion in its nearly thirty years as center of the town. Then, too, we had all those flowers from the *angelito* at Don Martín's. The fiesta began after the midday meal the day after the *angelito* and lasted well into the night. Night affairs were quite the thing in the days of Rosita because she owned a beautiful Coleman light. I would have given a new Coleman light to the school as a present long ago, but only Uncle Octaviano ever knew how to pump it up and generate it. It made a wonderful light for the fiesta; everyone called it *la luz;* even the faded roses in the wreaths showed up in its reflection.

My husband and I sat surrounded by the banks of flowers, as fine as any two *angelitos*. This was where we first got a taste of how well Rosita herself could dance and sing the songs of Oaxaca for the students and teachers of Los Angeles. All the Santa Cruz musicians were there to help her; the children did group dances in time to the town musicians. Nico and Juanita, both then about twelve, did the *jarabe*, which is the national dance of Mexico. Children very seldom get a chance to take a major part in an official Santa Cruz fiesta, as they did that night; in fact, this is the only time a fiesta in connection with our coming or going has ever been "school-centered."

All these performances by the children were followed by the usual adult speechmaking. I remember Rosita giving us a build-up. "They are teachers in schools with thousands of students. [We had both been teaching in Los Angeles' big city high schools.] They could have stayed all summer to dance in their own country. But they came to live with us, to help teach our children, to dance at our funerals." This brought rousing cheers.

Don Martín was acting as master of ceremonies. He introduced the school numbers and Rosita's dances. El Maestro recited a long historic poem about Benito Juárez. Then Don Martín unexpectedly said: "The next number will be a song by Crescencio."

Everyone clapped and laughed. We all knew, the whole town knew, just what it was that Crescencio could sing; and we appreciated Rosita's little joke. She had put Don Martín up to asking Crescencio as a last comic touch to the serious program.

Crescencio the Show-off climbed to the pile of adobe bricks used as the school stage, still in his ragged clothes, stomach bare. Rosita had that very day shaved his head clean to kill the lice, and his face looked more comical than ever. He planted his feet apart, smiled at the crowd, and opened his mouth to sing *cuarenta y uno, cuarento y dos.* But Crescencio the Shy One suddenly backed down. His more timid personality won out, and he fell to his hands and knees, scurrying off the platform like a frightened rabbit. The crowd urged him and urged him to come back out from under the stage, and he finally consented to try once more. The same thing happened again. Rosita gave up the idea of presenting him on the program, and the musicians tuned up for a dance.

Late into the night we danced, the children all still up watching us. Finally three of the musicians went home. The town-council members, who had been freely passing around the tequila, were determined not to let the party break up. They made a second round of lengthy and dignified speeches, thanking us for spending the summer with them. They offered five-centavo pieces to any school child who could sing. Chabella, Juanita, and two little girls I don't remember had the courage to do so, to the tune of Rosita's guitar. They were loudly applauded.

Then someone remembered Crescencio. He was found sitting in a fork of his mother's mango tree, looking down from the dark onto the lighted festivities. Someone held up a five-centavo piece so he could see it in the light; a second man held up another. I am sure Crescencio had never had a five-centavo piece in his life. He climbed down out of the mango tree and up onto the stage again.

But two failures had made him even more scared than before. He began to tremble and stood still as if glued to the spot. The audience was with him. More five-centavo pieces were offered, until every man left on the school porch had put up money to hear Crescencio sing. The money amounted to more than a peso. In those days he could have purchased a new shirt with it to cover his bare little brown stomach. Alas, no words, no numbers would come out. Finally, he "unfroze" and was able to get down off the stage, only to run home in tears at the struggle between his two personalities.

He was as much in evidence as ever the next day. I was packing our stuff while Rosita and some members of her Mothers' Club watched me. I was giving things away right and left, brushes and paint and paper to the school, mattress pads and dishes and knives and forks to Doña Rafaela, and to members of the Mothers' Club. For Rosita to use in the community I left all the first-aid supplies we had, some cotton, some needles, some scissors, and three cakes of Life Buoy soap. I have never been able to give so much away again, because I have always brought less in the first place and have always used more of it up. Perhaps the people have often been disappointed.

But to Crescencio that day, Crescencio who stood around so hopefully while I packed in public, I suddenly decided to give a whole package of safety pins. I held him still while my husband pulled his rags together and pinned them in four different places. He was so pleased with this gift, which we meant as a joke, that my husband felt ashamed of making fun of the child and gave him his jack-knife. No man carried such a thing in the Etla Hills; everyone had admired Don Enrique's use of it in cutting pinwheel sticks and whistles for the school children. Now it belonged to Crescencio forever; he still had it when I last saw him, in 1945, and doubtless still has it today. After the presentation of the jackknife, we gave him a silver peso, to make up for his theatrical failure the night before, with instructions to take it right to his mother for the purchase of a new shirt.

The last shots in the movie show us getting into the back of Don Martín's oxcart, stowing our luggage, and waving goodbye to everyone as we set off for the train. El Maestro kept the camera to take pictures of our departure, so we could both be in the movies, and then ran after the oxcart to return it to us. A month later we had the pictures developed; sure enough, we could see little old Crescencio, hanging on behind, trying to hold his balance underneath the moving cart.

We asked for him at Don Julio's in 1938. My brief diary notes taken then said, "Yes, Crescencio is still here, still shy, eating mangoes all day, peeking around the corners of the houses to watch us, only a little taller, that's all." But he grew up to be a very efficient woodcutter, a watcher of charcoal fires on whom many others depended, and finally to end up very far from Santa Cruz Etla. But that is all part of the account of the future of Santa Cruz, not of the past.

⤳ 5 ⤲

THE "DAYS OF ROSITA" were followed by the era of that *matrimonio*, the married couple who thought of Santa Cruz Etla as such a fine place to teach, a school through which the former teacher had received first a trip to the United States and then a promotion to Mitla. Disillusioned about their own professional advancement, they quit in 1939; and the rural school authorities ceased to think of the school as a prize job to be offered to the best available candidates. Mr. Ximello had been transferred to Mexico City; Rosita was

164

in Mitla. Though the new teachers forgot that Rosita had earned her reputation in Santa Cruz Etla, the town itself did not forget, and made odious comparisons with her methods in front of any new teacher who came. Anyone assigned to the Santa Cruz school heard about her successes there right away, from children and from parents, and would have had a hard time doing as well. For this very reason, as a friend of the famous Rosita I felt ill at ease in front of the later teachers, and I never tried to make arrangements to live as a guest in the school building again. It did not seem like home to me, and I did not feel any warm welcome there. Besides, no later teacher offered to put the primary-class desks out on the porch so I could have the primary classroom for my own private living room and bedroom, as Rosita had done.

By 1944 the school had gone downhill in other ways besides warmth and good will. There had been four different sets of teachers since the *matrimonio*. All idea of teaching there as a job of dignity and prestige was gone. A meek, mousy little primary teacher, Doña Ester Pacheco, lived in one of Rosita's rooms. A young Oaxaca man named Don Solomón, a good violinist, taught the upper class and was called principal of the school.

Everyone in Santa Cruz Etla liked Don Solomón. He played with the town musicians for all fiestas held on weekdays. He helped Chico and Don Fausto and Esteban to read notes, and he gave them much of his old music. The children learned group folk dances from him and many new songs. But the garden went to weeds, the *animalitos* were long since banished from the school, the painted designs chipped off and faded. When beams in the school roof sagged and Don Solomón took no interest, the school committee reflected his attitude, and none were repaired. When books wore out, none came to replace them. When there were no more paper and no more pencils, the children just quit having any practice in writing and arithmetic. Only thirty children were enrolled in the school, of whom only three had stayed to the fourth grade.

When I arrived for my visit with Doña Estéfana in 1944, Rosita was with me herself, having taken a day off her kindergarten job; and we came with the new rural director for Oaxaca in his *camioneta*, his station wagon. How we happened to do that is the beginning of another chapter; but suffice it to say here that Don Solomón's young wife, with whom he was none too happy, had just had a baby in Oaxaca City. For weeks he had been staying in Oaxaca at night, walking to Hacienda Blanca to catch the train; thus, he spent only about three hours a day in Santa Cruz Etla. He was not there, and no older students were at the school, when the director arrived with Rosita and me. Only the little Doña Ester was there, sitting on the school steps outside the locked doors, with a handful of primary children around her, all reading from one tattered book. I do not know what the director had to do with it, because of this bad first impression, but the next year Don Solomón left the school, his wife, and the new baby and went to the United States as a *bracero,* or field hand. No one in Santa Cruz Etla has ever heard from him again.

He did not really made a bad impression on me when I first saw him the next day after our arrival, or even all the following days that I stayed with Doña Estéfana. It was fun to be in his class, as a "student" or as a visitor. He did not have the fourth grade read out loud; instead, he lined everyone up on the porch to dance the *jarabe oaxaqueña* to the tune of his fiddle. Then they did a dance about the *carbonero,* the charcoal salesman. Each boy dances up to a girl in the opposite line, and as he jigs with his feet, he asks the "housewife" to buy charcoal. In the next "act" the girls dance to the boys and ask them to buy eggs and chickens. Then the boys come back to sell *sarapes,* and so on. Rosita, who was still visiting that second day and trying not to antagonize the two new teachers, could not resist joining in as one of the girls in line and teaching them three new verses.

Then Rosita asked them all out into the *campo,* the open ground between the school and the *municipio.* All ages, including Doña Ester the primary teacher, Don Solomón, Rosita, myself, and all the primary children, joined hands in a big circle. Rosita taught them more singing games, one a game like "Farmer in the Dell" called "Oh, Doña Blanca." Doña Blanca buys corn, the corn chooses the *metate,* the *metate* chooses the tortilla, the tortilla chooses the chile,

Crescencio (right) and his
brother Máximo, 1934

On the school porch:
Don Solomón playing the fiddle while the children learned folk dances, 1944

Eostolia, wife of Elijeo
and cousin of Chico and Nico

Eliseo and Elijeo Ramírez
the *analfabeto*

Fourth grade under Doña Ofelia:
Aurelia at left, Gerónomo in center,
Isaías Pérez at right, 1945

Perfecto, 195

Don Alfredo and
his wife with
the school
children in 1954

the chile chooses the bean, the bean chooses the new Doña Blanca, and so all over again. Then they played a "cat and rat" game she showed them. One child, playing the "cat," chases another, the "rat," in and out of a ring of locked hands, while the whole circle tries to help the rat. All this activity was very unusual, as the children never had a recess or played group games of any kind. Rosita had learned these games through her kindergarten teachers' meetings after she left Santa Cruz Etla. Cultural missions were the first to suggest taking the ideas of children's playgrounds and organized play into sierra villages.

Men of the public works committee were repairing the road near the *municipio* so the director's station wagon could come back for me at the end of the visit. They stopped to watch this unusual excitement, and soon were cheering for either the cat or the rat. Women from the nearby houses came over and clapped and sang with the crowd. I had enjoyed being in the ring, being chosen Doña Blanca, and holding hands hard to keep the cat outside the circle. But suddenly I was chosen cat and had to chase an eleven-year-old, third-grade girl in and out of the circle. Naturally I was exhausted quickly, and my failure almost broke up the game. Don Solomón himself saved the day by substituting for me.

When I joined the group of villagers who sat on the old stone church foundation watching the fun, a man I did not recognize spoke to me. "That is my Aurelia you chased, señora."

"Aurelia?" I asked, not remembering the name.

"Yes, I am Don Lalo," he said. "I brought my Aurelia every day to see you and *el señor,* your husband, when you lived in the school. It was then she learned to walk. Surely you know her, she is my only child." It was hard to realize, seeing Rosita so young and gay and playing with the children of Santa Cruz Etla, that ten years had passed since those days. The baby Aurelia was now one of the large girls in school. I met her, a dignified young matron, at Don Féliz' fiesta in 1954 and asked her if she remembered Doña Blanca. At first she hesitated, thinking I referred to some real person; then her face broke into smiles, and she began to sing the little tune of the Farmer in the Dell song.

⚜ 6 ⚜

BUT ROSITA WANTED the children of Santa Cruz Etla to learn something else besides singing games. Always concerned about the problems of Santa Cruz, no matter where she is teaching, she was particularly concerned in the spring of 1944 to hear from the Santa Cruz people, as they came in to the Oaxaca market and stopped to greet her at her "flat" or her kindergarten, that the school enrollment had dropped so badly and that the school itself was deteriorating. When I came to Oaxaca that year, she immediately thought up a scheme to get favors for the village because of my visit. We would go to the state rural education director, get him to assume responsibility for me, and thus bring Santa Cruz Etla to his attention. So that, you see, is how we both, Rosita and I, happened to go up to Santa Cruz Etla that year in all the imposing style of an official station wagon.

The chief rural school positions for the state of Oaxaca had almost become political footballs since the days of Mr. Ximello. New governors had put in new directors, regardless of their interest or experience in Indian education. But in 1943 came Don Luis Varela, himself an Indian from the north of Mexico, to the position of director; and he appointed a real teacher, a Señor Gómez, to be inspector general under him. Rosita, herself a city kindergarten director, had been delighted about these gentlemen and their interest in the rural Indian schools. But there are a score of village schools in the valley of Oaxaca alone. Señors Varela and Gómez had hardly begun to make the rounds. Certainly they had never heard of Santa Cruz Etla.

Rosita, as one director to another, made a formal appointment with Señor Varela to have him meet "her friend, the distinguished American teacher" who had "studied the rural schools near Oaxaca over a ten-year period." This friend wanted "official permission" to visit a certain school in the Etla Hills, a school, incidentally, in which she herself had started to teach, in whose townspeople, therefore, she still felt a great interest. It was an unusually friendly town, too; the people had a high moral character and a great enthusiasm for hard work. It was a shame that Señor Varela was not familiar with this community.

Don Luis Varela, who had welcomed the pretty kindergarten director and her "distinguished guest" most cordially, was full of ideas for the guest to visit model schools in the valley where his own new program already showed results. Wouldn't she like to stay a week in Mitla, a week at Teotitlán del Valle, a week at Tule? But as Rosita talked, he became involved in her web of intrigue, and before we left his office he had offered to drive us to Santa Cruz Etla himself in his official, specially-geared, mountain-climbing station wagon.

On the way we stopped at the San Pablo Etla school, that big, "modern" school with its large attendance, its running water, and its two fine teachers. After this stop Señor Varela was in an expansive mood about schools in the Etla Hills. But alas! Rosita and I and the townspeople of Santa Cruz Etla were badly let down. Unfortunately, we had sent no word of our coming, and that day turned out to be one of those days when Don Solomón had dismissed the school in the morning and had gone home to his sick wife in the city. The handful of primary children on the steps, all reading out of one book, the closed and locked building, the garden standing neglected in the weeds—what an impression for the state director!

Rosita was disappointed and chagrined, of course, but she rallied her forces and characteristically worked out a plan to take advantage of the situation. Leaving me alone at Doña Estéfana's, she went back to Oaxaca in the station wagon with the director, evidently turning on all her charm. She persuaded Don Luis to come back at the end of the week when he could see the "true character of the village people." Would he come for the day and bring the inspector, Señor Gómez?

With this arranged, Rosita excused herself from her kindergarten duties and came back the next day by train and foot to be with me in Santa Cruz Etla. Now she had to bring the community people into the plot, to get them ready to put up a good front before the director and the inspector. On every visit we made in the next few days, when she wasn't teaching Doña Blanca games, Rosita asked the people about the main "problems" of the town, what they thought should be presented as requests to the director. She had a tentative cultural missions list in mind herself, no doubt.

It seems unbelievable, but at first the people—Don Martín, Don Amado, Don Féliz León, Doña Estéfana—did not think the village had any problems. They could think of nothing to request. I saw many problems in Santa Cruz Etla which they *did* know they had. Doña Estéfana cried because she could not get along with her daughter-in-law. Doña Carmen lived alone and brooded over the thoughtlessness of her daughter. Don Amado gave his life to public betterment and would get no appreciation until they gave him a fine funeral after he was dead. Don Florenzio worked hard to build up a fine orchard and had no child to whom he could leave it. Don Féliz Jiménez sought solace from a nagging wife in raising Kentucky Wonder beans. The old people thought the younger ones were forsaking the old customs and were changing too fast; the young ones thought the older ones did not change fast enough. Well, these are all problems of far more sophisticated people than Rosita's people of Santa Cruz Etla, and it takes more than a rural education supervisor to solve them.

Rosita, though, could think of hundreds of things Señor Varela could do for Santa Cruz Etla, and she kept slyly making suggestions on our visits so that the people would think they had thought of the ideas themselves. Finally she got Don Esteban, then president, to call a night meeting. It was the only large mass business meeting I ever attended in Santa Cruz Etla; and it was held in the schoolhouse, as the *municipio* was too small for the crowd of sixty or more people who came. Since the meeting concerned problems of the school, women came as well as men, and they took active part in the discussion. Rosita was staying at Patrocina's the few nights she stayed over, and I was alone up the hill at Estéfana's. Rosita had already taken Chico's lantern and opened the school when I arrived "by flashlight" with Don Pablo, Doña Estéfana, and Don Amado. We kept the kerosene lantern going and lit two candles besides; the Coleman light had gone back to Oaxaca with Uncle Octaviano ten years before. With the kerosene lantern we could not see the faces of all the people who sat on the benches, on the school desks, and on the floor. It took an hour for the crowd to gather after *cena*, so we sat chatting with old friends and waiting, while Rosita carefully planned her campaign.

Don Esteban (too bad that Don Amado had sponsored such a shy young person as president that critical year) opened the meeting, introduced Chico, the *alcalde* of the school committee, who introduced Rosita. She took over from there and kept the floor all evening, starting with one of her usual long speeches.

The village was honored; Doña Elena was here again. She had come with splendid introductions to the state director, who had made plans for her to visit prosperous villages in the valley. But Doña Elena had insisted on coming here because she was a friend of Santa Cruz Etla. At this point Rosita urged me to say something. I spoke a few poorly chosen words in bad Spanish about how glad I was to be there and how nice everyone always was to me. This over, Rosita got to the heart of the plot. She had given the director a big "build up" about the town so that he had come himself to bring Doña Elena. When he got there, there was nothing to see, no students, no garden, no friendly spirit. On the way back to Oaxaca, she had pleaded with the director not to misunderstand. The people of Santa Cruz Etla were a wonderful people. The director had listened to her pleading, had promised to come to dinner sometime while Doña Elena was there. What an honor that a Oaxaca State school director should have dinner in the home of a Santa Cruz Etla family!

Now the rest of it was up to them. They must take advantage of this opportunity; they must put on a fine, fiesta-type meal, present a good appearance, and if all was favorable and the director was impressed, they could tell him their problems and make definite requests to him for help.

Doña Patrocina rose to offer her house for the dinner; other women promised *gastos* of food and help. Chico offered the musicians for the day; Don Féliz León, then public works *alcalde*, offered to get the road repaired so the station wagon would have an easier trip. Most assuredly Santa Cruz Etla would turn out to entertain the supervisor. There was great enthusiasm among the men for the "entertaining" project.

Now Rosita had to steer them back to the "problems." They should discuss them, and then pick out the five most important ways the director would be able to help them. They were all quiet a long time, and I stirred uneasily as I sat near the lantern on the floor. Finally Don Féliz Jiménez (the first time I remember him taking part in politics, by the way) rose to speak. He thought their great need was for pure water. If they could get a tank for filtered water which would run the year round, water could be piped into the schoolyard, as it was in San Pablo. He knew that many children died in the dry season because the water wasn't filtered, but such a project was impossible for the people to build themselves. They needed technical help and money. If the townspeople would show the director that they had integrity, good character, he would trust them.

Chico seconded this ambitious idea. If they had water piped in the year round, they could have a school shower bath. Children and grown people would not have so far to go to bathe in *el río*. Don Florenzio then spoke about the need for windows in the schoolrooms. They had chosen Doña Patrocina's house for the dinner because one of her rooms had a window with shutters. But the children went to school where it was as "dark as a cave," so that reading classes had to be held near the door or on the porch. Why not ask the director for glass windows for the school? I thought how fine it was that Don Florenzio, with no children of his own to go to school, was so concerned for the conditions under which children learned to read, and he himself illiterate.

Doña Enriqueta thought of asking for more books, pencils, and paper. There had been nothing new brought to the school in more than three years, and everything was worn out. Don Marcelino, whose intelligent son Perfecto had finished the four grades provided in Santa Cruz Etla and longed for a chance at the fifth and sixth year provided in some larger towns, made a speech about the need for advanced education. There should be a third teacher who did nothing but teach the older students. If Santa Cruz Etla had such a teacher, San Pablo Etla children would come to Santa Cruz Etla.

San Pablo Etla had no opportunity to ask favors of any director, so here was one chance to get something the larger town wanted.

Then Don Amado, an active leader still in that last year of his life, made a speech scolding Santa Cruz Etla. Here they were asking favors of a stranger, and they had *la parcela,* the school-owned acreage, and for a year, what with the lack of interest in school affairs in general, no one had worked it. Last year's school committee had let it lie fallow, saying it would be worked when an emergency, a "problem," for the school arose. And here they were discussing what their problems were. Their problem was to work the public-school land, make seventy or eighty pesos a year, and buy the school what it needed themselves. Don Martín seconded this motion with a long speech on cooperation and self-help; and Chico, the school affairs *alcalde* who had been too busy courting Esperanza that year to worry much over the school, promised to get the land planted right away.

Rosita had not meant the discussion to take this turn. She let the motion pass that *la parcela* be planted, and then made a speech herself about the five most urgent problems. They would have the director welcomed on the school porch before he went to Doña Patrocina's. When he was introduced to the council, chosen people would make speeches. Don Féliz Jiménez would ask about the tank, and Chico about the shower; Doña Enriqueta would ask about the books and supplies, Don Marcelino about the advanced class teacher, and Don Florenzio about the glass windows. Rosita did not want to bore the director with fervent speeches by *campesinos, los pobrecitos* who fawned on public officials asking for favors. She called the chosen speakers to her as the meeting broke up and told them to plan what they were going to say and to get right to the point.

On the day Señor Varela was to come, Rosita and I spent the morning helping at Doña Patrocina's and watching the committee of public works repair the road by filling in chuckholes and removing the rocks. Perhaps this was the last time it was so well repaired, until Don Féliz Jiménez was president ten years later, and we tried to come in with a car.

Doña Estéfana, Doña Margarita, Doña Rufina, and Doña Sofía

worked at Doña Patrocina's all morning. Two chickens were dressed and put on to boil. An *olla* of rice and one of squash were cooked. More than one hundred tortillas were made, and a great bowl of hot dark chile *mole* was mixed. Beans were prepared at Doña Angelica's and brought over at the last minute. Don Julio's *gasto* was twenty bottles of strawberry pop. Rosita made orangeade with oranges from Don Florenzio's orchard, and I helped set up the table in Chico's little room where the window opens. That is how I happened to realize how nice a room it was and to plan on staying there when I came the next summer, though Chico and his bride occupied it by then. We brought over a table from the school and put on a red and white tablecloth loaned us by Doña Ester, the primary teacher. School children brought over benches for all the guests to sit on. Everything was in readiness by one-thirty. There was a great crowd on school steps, waiting for news of the station wagon to come from the runners posted all down the road to San Pablo Etla.

Of course the director was two hours late, but that never seems to be a cause for worry in rural Mexico. At three-thirty he alighted from the station wagon, accompanied by the inspector, Señor Gómez, and the young man secretary who drove. Don Esteban, with clean, white clothes prepared for him by his sister-in-law Elodia, who kept everything at Doña Paula's cleaner than in the days when we knew his little brother Crescencio at the school, welcomed the director on the school porch and introduced the council. He mumbled a few words about the shame the village had felt when the director had come the week before and had received no welcome. Don Luis Varela sat down on a bench on the porch, and there was a long pause.

Finally Doña Enriqueta, taking her courage in her hand, rose to ask about the new schoolbooks. The others followed in quick succession, each one to the point, each "problem" concisely stated. Then the visitors were led to Doña Patrocina's for dinner. Here Don Esteban, who had disappeared as soon as his speech was finished, showed up as flutist with the musicians on Patrocina's portico, playing the Mexican national anthem as the visitors approached. Don Solomón, whose absence had created such a bad impression a few days before, was there also, dressed in a black suit, with shoes, and playing the fiddle for all he was worth. I am afraid, however, that Señor Varela never connected him with the missing teacher, as school had been dismissed for the day and there were no classes to visit.

Both the municipal president and the principal teacher being occupied with the "dinner orchestra," Rosita and I were the only ones who sat down with the three city men. There were dishes, but few forks or spoons. This embarrassed me, but not the director, who dipped up his chicken *mole* with pieces of tortillas as he had doubtless done all through his childhood. Most of the dinner conversation centered round Rosita. I made the mistake of saying that I had lived in Santa Cruz Etla ten years earlier, when Rosita was teacher there. How could she have been a teacher ten years earlier, joked the visitors, when she was even now only twenty? Rosita coquetted enough to get the director in a generous mood, and then she brought up the "problems." Go ahead, the director implied, tell us again what your people want, and we'll do anything we can.

He turned down the shower and tank, however. The ditch provided the best running water he'd seen in any village. Governmental school funds provided pipes for water only when a whole village had to walk some distance to the water supply, or had to dig deep wells. Rosita and I should know that a filtering tank would not purify the water nor provide water in the dry season. As for the shower, why not construct a wooden tank, drill holes in the bottom, bring in water from an uphill point in the stream with an easily constructed tile conduit—well, he had printed plans for making such a shower, and he would send up the plans. As for the supplies, Rosita could come to the rural education supplies office and pick out anything there was extra, if only some man in the community would send in an oxcart for it.

He said that, in his experience, these *campesinos* seldom sent their children beyond the fourth grade. Only half the children got that far. Let the ambitious youngsters go to that larger school down the hill; there should be a third teacher there before there was any fifth and sixth grade in a little place like this. (Poor Don Marcelino!

Fortunately, he didn't hear the director say this!) But the windows —he could do something about windows. There was a set of large windows in a school-supply office, frames that had been made for an office building which was never built. Santa Cruz could have the frames, if someone would come and get them.

We finished the dinner in great good humor, having accomplished something, at least. We drank the last of the pop and walked out to join the crowd which had been patiently waiting in Doña Patrocina's yard. I asked Señor Gómez, as we left, what he thought of the dinner, and he said it was *regular*, which is a very common Spanish word. He could have meant that it was ordinary, or up to a good standard, or just about what he expected, or just as good as he was accustomed to, or any one of a number of things. I don't know whether he meant to compliment Doña Patrocina's committee or not.

Out in the houseyard the long flowery speeches Rosita wanted to avoid started before she could stop them. Don Amado vied with Don Martín in thanking the visitors and rehashing the problems. Rosita made a little speech; I made a little speech. Then the director himself talked in a very friendly fashion, while I took pictures. He said that it was a very nice dinner, and he was glad to have the problems brought to his attention. Meanwhile, the people should cooperate with all the teachers who came, help them with contributions of work in the public fields, and make them feel a part of the community. Inspector Gómez talked, too, saying that he would come again, that he wanted to be able to report improvement to the *profesora americana*, that he and Señor Varela thanked Rosita and the visitor for bringing this fine town to their attention.

A whole hour was consumed in this speechmaking, and it was getting near sunset. The families brought the visitors presents of eggs, flowers, squashes, avocados, and mangoes. Rosita also received baskets full of presents, including two live chickens, for she was to go back to the city with the officials. The kind, young secretary offered to come back up to get me whenever I was ready to go home, and to bring my husband up for the day when he came. So the school officials left, with the air filled with friendliness and hopes for a great future for Santa Cruz Etla. All the most pressing problems were going to be solved.

Rosita felt she had accomplished a great deal for her beloved town. She came back by train and foot the following week end and called one more meeting of the whole town council. She told the men that Don Amado had been right, that they must help themselves to improve their own school and community. They promised her to plant *la parcela* to beans right away, as it was then July and too late for corn. Ten men would plow the land in two days. Another committee would plant, and a third was listed to weed and cultivate, even though this was a busy time of plowing for every man at home. The bean crop would be harvested in October, and it should bring the eighty pesos they hoped for. Rosita glowed with pride at their sincerity and their affection for her.

She went back to her city kindergarten. The station wagon came with my husband and got me, and I went back to the United States. Don Luis Varela, having done a fine job during his two years in Oaxaca, was promoted to Mexico City. Señor Gómez was sent to found an office for school inspection in Tehuantepec. Don Esteban lost his lovely wife María, daughter of Doña Angélica, in childbirth; and distraught, he left the town and went to work alone in Oaxaca. Don Bartolo the Comical became president. Chico got married and did not run again as school *alcalde,* working instead for the election of his father-in-law, Don Melitón Arroyo, who lived way over on the San Lorenzo ridge and sent few of his children to school.

But *la parcela* was planted, and the beans were harvested, and the sacks of beans lay stored in the jail more than a year until prices should be better. Rosita had remembered, in September, 1944, when I had long since left Santa Cruz Etla, to pick out what books and supplies were left over in the office and to send them up with the León boys when they brought their oxcart into town with wood. These were the books with the silly little citified stories which had replaced Firmín, but better than no books, of course. If any blueprint for a shower bath was sent up, it got lost among the books and the papers.

And, O unexpected and unjust result of my visit! fifth- and sixth-grade classes were established in San Pablo Etla before Don Luis Varela left the valley. Fortunately, it was after Don Amado died, and he never knew about that boost to the rival town. Perfecto, the son of Don Marcelino who had spoken to Don Luis so eloquently about the need for advanced grades in the hills, compromised finally and went with Doña Estéfana's grandson Aurelio down to the San Pablo school for the upper two grades of work.

But the problem of the windows was solved. Before Señor Varela left Oaxaca, he contacted Rosita to remind her that the windows were still lying useless in his building. She got a message through to Santa Cruz by the charcoal sellers, and Don Martín brought the oxcart in to get them. There were five large windows, each about three by six feet, divided into nine small panes apiece. They could be hinged like a door to open in or out. But alas, they were wooden frames only and had no glass. Each small pane would cost two pesos, a total of ninety pesos to get the glass for the five windows. The window frames lay piled in the jail, objects of great pride and of some bewilderment to subsequent councils.

Don Bartolo told me in 1945, as I sat chatting with him on the portico of the *municipio,* that they were holding the beans from *la parcela* till they could get ninety pesos for them. Meanwhile, they were planting corn and hoped for fifty or sixty pesos from that crop. Then they would buy the glass, though how they were to get forty-five panes of glass up to Santa Cruz in an oxcart without breaking half of them, I couldn't see. Maybe they eventually came up on the truck which delivered flour to Don Martín.

But who was to put in the windows? There was no experienced glassworker nearer than Oaxaca City. Such a worker would charge by the day to fit in the glass, would take many days, and would use much time coming and going. The public works committee would have to tear out adobe bricks along the rear of the school and build wooden frames the exact size to fit the windows. Don Bartolo meant to be progressive, but: "Frankly, Doña Elena, this problem presents us many new problems. The windows are too big for the school and should be put in the municipal building. The beans will probably sprout before we get a better price. Besides, the corn planted in *la parcela* is not doing well, for this dry July shows that it surely is not a good corn year." Another time he asked me: "What does the Señorita Rosita say about us and the glass? Does she think we are backward to have done nothing?"

I went into the city with Chico and Esperanza to see the regional dances at the great *Lunes del Cerro* fiesta of 1945, just after this talk with Don Bartolo, and stayed over at Rosita's "town house." When I told her about all the problems presented by the windows, she sighed with discouragement. "How sad there was no glass in the windows in the first place! Don Luis Valera should not have promised the windows if there was no glass. It would have meant so much to their pride for my people of Santa Cruz Etla to have those fine glass windows in the school. They are not lazy; they just have no initiative about glass."

Neither she nor I could foresee that Don Martín, full of initiative, would serve anther term as president in the early fifties, that he would be followed by Don Féliz Jiménez, without a lazy bone in his body, that during those two terms glass windows would go into the school building, roof beams would be replaced and the porch strengthened, a shower would be built at the back, and the whole chapel project would be started as well.

⚜ 7 ⚜

When I returned to Santa Cruz Etla in 1945, none of these future improvements having been organized yet, I noticed only that the outside of the school had been repainted pink and that inside the gloomy, windowless classrooms the walls were a dark green that reflected no light at all. The tables and benches were clean, however, and there were the new books from Oaxaca stacked on the tables. The garden was weeded, rose bushes were blooming in it, and green beans were up. And far down the hill at the end of the garden had been built a real outdoor privy made of adobe. Building outdoor privies was a thing the cultural missionaries were to do for

179

mountain villages, said the government in comfortable, sanitary Mexico City; but it will probably take rural teachers a whole generation to put over the idea. Unfortunately for me, this new privy was nearly a city block from Doña Patrocina's; but at least it was there, the only thing of its kind I have ever seen in Santa Cruz Etla. I arrived on a Saturday, and the teachers were gone for the week end; but things at the school looked so much neater than they did the year before under Don Solomón that already I had a good impression of the 1945 teaching staff.

Monday morning early I went to introduce myself at the school, since Don Bartolo was still too "sick" to do the honors for me. I waited half the morning, and no one came save a few shy children. About noon, one of them remembered it was Benito Juárez' birthday. Of course it was; the teachers would not come back from Oaxaca City before Tuesday. I remembered the singing and marching and flag saluting on Juárez' birthday in 1934, and my idea of the teachers went down.

The next morning about ten-thirty they came up the hill. The new principal, Doña Ofelia, sat primly on a burro, while little Doña Ester, a trifle gayer and more poised than in the year of Don Solomón, came along behind on foot. Isaías Pérez, the boy with the sore eyes, urged the burro along and tried to hold a black umbrella between Doña Ofelia and the sun. He stopped the burro in front of Doña Patrocina's, where I stood with Esperanza watching the caravan. Esperanza, though illiterate, having stayed in Rosita's class only one year, was the daughter of the 1945 *alcalde* of the school committee, Don Melitón Arroyo, and as such deserved the courtesy of the principal. She received a scant nod.

"Here is the *señora americana,* friend of Doña Rosita, our beloved former teacher," said Doña Patrocina, calling from the portico.

Muy buenos días, said Doña Ofelia coldly.

I felt rather timid. She was past fifty, her hair was slicked back into a knot, her dress was black cotton with a high neck. She had on black cotton stockings and black shoes, unusual because Rosita and Doña Ester had both gone barelegged and all the teachers had worn sandals, even Don Solomón. I could see that this lady considered herself one of *los correctos,* the better class of people, the "right ones," and considered Santa Cruz people among *los tontos,* the ignorant ones.

I wanted to feel welcome at the school, so I asked her if I might visit. Of course, I looked very shabby in my old khaki clothes, not at all like one of *los correctos* myself. "Visit the school any time you please," she said over her shoulder, as she signaled Isaías to urge the burro forward.

I put on a clean blouse and went over to the school later in the day. She was probably surprised to see the enthusiastic welcome the children gave me, children in whose homes I had already been visiting three days, who remembered me in the exhilaration of the cat and rat games of the summer before. Doña Ofelia nodded to me pleasantly enough and had the children continue reading. During a lull I complimented her on the new garden and the paint job. To explain myself and my presence in the community, I spoke about the campaign against illiteracy and my willingness to help with the teaching of reading and writing to adults.

She showed the first spark of interest in me. *¿Puedes tú escribir?* "Can you write?" she asked in a surprised tone.

"Well, I can write well enough to help the illiterates," I said.

"Then we can use you; we get little enough cooperation from these *tontos* on that program," she said.

When I told Rosita about this incident, expecting her to be very amused and to act it all out many times to tease me, she surprised me by being angry—angry not because Doña Ofelia thought I could not write, but because she had called me *tú,* as to an inferior, instead of using the polite pronoun *usted.*

Doña Ester was much more friendly than Doña Ofelia. I had had long chats with her in 1944 about ways of teaching beginners to read. I felt always welcome in her class and came again and again through the summer of 1945, sometimes stopping there on the horse so Doña Sofía's Leopoldo and Doña Rufina's Margarito and Don Bartolo's *chamaquita* could pet the nose of *el caballo.* Don Marciano considered the horse so ferocious, of course, that no child could take such a risk when he was riding it.

181

Doña Ester's little charges took turns sweeping the school porch and classrooms and watering down the tile floor with an old-fashioned watering can. Their names and their responsibilities were listed on a chart on the wall, neatly printed by Doña Ester. She worked very hard at making *planos,* copies of letters and simple words, so that each child had something of his own to copy. Her little beginners had no books at all, only pencils and paper, and most of these the families had to supply themselves. I would help her make these copies and spent many mornings making beautiful sentences about cats and goats and burros for Leopoldo and the others. We sometimes used the books provided in the campaign to teach illiterate adults, as they were much better than anything provided for the primary grades. I would like to have been there when Chabella's Margarita, Don Martín's oldest grandchild, started school in 1946, for she was already so cute and bright at five.

The advanced primary class had a reader. It was full of Aesop's fables and prosy little stories of good city children who loved their dollies and played with their tin soldiers. Such things Santa Cruz Etla second graders of the 1940's had never seen. I longed for the old tattered books about Firmín and his burro and his tortillas. Rosita had found these citified little books in Don Luis Varela's supplies and had sent them up. They were at least better than the single copy Doña Ester had had the year before; anything was better than the almost complete lack of books in Don Solomón's time. The trouble was that Doña Ester had eighteen pupils in the first grade and fifteen in the second grade, on the average. She could give any one child about twenty minutes a day, and perhaps he came three days a week. No wonder that it took the Santa Cruz Etla children two years to do the work for each grade and that so many were still in the third grade when they became discouraged and quit at twelve or thirteen. Many parents considered that a child knew enough when he could read a little and write his own name. Many children dropped out at the end of Doña Ester's classes, too, because they liked her and were afraid of Doña Ofelia.

I saw the petite Doña Ester in Oaxaca City on a Sunday at the end of that summer. She had on high-heeled pumps and silk stockings, a stylish black and white suit, and black ribbon-and-veil hat. She stopped to remind me of a promise to send colored magazine pictures to the school in Santa Cruz Etla throughout the coming year. I almost told her that she looked as strange to Santa Cruz in that stylish outfit as any colored magazine picture would be, and that I could see her getting married to some well-to-do Oaxaca man and never staying in Santa Cruz Etla long enough to receive any pictures from me. Though this marriage actually happened, my judgment did her an injustice. She had stayed in Santa Cruz three years, longer than any teacher since Rosita; she had made the children love her; and, although I have never seen her since 1945 myself, Leopoldo told me that she came up to visit the town two times on fiesta days after she had a nice, new husband.

Doña Ofelia, with no hopes for a husband, stuck forever perhaps in some lesser place even than Santa Cruz Etla, ground away at teaching the third and fourth grades. The third-grade reader had stories about Mexico's heroes—Hidalgo, Morelos, Juárez, Madero. It had the words of the national anthem and the pledge of allegiance to Mexico. There was a long chapter about the Aztecs, who seemed to live still in some strange world and to have no connection whatever with the Mixtecs who built Monte Albán or the Zapotecs who built Mitla. The third-grade reader, the only glimpse of the rest of Mexico that most of Santa Cruz Etla would ever get, did not even mention the romantic ancient history of the valley of Oaxaca. Time not used by Doña Ofelia with the third graders in reading this book aloud, each at his own speed, was spent teaching multiplication and long division. There was only a square of black oilcloth used as a blackboard, and that board and Dona Ofelia's stubs of chalk made up the only arithmetic textbook. The reader itself had rather difficult words and stories, material we would expect fifth or sixth graders to read in the United States.

Doña Ofelia had two boys and three girls in the fourth grade in 1945—Isaías Pérez, Gerónomo Méndez, Chabella's little sister Adelita from Doña Rosario's house on the trail to the San Lorenzo *loma*, Don Marcelino's little Teresa, almost as good a student as her famous brother Perfecto, and Don Lalo's Aurelia, then twelve years old.

These children cared for the garden, watched the younger children as assistants to Doña Ester, doled out the few sheets of paper, and kept the teachers' living quarters clean. But they had a harder time financially than the younger students, because they each had to buy a book. They had the regular fourth-grade reader which has to be "passed" in order to get out of the last year of school, readers which were sent free to Santa Cruz Etla after our visit in 1944. But in addition each child had to spend three pesos of his father's money for the *Libro General,* the "Book of Everything," for the fourth grade. I took Adelita's book home and looked it through. It was a big book with half-tone cuts from photographs, a better printing job than the little readers. It had two hundred fifty pages and was divided into sections on natural science, Mexican geography, hygiene of the body, description of Mexico's constitutional government, and products of the various states of Mexico. Only seventh or eighth graders here in the United States could tackle that mass of detailed subject matter. There is a Oaxaca State regulation that an examination on this book must be passed in order to earn the fourth-grade "certificate of completion of a rural school"; but the book was never seen in Santa Cruz Etla before the days of Doña Ofelia. I am sure Don Solomón didn't know all that stuff himself. Only Isaías Pérez and Adelita had any hopes of being *certificados* at the end of the school semester in 1946. Then Crescencio's little sister Alicia and three others from the third grade came on up, bought the books, and went plugging along. I surely hope this erudition did Santa Cruz Etla some good, but only the part about hygiene seemed to me to have any bearing on the existing "problems."

Although I did not have the friendly feeling of "home" about the school that I had when I lived there with Rosita, I came to know these children almost as well as I had those of 1934, to feel a kinship with Gerónomo and Isaías, Adelita and Teresa, Alicia and Aurelia, Leopoldo, Margarito, and Martiniano, these last two the fatherless little sons of Don Amado. Twice we played ring games such as Rosita had taught us, even through music and singing and folk dancing had been exiled from the school forever by the "academic" Doña Ofelia. I was surprised also to see the boys play with homemade tops and marbles for the first time. They played marbles in a circle drawn on the ground just as boys play marbles everywhere.

"Do you play marbles like this in your country, Doña Elena?" asked Gerónomo. I described our game, telling them about the beautiful glass agates boys have in America. Their faces fell, and I was sorry I had said it. They had thought their little red-clay marbles so fine.

Doña Ofelia did not mean to be a purely "book-learning" teacher, and she had done more with the garden than anyone since Rosita. There were five irrigated plots of squash, corn, and green beans; in fact, the school garden looked better than anything else in Santa Cruz Etla in that very dry year of 1945. Doña Ofelia told me, when she became chummier after our weeks of night school teaching together, that the children could sell the vegetable crop and buy some rabbits again. She hoped the present third graders would be concerned enough for the garden to keep up the irrigated plots during the dry season when she would be gone on vacation.

So I guess she did have some interest in the children. But she surely was scornful of the adults in the community, especially of *el Presidente* Bartolo and the council. She spoke crossly of their small crop on *la parcela*. There was that project about the windows for the school room. How stupidly these *tonto* people had handled the whole affair! Why didn't they raise two hundred pesos by growing a better crop, and put the windows in right? (This when Don Martín and Don Melitón, the school *alcalde*, had both spoken with pride of how they had worked on the school land in spite of the dry year. I wonder where Doña Ofelia had taught before.)

She also wanted new desks and tables. The chairs and tables, made of rough lumber when the school was built, were all the same size, all too small for Gerónomo and too large for Leopoldo. "These people are clever enough with their tools when they want to make something for themselves, or for sale. They could set in the windows and make the benches. But they will not. Under this president and this school *alcalde*, they never will."

At the end of the summer I asked Doña Ofelia my question. "Does a school in a community, the first school ever built in a primitive rural community, raise the standard of living in a ten-year period?" Of course, I didn't say it just that way, but I got the general point across in a roundabout fashion.

"Not in this community it won't," she snapped, "not with *la gente,* here. They are a dirty, lazy people."

"Oh, no! Oh, no, they aren't! You just don't know them," I thought as I walked sadly away.

But that was the year I was so "scientifically" trying to find out if a rural school *did* change a community in a decade, and I was determined to get some scientific sociological answer. So I asked the town council my question one day, when I appeared at a last meeting to thank them for the summer. I couldn't put over to them the idea of "raise the standard of living." Of course, they thought they had been doing very well, especially in good corn years; and they have such pride in their community that they never think in terms of personal improvement. So I asked: "Are the young men who were in school ten years ago better gardeners and farmers than their fathers?"

This idea just produced polite laughter. "How can any young man be a better farmer than his father, Doña Elena? Surely that cannot be true, even in your country," said Don Martín.

"Well, can they raise more corn per acre?"

"In good years, yes; in bad years, no. One year in this last ten came a pest which destroyed a great deal of the crop. In another, a great rain washed out the seed. This year, you know yourself, Doña Elena, how dry it has been. Both the fathers and the sons do the best they can." No answer to my question there.

Doña Estéfana had the same reaction. Could the girls who were in school ten years ago keep the houses cleaner, keep the babies freer from sickness? "No, of course, *seguro que no,* Doña Elena. How could any young girl raise babies better than her mother? For all of us some live, some die."

So I looked for an answer in the school itself that year, and found it a stuffier, less vital school than ten years before, although an improvement over Don Solomón's year. Here also the answer seemed to be: "In good years, yes; in bad years, no." Then I thought of the children who went to school to Rosita—Chabella whose four children were so clean and sturdy, Eduardo who knew so much about the mill, Juanita the prosperous, tidy, little wife in San Pablo, Joel who already was taking responsibility in running Doña Estéfana's wide lands, Nico such a good farmer, Chico who did the writing for the town after the death of Don Amado, Cassiano who gave so much time in a program to teach the illiterates. Who was to say they were not doing these things better because Rosita once taught them? I note that I closed my solemn sociological notes of 1945 with this statement: "Perhaps it is not the school, nor the land, nor the home life which indicates the progress, but the good students of the good teacher."

🐾 8 🐾

BY THE TIME OF MY 1954 VISIT I had given up "profound sociological studies" both at home and in Santa Cruz Etla, and I had no scientific approach one way or the other to the problem: How has a school helped a community in twenty years? As for Doña Ofelia, Don Martín and Don Féliz knew only that she had gone, they did not remember how long after 1945. "A long time ago, Doña Elena, who knows what year, one year or another."

Then there had been another *matrimonio* for two or three years; we met the couple briefly on our daylong picnic at Santa Cruz in 1951, without even noting their names. They had evidently not worked the garden, for the whole area of the garden had been cleared of growth in 1952, with no one having a thought as to long-term values of school gardens; and the new chapel had been built on the site, occupying half the garden space. I was disappointed to see no garden. I wondered whether in the long run the garden did not accomplish more for Santa Cruz than the empty chapel, which would probably never have a resident priest. But perhaps the example of the garden—the cultivation of many kinds of green vegetables, the careful choice of the best seeds, the banking and channel digging for small-scale irrigation, all the things which Rosita and El Maestro and Doña Ofelia had taught—had already become such a part of the community, which had always loved gardens anyway and needed only the incentive of better methods, that the school garden itself passed into oblivion without anyone's remarking it.

With the 1953 session came Don Alfredo González as school principal and his wife Estella as primary teacher. Small, slight, dignified, and conscientious, himself of Indian stock from a distant town at the dry end of the valley, Don Alfredo was pleased with his assignment to Santa Cruz Etla, because, as he himself said, "It is so green here the year round, so much grows, and the fruit trees. ¡Qué magníficos! Besides, this is a good people, an ambitious town, such fine municipal presidents!" Doña Ofelia may have taught in better villages, but evidently Don Alfredo had taught in worse ones, with drier fields, less spectacular views, and less cooperative townspeople. "The first thing the president and council did when the new session started was to put glass windows in the school building. Imagine that! What other mountain school has glass windows?"

Naturally, it had taken another term in the presidency by Don Martín to get the glass project started at last. But there had been two good years, the price of both corn and charcoal had gone up with the general rise in the standard of living all over Mexico, and the townspeople had voted to get the windows in the school before they started the church. The glass and the skilled labor cost one hundred fifty pesos, but there were twice as many pesos then for one load of firewood or charcoal. A single crop on la parcela paid the bill.

With the new school windows letting in the light, Don Alfredo suggested that the inside be painted a soft light green instead of the dark green it had been for so many years. The outside was also newly painted, a cream color; and, for the first time, the name Don Amado had given it, Escuela Federal de Benito Juárez, was painted inside the arcade in letters a foot high. This last was another work contribution by Perfecto. Don Alfredo also purchased blackboarding such as one sees in schools in the United States to replace the small pieces of black oilcloth used in the school since Rosita's day. Don Alfredo bought it at his own expense in Oaxaca and had it brought up on the San Lorenzo bus, fifteen feet of it, three feet wide, in two sections. He got Joel and Nico to help him mount it in wooden frames attached to the wall, one in each of the school rooms, where the light came in bright for all to see it. The desks and benches were repaired, there were new colored pictures of Cárdenas and of Ruiz Cortines up on the wall next to Hidalgo and Júarez.

The day we arrived in 1954, our car pulled by oxen into the schoolyard, the children were at home for the midday meal, and school was not reopened for the rest of the day. Instead, the official speeches of greeting were held right up on the school porch, not out on the steps as they had been when the schoolteachers were less a part of the town's life. While we ate lunch at Don Martín's, Don Alfredo joined with Don Féliz in summoning the town band, which then sat on the school benches on the porch all the rest of the afternoon, playing its entire repertoire over and over, no matter with whom we were chatting or what speeches were being made. I could see from the whispered conversations and the "scurrying-arounds" of Don Féliz and Don Alfredo that this teacher was a member of the community more than any man teacher had ever been. His wife, twice his size in girth and not much more than half his age, had a little group of primary children fluttering round her all afternoon like chicks round a young hen. Evidently Santa Cruz had at last got over the nostalgia for Rosita and had found a pair of teachers it could take to its bosom.

But if I had come that time to analyze the school for "improvements in *two* decades," I would have found little to encourage me beyond the beautification of the building. What teachers can do a good job with only the equipment they or the parents can afford to purchase? In the days of Rosita, the Firmín books, the paper and the pencils, and many crayons, colored chalks, sewing materials, and such things had been provided by the Mexican government, anxious to make the rural schools a success. Don Luis Varela's interest had provided new books, however inadequate, and some small supply of

189

paper and pencils, in the mid-1940's. Now since the beginning of the 1950's, anything that the school has above the teachers' salaries must be provided by the community itself. The Mexican rural schools are beginning to be an old story, while the official interest of the nation centers on the new industrialization. The federal government gave the impetus, maintains the staff; let the towns carry on from there. Fair enough!

Santa Cruz Etla had fixed up the school building, then had taxed every family heavily, one hundred pesos, to build the chapel. When Don Alfredo reported that the books had disintegrated and that there were no writing supplies to be found, the school committee called a parents' meeting. It was decided that every family with children would purchase books and supplies for its own, the stores in Oaxaca being so accessible these days by bus. Seemingly a wise enough decision, but nonetheless responsible for the practical failure of Don Alfredo's program.

Nico's little girl and Chico's little boy were in the first grade in 1954. For an outlay of five pesos, Doña Patrocina's family purchased for each child one copy of the most namby-pamby little reader I ever saw, and a "copybook" of about thirty blank sheets with a pencil attached by string. When the sheets were filled with the childish attempts at writing, the paper was turned and the new writing went across the old. When my husband came back with the car on the second Sunday, he brought a new copy book and a dozen pencils for each child in Doña Patrocina's family, as well as gifts of pencils and paper for many other children we knew well in the community. But such artificial irrigation does not water the vineyard. What of the children from San Sebastián and San Lorenzo whom we do not know well, who months before had dropped out of school when the first family purchases were used up, when the pencils were lost or the copybooks inadvertently left out in the rain? Or what of the children who were to enter school at six, near the end of the year when the crop was long since exhausted and all money from it spent—and so never entered school at all? And how about the third and fourth graders, whose books were so expensive, who needed more than one book apiece and a great deal of paper?

Don Alfredo was not so concerned about all this as I. He had started teaching as a tutor in a private Catholic boys' school, had been eight years in communities where there were even less supplies than in Santa Cruz Etla, and had had no experience with a regime in which a benevolent central office sent out supplies. As academic as Doña Ofelia in the classroom, he scared away the older children by his insistence on rote learning, and he was almost as responsible for the small enrollment in the fourth grade as was the expense of the books.

There were three boys and four girls in Don Alfredo's fourth grade, not much better a survival rate from the lower grades than in Doña Ofelia's time. Don Marciano's youngest girl, Chabella's second daughter, Adela, and a brother of Esperanza were the only ones from families I knew well. Living as I did in Don Martín's house, I could look over Adela's books every day and "pump" her on the value of what she was learning. Bright child in a bright family, though not up to the brilliance of her older sister Margarita, Adela found the fourth grade a disappointment and talked wistfully of going down to San Pablo to school. This was a thing no Santa Cruz girl had ever done, although Margarita had the fifth and sixth grades with the nuns in Oaxaca on a sort of scholarship. The same *Libro General* was used as in Doña Ofelia's fourth grade, and Adela's copy was in shreds from many different users, with pages missing and the binding gone. The "little red school house" on the mid-western prairies in the days of our grandfathers had the same problems about the providing of books and their disintegration and obsolescence as they passed through a family.

However, no one in Santa Cruz was complaining about the books in 1954, or about the teaching either. There were fifteen third graders, twenty-two second graders, and thirty-one first graders to be lined up in groups for me the day I took photographs of the school. Don Alfredo and Doña Estella are still happy in Santa Cruz Etla as I write this, according to my correspondents, and have no idea of leaving unless a new director shifts them arbitrarily. Little bank drafts or international money orders sent down from time to time, at twelve pesos to the dollar, buy quite a lot of pencils and paper for a very little; and Rosita and I can be sure that with the new mail system coming up to San Pablo, these little sprinklings get directly into the hands of Don Alfredo whom we can trust to spend the money wisely in the Oaxaca school-supply stores. Materials sent from here—bright magazine pictures, colored papers, watercolor paints—if carefully packed and labelled "Educational Materials," have eventually reached the Santa Cruz Etla school, but the outlay of money goes five times further when spent by Don Alfredo. Our own little red school houses improved as the United States became industrialized and rural standards of living raised over a fifty-year period, so I do not mean to be too impatient with Santa Cruz Etla.

9

AT ANY RATE, most of the younger people of Santa Cruz Etla have learned to read in the school. But what of the adults? Rosita had learned in her own normal-school training that the good rural teacher organizes night school classes to "reach the older people who are hungry for book learning," and surely "teach the illiterate adults" was another "must" on the cultural missions list from the time of the first cultural mission.

So Rosita had bought her Coleman light and kept Uncle Octaviano to manage it for her when it began to sputter, and she had held night classes for adults three times a week on the school porch. Twenty of the now middle-aged men had learned to read from her. Chico who became town secretary, Eduardo who was fourteen in 1934 but not allowed to attend day school by the hard-driving Don Julio, Don Pablo who married Sofía and then went to work in the United States, Esteban (oldest of Doña Paula's neglected brood) who was municipal president in 1944 when he was only twenty-seven—all these we can count as Rosita's children, for she taught them to read under *la luz* and by the sweat of their brows. I noted them bent over the paper, writing with stub pencils from the children's first Firmín reader, and remarked in my 1934 diary, from the experience of my own twenty-five years of life: "This attempt at writing is the hardest work undertaken by these sons of toil." But they did learn to write, in Rosita's own *campaña contra analfabetismo,* her "campaign against illiteracy," and they used their learning in later years. After Rosita left and took the Coleman light away, no teacher in the next ten years even tried such a program.

In 1944 all Mexico was electrified by the dramatic program of the Education Minister, Dr. Jaime Torres-Bodet, called the "Each One Teach One Plan." Everyone was talking about it in Mexico City, on the trains, in Rosita's school meetings which I attended with her in 1944. Half the people of Mexico were adjudged illiterate in that year, and under a war emergency law President Ávila Camacho ordained that all illiterate adults must learn to read and write. Dr. Torres-Bodet said that this could be done by a nation-wide publicity campaign, by urging all who could read and write to help teach those who could not.

The education ministry printed a booklet as a standard text which was distributed free by the millions of copies. A registration of literate persons was held nation-wide, through the schools, the various civil service offices, the bus and railroad ticket agencies; it was a fairly simple problem to get the booklets widespread among the literate. In each booklet was a coupon to be signed and sent to the Department of Education by everyone who could read. On the coupon he listed the name of the person he was teaching. When the booklet was mastered, the learner filled in a second coupon from the book and sent it in to be matched with the first. Trained teachers and special volunteers were to take thirty or forty booklets apiece.

The idea spread like wildfire in the summer and fall of 1944. Some bus companies near Mexico City would not sell a ticket unless the prospective passenger could produce a yellow card showing that he was either teaching or learning. Any university student who taught fifty illiterates would get a scholarship for the rest of the year. Persons who taught five or more received a gold seal from Mexico City. In all the attendant publicity throughout the ensuing two years, the state of Oaxaca was cited as the center of enthusiasm. The valley market town of Etla was mentioned in an

193

American magazine as being one of the first towns to establish
100 per cent literacy. Señor Torres-Bodet himself visited some mountain towns in the upper valley of Oaxaca and reported amazing progress. He told an American reporter (Amy Vanderbilt, writing in
Collier's, December 14, 1946):

A poor Mexican living in his adobe hut in a little unpaved village . . . has nothing very different from what he had when the
Spaniards came. Of what use is it to tell him why he is so poor? . . .
why the babies he loves so much must often die young? He has
no real contact with the world. He doesn't know how to live better,
and improvement can't be forced upon him. But if he learns to read
and write Spanish, he becomes a unit of our society, and the possibility of his human and social improvement is limitless.

Mr. Torres-Bodet could report three million illiterates taught
throughout Mexico by the end of 1945. He himself went up to a
higher cabinet position, and from there to the world chairmanship
of UNESCO, the United Nations Educational, Scientific, and Cultural Organization, where he introduced his "Each One Teach One"
program for all backward peoples, and eventually resigned in
protest over the small funds granted for this work in the United
Nations budget. But he left in Mexico a permanent office staff and
a detailed plan to keep up the program there.

It sounds too good to be true, on the face of it, but the same
missionary spirit which had made school buildings and teacher
training possible in Oaxaca fifteen years before made this new plan
work with surprising efficiency. Rosita and her kindergarten assistants in Oaxaca City had a class of forty poor working mothers
who came to the kindergarten when the children were dismissed,
who sat at the low tables in the tiny chairs and struggled to write,
while the teachers volunteered the extra hours without pay. Two
Indian servant women in Rosita's block came three times a week
to learn from Rosita's mother at her home. Even the current little
"Augustina," a twelve-year-old Indian boy from Mitla who washed
the dishes at Rosita's town house, had a lesson every day in reading

and writing so that he could enter the city schools at his own age level in the next year.

Who was I to resist such pressure? Was I not a "lettered one," obligated to teach one or more "unlettered ones" to read and write? If I wanted an excuse to go back to Santa Cruz Etla in 1945, after my short, "scientific," ten-year-study visit of 1944, I need only think about the spectacular and successful work of the *campaña contra analfabetismo.*

Things always go a little slower, a little less spectacularly, in Santa Cruz Etla. There the illiteracy rate is a good deal more than 50 per cent. Only the people who were ten or younger when Rosita first came, and then that handful of adults under the Coleman light, had had any chance at book learning; and not half of those really had had two years of schooling. Even Esperanza, pet of the school's primary class in 1934, had quit a year later because of the illness of her mother and had forgotten everything she had learned. Oh, illiterates there were in plenty, and the town was anxious to do its part in the campaign.

In February of 1945 Don Bartolo was summoned to a meeting of "heads of municipalities" from the hills above Etla. The governor of Oaxaca spoke to them. He told them that each president must make a roster of all those in his municipality who could read and all those who could not and bring it into the city. The mountain communities must do as well as those in the valley had done. Two books for each lettered person would be sent to the school. The rural teachers went to a meeting about it the next week end, and they were urged to assist the presidents in handling clerical details. Doña Ester, the meek little primary teacher, signed a receipt for thirty of the booklets.

Don Bartolo, with no great personal enthusiasm for the project, called a meeting of the householders of Santa Cruz Etla. Cassiano, Eduardo, Joel, Aurelio, Adolfo Soto, Chico, and Nico all signed the roster as "literate ones," *alfabetos,* willing each to teach two *analfabetos.* Two-thirds of the coupons were returned, Doña Ofelia and Doña Ester taking the responsibility for three *analfabetos* apiece. At the mass meeting it was voted to have classes for women

195

in the afternoon and for men at night. Don Bartolo had heard the new regulation read out loud at the meeting for municipal presidents: "Be sure to start the classes the closest Monday," so it was decided to hold classes on Mondays, starting about the middle of April. Surely the authorities had meant Monday, Tuesday, Wednesday, and so on, every week night.

Doña Ofelia had misunderstood something, too. She thought the education director had said: "Do not go on in a new lesson till the previous lesson is learned perfectly." She taught the Monday class like a modern school. The literate ones prompted and helped each backward pupil, but all worked together, and the entire group waited till each "unlettered one" had "learned the previous lessons perfectly." Naturally, everyone started over at the beginning again every Monday.

The council had also voted that each *analfabeto* should bring his own candle, that no money for candles or kerosene lanterns should come from fiesta funds—and of course there was no Coleman light. A candle is a luxury in Santa Cruz Etla. Before I brought candles to Doña Patrocina's house, her family had eaten *cena* by the light of a pine torch. Chico used the kerosene lantern at home only that one time the ox was sick. Candles are not made in Santa Cruz, because there is no beeswax or tallow, and store-bought candles are used only for weddings, *baptismos,* and *angelitos.* Many *analfabetos* did not come at all in those first months because of the "bring a candle" ruling. They wanted education, but not that badly.

Don Bartolo was asked to report on progress the first of June. His own personal progress was zero; that of the *analfabetos* averaged two lessons. Don Bartolo certainly did not like to lie about it all, and anyway a careful check was to be made at the end of two years, so he promised that Santa Cruz Etla would do better. The whole community was doubtless glad to be able to tell Rosita three weeks later that classes were being held "three nights a week now," and that women had at last begun to come for help from Doña Ester in the late afternoon.

After my arrival that summer of 1945 and as soon as the classes started again after Doña Ofelia's absence over Juárez' birthday, after

196

Don Bartolo was up and around after the "hangover" sickness, and after I began to rally from my first bout with the "water sickness" —then the work with *analfabetos* in Santa Cruz Etla took a new lease on life. Everyone ate *cena* after dark, and it was better to wait until the moon and stars were out before going anywhere up and down the ridges and ravines in the evening. My first night Chico took me over to the school with the lantern, but he put it out at the school door and left it outside. I brought three candles, a pad of notebook paper, and a pencil. By August I had sent for more candles every time I could arrange for Oaxaca City purchases, had broken all my drawing pencils up to make each into three short pencils, and had used up all the diary and note-taking paper I had brought to Santa Cruz Etla with me.

That first night I attended, nineteen *analfabetos* were present. Don Bartolo should be counted as the twentieth, for he was certainly there. He opened the class like a professor, and asked Doña Ofelia to call the roll. His own name was not listed, and as soon as the "business" was over, he disappeared into the shadows. He came every Monday in this way, but he never brought a candle.

I did not want to run afoul of Doña Ofelia again right away, and I stayed back behind my candles with Joel and Cassiano. Don Bartolo called me out, however, and asked everyone to clap for me, while Chico told Doña Ofelia how Rosita had promised I would help. Doña Ofelia really did not like to teach the grown men, anyway. All those who were there, averaging around thirty years of age, did look very *tonto*, with scraggly beards, uncombed mops of hair sometimes halfway to their shoulders, horny bare feet, and clothes dirty and torn after a long day with the plow or up in the sierra. She just oozed scorn of them. When Don Bartolo told them to thank me because they "needed my help so badly," Doña Ofelia just said, *Seguro que si*, "surely we do." Then she retired with a long, new candle to a corner table and devoted herself to helping two well-brushed students who had advanced three lessons. Doña Ester and I went on most of the time without her after that. It was that first night when I saw how the "don't advance till everyone is perfect" system had retarded everyone. The little booklet itself was so simply written that it was easier to learn at one's own speed than by working in concert.

The lesson they had all learned was about the vowels. The booklet, *La Cartilla,* was printed cheaply on newsprint paper. It began, after fifteen discouraging pages of explanations to the teacher, with a lesson on the vowels. Here was a picture of a squeaking mouse saying "i-i-i-i," and after him the capital *I* and small letter *i* in both printing and script, for *I* is pronounced only as "ee," and no other way, in the Spanish language. Next came a black and white line drawing of a train, with a cloud of steam, whistling "u-u-u-u," followed by *U*'s. Now even Santa Cruz Etla people know that a train goes "oo-oo" for they can hear the valley train on windy days, and in Spanish *U* is always pronounced that way. *E* was illustrated by a deaf man holding his hand to his ear and saying "e-e-e-e-e." Deaf people everywhere in the world say something like "eh," or "hey," which is quite similar to the only way *E* is pronounced in Spanish. Then there was the sketch of a horse rearing high while its rider cried "o-o-o-o," a sound like our "whoa"; and a drawing of a pleased child launching a model airplane with cries of "ah!" or "a-a-a-a," the standard Spanish *A*. Santa Cruz children have never launched model airplanes, but they said something like "ah!" when they first saw the pinwheels my husband made for Crescencio and Augustina in 1934.

Thus, the great joy of the Spanish language to a person who has struggled all his life with English—the fact that vowels, and most consonants too, are pronounced always the same—made the first lesson in the *Cartilla* an immediate success. The only delay waiting on "perfection" was in writing. At the end of the summer one of my own pupils was still trying to learn to write a capital *I.* My handwriting is so bad, and my capital *I*'s so strange looking, that only those men who had got beyond the letter before I got there, or who copied Cassiano's capital *I*'s, ever reached "perfection."

The second lesson was also clearly understandable to Santa Cruz Etla. It introduced the letter *L* by means of a youth named Lalo. Here was a picture of a young *campesino*, badly in need of a haircut, a striped V-necked *sarape* over both shoulders, puzzling

over a printed book. In printing and script it said, *Lalo lee; leo a
Eulalia* (Lalo reads: I read to Eulalia). In Santa Cruz Etla, in the
ravine just below the school, lived Don Lalo, father of the child
Aurelia who learned to toddle while we watched in 1934, and
whom I chased in "cat and rat" in 1944. Lalo was himself illiterate
and came to class several times when he learned that the lesson
was about him, but he told me he was "too old now to learn." To be
sure, "Lalo" is not an actual baptismal name, but a *paisano* shorten-
ing or nickname, based on "Eduardo." Lalo was probably always
sorry he bore that name from then on, for it came to be a slander
among the forty or so men who came to the classes from time to
time. One would say: "You? What do you know? You never got
beyond Lalo!" Or: "Why aren't you at the school at night? If you
forget you will have to go back to Lalo." Or: "Remember the days
before Doña Elena came? We none of us got beyond Lalo."

Everyone who got beyond Lalo went on to the S lesson. Here
were words and sentences using S and L with the vowels. The story
told in S and L that the sun comes up at six, and then Lalo, just
like Nico and Chico and everyone else, washes himself. *Lalo se
asea a las seis.* The *a las seis* needed a little explanation, because no
one in Santa Cruz knows whether he gets up at six and washes
himself, or maybe at five or at seven. Luisa and Luis entered the
lessons, along with Lalo and Eulalia. Then there was an *M* lesson about the Mama that ground the *mole* when Lalo went to the
lomas. The *tía* or Aunt Tomasa, the papa named *Pepe,* and the rest
followed lesson by lesson and letter by letter. So went the lessons
through the alphabet, *el alfabeto para los analfabetos.* Only Felipe,
who was *firme* and *formal* and went to study at the *colegio* in
Mexico City in the middle sentence of a lesson, was beyond the understanding of Santa Cruz Etla. But since the *F* came as far along
as page 59, very few of my people were advanced to *F* by the end
of August.

After my first night, Doña Ester and I divided the men by
tables, four or five men, two candles (no matter who brought the
candles), two pencils, and three pieces of paper to a table. At first
she and I would begin the new men, get them to "Pepe," and pass

them on to Cassiano or his friend Perfecto. Those two boys were the only ones who had patience to stick all evening and do three or four lessons over and over. Eduardo, Aurelio, and Chico could go on with the faster students, but Nico and Joel would forget about the teaching and laugh and talk with each other. When special friends of theirs came the second week, though, they were willing to start with the vowels and see their friends right through to "Felipe." Thus, we were soon all helping our own pupils. I started almost everyone, but hung on especially to four: Ceferino Jiménez, who played the bass viol (under obligation to his teacher, he danced with me all afternoon that time at the *angelita* when his string broke); Bernardino Méndez, who started with me on the L lesson and took all summer to get to "Tomasa"; and two brothers named Elisha and Elijah, or Eliseo and Elijeo Ramírez, who were already friends of mine through Doña Patrocina's family.

I learned the last names of the students, although before then I had known few last names in Santa Cruz Etla. As I helped everyone get started, I wrote models of their names, so that they could practice writing them as soon as they got a good start with the lessons. Since there are so few families and there has been so much marrying between families through the years, almost everyone seemed to be named Pérez, Méndez, Ramírez, Sánchez, López, Jiménez, or García, the common family names of half the people of Mexico, the Smiths, Joneses, and Browns of Latin America.

Doña Ester and I had them write their names because we couldn't interest them in writing any other way. They would read with ease and enthusiasm; all the literate boys were willing to sit and pronounce the words and have the "pupil" repeat after them. The table with Joel and Nico got clear through to "Pepe" before anyone had written a word. Cassiano was the best writing teacher. Even Don Amado would have been pleased to see his son's neat writing and his shy eagerness in the teaching. His best pupil was Doña Rufina, his own mother, whom he helped at home every day after he came in from the fields for dinner. She was at the "Felipe" lesson when I left Santa Cruz Etla.

I would have said: "Why bother with this perfect copybook

writing? Who in Santa Cruz Etla needs to write so much? Only those who keep the town records and serve as municipal secretary; surely not all these people." But I knew the inspection at the end of the first year would include a written test for all those names sent in to Oaxaca on the coupons, and I wanted Santa Cruz Etla to shine on the examinations. Even Doña Ofelia wanted that. She made a little speech one night about how all the literate teachers must try as hard to teach writing as Cassiano was trying.

It is true that all the students were plugging hard at some phase of the learning. They would work more than two hours without a pause, and for them it was really harder work than plowing land or cutting wood. Cold as the night is at that altitude, beads of sweat would stand out on their faces as they read, *Tomasa toma los tamales* (Tomasa takes the tamales). I had noted this extreme effort, and the sweat on the faces, when I saw Chico and Esteban learning to read in 1934, and they had the Coleman light and Rosita to help them.

In 1945 our light was so poor. We would work until the candles burned down into the rough tops of the tables. Don Ceferino would gather the melted wax from the table top and feed it into the quarter-inch of candlewick still burning, just to make light enough to read *Pepe es el papá* one more time out loud. (Of course, everyone was reading something different out loud all evening; it was hard to concentrate on "Pepe.")

Doña Ester or I would have to say: "The lights are dying. Do you not have to go to the sierra early tomorrow?" Then they would take their booklets (for all kept them to read aloud and show off to their wives) and save the papers with their name patterns, and go off down the ravine or up the hill. There was no problem about my getting home on moonlight nights, nor on the nights when Chico would put kerosene in the lantern and let us use it to guide us home. One night, when we stopped to chat on the steps, Aurelio guided me home with a flashlight, one that Sofía's Don Pablo had left when he went to the United States. But the night Cassiano, Joel, and I stayed late to help Elisha and Elijah, it poured rain, and we had no light at all. We formed a chain holding hands, and they got me down the trail to Doña Patrocina's, where I stumbled, cold and wet, into the dark room and to my *petate*. Cassiano and Joel must have found the way back up the trail to Doña Estéfana's, for they were both back the next night in the light of the full moon.

There were no lighting problems with the classes for women; but then, there were no helpful Cassianos either. Juanita and Chabella and the other "doll dressers" of 1934, who might have helped, had little children to dress in 1945 and many tasks at home in the daytime. It would not have been seemly for a young matron to leave home, bring her suckling baby, and come to teach others on the schoolhouse steps. Even few *analfabetas* thought it seemly to come. Chico and I struggled with Esperanza day in and day out, and never got her really beyond "Lalo." Doña Ofelia was graciously willing to help the women and worked with the industrious Elodia from Doña Paula's and with three other young married women. I did not go to the school porch to help every afternoon, as I was often riding *el caballo,* sketching, or just visiting.

But I took one of the spare booklets with the coupon unsigned and registered Eostolia. She was a round-faced, pleasant woman the age of Nico, an only daughter of his father's brother. Such a close cousin is called a *hermana prima,* or "cousin-sister," and the relationship was even closer in this case, for Nico and Chico had no sister. It was because Eostolia was the wife of the older Ramírez brother that I tried so hard to help Elisha and Elijah. She had been twelve in 1934, had come to watch us sew doll dresses, but had not been able to come to school because of the long illness of her mother, who died when Eostolia was fourteen. Now she was determined to learn faster than Elijeo. She often came to Doña Patrocina's house and had "school" there with Esperanza and Hipólito Arroyo, Esperanza's next younger brother. Though she was there less often, she learned twice as much as they did. Altogether, at the school we taught eight young women the first half of the book that summer, but we taught thirty-five young men.

Eostolia and the Ramírez brothers invited me to come and visit them after they all had advanced through the "Tomasa" lesson. They lived with the boys' old mother in the ravine above the *Co-*

operativa and near Don Féliz' irrigated garden. Here was an old bamboo and adobe hut, a one-room shack under straw thatch, and Eostolia had moved into it with *metate* and bridal chest. It seemed a very happy family. They were all great jokers, and their only sorrow seemed to be that after five years of marriage there were still no children.

It was difficult to get to Eostolia's house down in the ravine, such a slippery trail when it was wet, such a "caving-in" and "crumbling-off" trail when it was dry. It was hard even for Eliseo's donkeys to step out of the ravine in the morning when they had to go to the sierra. Elijeo worked the fields and went to market, and thus had more time with his wife. When I first saw them both, the night they were turned over to me by Doña Ofelia, they looked like a tourist's wildest idea of marauding bandits, they were so unwashed and uncombed. The day they asked me to visit, they had both been to Oaxaca, had had some of their hair trimmed and had been shaved by a barber, of all things! So they did not look at all wild in the photograph I took of them.

I wrote enthusiastically about them in my notes of 1945: "I shall always remember Eostolia, Elijeo, and Eliseo, *los analfabetos de Santa Cruz Etla*, as the best students I have ever had, in many years of many kinds of teaching. They truly appreciated what little time I spent with them; they made the fastest progress in the subject they were trying to learn; they and I all had a feeling of accomplishing something important." I took this teaching of the illiterates very seriously in 1945, and thought I was "advancing a whole family a hundred years," to quote myself at the time, simply by teaching them to be "literates." No doubt that was an exaggeration, but there is that much difference in the minds of many Mexicans, in the eyes of the Mexican law and society, between "unlettered ones" and "lettered ones."

Eostolia served me strawberry pop which she, one of the poor little ones, the *probrecitas* of Santa Cruz Etla, had had Elijeo bring from Oaxaca. She gave me three fresh eggs; she had no other gift, for there were neither flowers nor fruit trees on the Ramírez brothers' land. The morning I left Santa Cruz, when I was trying to get away without any fanfare and ceremony, Eliseo heard about it and de-layed his trip to the sierra to come with his brother and sister-in-law to bid me good-bye. They were full of thanks for the teaching, but Eliseo said, "I want to press again the hand of Doña Elena, the fearless one."

"Oh, oh," I thought, "fearless to pull myself up the trail in the rainy dark when I had the water sickness, to teach uncombed moun-tain Indians to read about Tomasa and Lalo and Pepe? Well, I'd hardly call that fearless, Eliseo."

But I said out loud only, "Why fearless, Eliseo?" hoping for some compliment on the tremendous "difficulty" of the job.

"Fearless that you ride the horse of Don Marciano to the sierra," he answered, putting that feat above any mere teaching of *analfabetos*.

I had other pupils besides these. Don Ceferino was the good musician, the player of bass viol and flute and fiddle, all three, who could read music long before he could read words, and who after-wards trained his two young sons to be musicians also. Pedro Sánchez from the San Sebastián *loma* got to "Felipe" with me and Doña Ester. Luis Jiménez tarried long on the capital *T*'s and finally went on to the *C*'s, one of the most difficult letters because of the con-fusion with the *Q*-sound in Spanish. Cassiano, Eduardo, and I shifted many of them back and forth between us, according to the number of candles we had to the table. No one in any helper's group got beyond the twenty-five lessons which introduced the letters. Elijeo promised that he would read the whole booklet if I would come again.

"The next twenty pages have an educational value beyond lit-eracy itself," said an American educational journal in 1946, describ-ing the booklet as a "splendid educational experiment in our neigh-bor republic." I almost have to take this statement as to educational value for granted, because I never got around to teaching anyone the second section. These latter pages, written it is said by Dr. Torres-Bodet himself, consisted of brief reading sections of one or two pages each: on public health, the family, the soil, biographies of famous Mexicans, and the Mexican constitution. The booklet ended with the complete words of the Mexican national anthem. I read this last part through only once with Don Ceferino, and I'm sure he didn't follow me. Some of the Spanish vocabulary was over my head, although Don Ceferino nodded wisely as we read the words together. I had a message the following winter from Chico, via Rosita, that Doña Ester had taken twenty men and five women through the last part of the book, and that Santa Cruz Etla was "ready for the inspection."

I am afraid this "inspection" was not as serious nor as thorough as we had expected it to be. Evidently Doña Ester finally took fifteen of our people down to Oaxaca on the San Lorenzo bus on a Saturday, and they were given a very cursory examination in the office of rural education, which is always worked to death anyway with the problems of regular rural schools. They read out loud from the book (by then they knew every page by heart), and then they answered written examination questions. Rosita wrote me only that this had happened; she did not say what the questions were. It seems that the group rallied first at her "town house," and she went with them.

The examiner matched the coupons turned in at the beginning to the learners' books, accounting for each one, filled in and tore out the second coupon remaining in the book and gave it to the *aprendedor,* the learner. The coupon left in the book at last, bearing a serial number, was signed by the learner and by the teacher (who signed for my people when I wasn't there?) and filed away forever. "All fifteen of your people passed," wrote Rosita, "including your Ramírez family, those cousins of Chico." She did not say whether Cassiano and Doña Ester got gold seals. I know nobody sent *me* one.

But we had checked out thirty books in the first place. I wonder what became of the certificates of my other people, whose first coupons I signed, and who, after they had learned the alphabet, had no one teacher, but probably listened in on everybody else for the hard last twenty pages? And what about Esperanza, who gave up along the way, and whose book, with Coupon One long since sent in under her own name to the authorities, was given me by

Esperanza as a souvenir and was brought back here to Los Angeles? And what happened to Pedro Sánchez and Bernardino Méndez and those two friends of Joel and Nico, who undoubtedly did not finish the book and pass? Didn't they get even any gold stars for trying? No one remembered the answers to any of these questions by 1954.

And how about the people who did learn, who "advanced one hundred years"? It was announced in the fall of 1945 that the municipal president (oh, oh, Don Bartolo! and you never on any list yourself, either of literate ones or of book holders or of examination passers), the municipal president must "send the results of his area to the Secretariat of Public Education in Mexico City." Then the federal secretariat would distribute second-grade pamphlets to the new "literates." These pamphlets were called: "How to be a Better Farmer"; "How to be a Better Citizen"; "How to Care for your Baby"; "How to Avoid Disease." Because of the campaign, fifteen more people in Santa Cruz Etla were supposed to be able to read about these things than had been before.

Whenever people meet on the trails in Santa Cruz Etla, they say to each other, *¿Como lo va?* (How goes it?) During the summer of the *campaña*, the answer would not be the usual *muy bien*, among the night school students, but often, "It goes as far as 'Tomasa,'" or "Pepe," or even "Felipe." We "lettered ones" would often give this answer too, referring to our current learner. I noted this fact in my diary notes of 1945, and remarked (oh, so optimistically!) in describing what I had heard about the second-level books that were to come next: "When the second-level books come, and they say to each other, 'How goes it?' if they get the custom of answering, 'It goes as far as being a better farmer,' or 'It goes as far as giving better care to babies,' then will the hundred years move forward faster."

Too idealistic, too optimistic for Santa Cruz Etla the reader will say; and I, myself, now the reader twelve years later of my own 1945 notes, say so too. But no one in Santa Cruz Etla is discouraged. The people remember the campaign with pleasure, and the town leaders mention with pride that fifteen people passed. Even Don Bartolo, unchanged in 1954, said: "Remember the *campaña contra analfabetismo,* Doña Elena? How well we did here in Santa Cruz Etla!" He remained president until the New Year in 1947, so naturally no second-level books came through any initiative of the municipal president. Doña Ester, the only one of the teachers interested, was married and gone by the time another president came in; and the new teachers could not be expected to carry on something they did not even know had started. Cassiano, Joel, Nico— then so young, so shy of city ways and official contacts, unwilling to take any action that the men of the council did not request—well, no one could expect them to send for the other books. In everyone's experience it was almost impossible to get any schoolbooks, anyway, so who would try?

That left only me, busy in Los Angeles, traveling and studying far afield from Santa Cruz Etla in every subsequent summer until 1951. So I have to question my own conscience, if Santa Cruz Etla people never answered each other on the trails about the "Better Farmer" and the "Better Babies" booklets. Was I really interested in getting my *analfabetos* ahead a century, or wasn't I just interested in an excuse for having a nice summer in Santa Cruz Etla, a story to tell teacher and student audiences in the United States about "the splendid campaign against illiteracy" and my own part in it? If none of the second little books ever got into the Etla Hills, the fault is as much mine as anyone's.

On a nation-wide scale the *campaña contra analfabetismo* still goes on. In 1953 President Ruiz Cortines asked for a complete new evaluation of the program, and his committee then decided to continue it by means of special, paid teachers. The *Cartilla* was reissued to all regular teachers, in the cities at least, though Don Alfredo never received one in Santa Cruz. The new edition had pictures in color, contained some easier stories in the back about health and agriculture, and included much of the material meant for the second-level books before. Rosita attended a special meeting in Mexico City in June of 1954 that was called for teacher volunteers and received several copies of the new edition, without the formality of signing for them. When I came back through Mexico City in August of that year, she had already launched her own little new *campaña* and had three kindergarten mothers busily at work on "Tomasa" and "Pepe." She says that some cynics in Mexico think the "Each-One-Teach-One" program fell down, that "each one" is not necessarily a good teacher. Naturally Rosita is not cynical about anything, and she tells success stories of the city mothers she taught to read in 1945 and 1946 in Oaxaca, of the little Mitla Indian servant boy in her house then who is now teaching school himself in the hills behind Mitla.

So I looked again to see what the little learning they had received meant to some of the *analfabetos* in Santa Cruz Etla. Are they, and is the town, better off because of Tomasa and Pepe and Felipe? I got around to answering this question when I checked on the future hopes of those who had ever been to any kind of school class in Santa Cruz Etla.

PART FOUR

Send On Another Benito Juárez

1. **DON AMADO'S DREAM:** *A future leader should come from Santa Cruz Etla.*

2. **CHICO AND ESPERANZA:** *They are happy and they are still in the hills.*

3. **THOSE OTHERS FROM UNDER THE COLEMAN LIGHT:** *They were all grown men when they learned to read, anyway.*

4. **DON PABLO EL BRACERO:** *He went to work in the United States.*

5. **THE RAMÍREZ BROTHERS AND DON CEFERINO:** *What became of the young men I myself taught to read and write?*

6. **NICO:** *Would Don Amado have been pleased with a fine young farmer?*

7. **THOSE OTHERS WHO WERE CHILDREN IN 1934:** *What did they do for the village?*

8. **THE CHILDREN OF THE DAYS OF DOÑA OFELIA:** *All these are grown men now.*

9. **DON AMADO'S OWN SONS:** *They gave up the dream and went to the city.*

10. **MARGARITA:** *Our public health project failed.*

11. **SANTA CRUZ ETLA ITSELF:** *It is an "awakening village."*

❧ I ❧

Don Amado had not been satisfied to have just an ordinary school in Santa Cruz Etla, which would do the usual routine educating job. He deplored the end of the night classes after Rosita and the Coleman light left; he would have been delighted at the *campaña* against illiteracy. All to the same end. He wanted Santa Cruz Etla to "send on another Benito Juárez."

Benito Juárez, the reform president of Mexico in the days of Maximilian and Carlotta, had been born a full-blooded Zapotecan Indian a century and a half ago in the sierra of Ixtlán fifty miles back of, and beyond, Santa Cruz Etla. Orphaned early, abused by his ignorant *tonto* Zapotecan relatives, he ran away at twelve to the "great metropolis" of Oaxaca, which had then perhaps ten or fifteen thousand inhabitants, most of them Spanish-speaking colonials. He was taken in as an "Augustina-type" kitchen slavey by a well-to-do family; for the first time he heard there the Spanish language spoken and learned of the existence of writing and books. Adopted by a kind friend of his employer, he was sent to school and then to college. He became a lawyer and a champion of Indian rights in the new republic, and eventually became governor of Oaxaca, member of the national congress, chief justice of the national supreme court, and then president of Mexico and personification of the rights of the *pobrecitos* against the landlord class. He is called the Abraham Lincoln of Mexico. Every Indian village, every person of Indian blood in Mexico, is better off because he lived. Don Amado was expecting a great deal of Santa Cruz Etla when he hoped the town and the school would produce another Benito Juárez.

When he spoke of this idea so fervently that night at Doña Estéfana's in 1944, I asked him if he wanted such a heroic person to work for the improvement of Santa Cruz Etla, or for the fame of the Etla Hills throughout the nation. Did he want personal betterment, community-wide improvement at home, or national leadership? Perhaps he himself had not thought that far, as he floundered around answering, with a great deal of high-flown prose, and I was very sleepy. But he spoke of the older fellows who had learned to write under Rosita's Coleman light: Esteban whom he had pushed as president; Chico who had helped him with town records; Panfilo, Don Marciano's eldest; Eduardo the mechanically minded one; and Pablo Bautista who had married Doña Sofía. There was still time for all these to do something spectacular.

Then he had hopes for Rosita's own students whom we had known in 1934; the boys Nico and Joel and Crescencio and, though he did not mention them, the girls who might also (it seemed to me) do something for the village: Esperanza, Chabella, and perhaps Juanita. Speaking in 1944, he was hardly conscious of the work for illiterates which had just been launched in Mexico City the same month he was talking to me at Doña Estéfana's. But if he had, he would have leaped to make plans and to have hopes for Elisha and Elijah and Don Ceferino.

Closest to his heart was his own son Cassiano, fifteen when Don

Amado died, a student of Rosita in the primary class before she left Santa Cruz Etla. In Cassiano's generation other bright boys, such as Aurelio, Doña Estéfana's grandson, and Don Marcelino's Perfecto, that good, good student, would have appealed to him as possibilities of the Benito Juárez type. There was a younger bunch of children in school when I was there in 1945, fourth graders like Gerónomo and Aurelia and Isaías Pérez, and the little ones like Doña Sofía's smart little Leopoldo and Don Amado's other sons, shy Martiniano and bold Margarito, all then in the first grade. Waiting to go into the first grade in 1946 was the brilliant little Margarita, daughter of Chabella and granddaughter of Don Martín—and they are still coming on, Don Amado. There is Esperanza's little son and Joel's two children, and Aurelio's much beloved baby boy. Surely in all these there will be someone to please you, Don Amado, to carry the torch for Santa Cruz Etla. The school itself was named *Escuela Federal Rural de Benito Juárez.* Through its portals all these young people passed or will pass.

Can you be satisfied, Don Amado, that most of them lived happily and brought joy to their own families, and in many cases some improvement, and that they produced fine children, and cut more wood or raised better corn? And those that left home, as did Benito Juárez, longed to be back in Santa Cruz, with few exceptions, and came home sometimes to bring new ideas. Who is to say that Benito Juárez himself would not think they were "carrying the torch"?

≈≈ 2 ≈≈

IF I WERE TO ANSWER the questions I pose to the spirit of Don Amado, if I were even to set up aims for cultural missionaries, should I seek out those of the second generation in Santa Cruz who are most successful, or those who are happiest? Isn't happiness success? And being happy is to have founded a happy family. And Chico, from Rosita's first night school class, and his little wife Esperanza, from Rosita's primary class in 1934, have surely done that.

In addition, Chico (Don Francisco López in the eyes of the newest new generation in Santa Cruz) is a great credit to the town. For years after the death of Don Amado and before Cassiano and Perfecto could take over, he kept all the written records of the town. He served as *alcalde* of the school committee in 1944 and again quite recently (I didn't check what year), and he did a better job the second time, now that his own little son is in school. Without a doubt, he will some day be president. He went to work one short season, just before his marriage, on the Pan American Highway as it was being worked through the valley into Oaxaca, but he preferred to return to the village and spend his energies there. He is the head of a household, and can command his mother, his wife, and his younger brother's family. This is purely theoretical, however, or at least it was when I lived there, for Doña Patrocina ran the house and surely Esperanza commanded Chico. But he was the highest ranking man of the young generation left in Santa Cruz Etla after Esteban withdrew from "politics." He was also a musician, which was even more important, and a regular liaison officer between Santa Cruz Etla and the Oaxaca market.

This last activity was so important to me and my life in the village in 1945 that it is worth digressing from Benito Juárez to tell about. Chico could get candles and embroidery thread, turpentine for the oil paints, white cheese for *cena*, all these things within two or three days from the time I began to want them, because he went so often to market. He did not have to wait for Saturday, but could sell his charcoal any day at private houses, where the *señoras* knew him, and where, he told me, he was always sure of a good sale.

Sometimes he sold loads of unburned wood, and on those days he would take an hour getting the load ready. He would put green alfalfa across the burro's back, then cushions made of old *petates* stuffed with straw, and finally the pack harness made of century-plant fibre. The week before my 1945 visit he had just paid eighteen pesos for new harnesses, cinch straps, bags, baskets, and the ropes. Chico's burros were always so carefully packed that they never had the sore backs you so often see on the poor little pack-burros of Mexico. Chico's burros had been working the trails between Oaxaca and the sierra for ten or twelve years, and he told me he figured on them lasting twenty. Everything that came from the city to Doña Patrocina's house came on their backs.

Chico needed the money he got for the wood to pay installments on his wedding clothes and his part in the fiesta taxes. But it is surprising how much buying and selling goes on in Santa Cruz Etla without any money or any trips to market. During the summer we had the mangoes to offer for eggs, in a ratio of about six to one; and for tomatoes and onions, three to one; and for avocados, just even. When Esperanza's brother, Hipólito Arroyo, chased our runaway burros for us, we gave him three mangoes. When Chico sent the burros home from market early by Don Marciano's third son, we gave him six mangoes for the errand. I don't know what Doña Patrocina does in return for small favors in the dry season when the mangoes are not ripe. I know that we had flowers from Doña Paula's garden on our altar every Sunday in return for Doña Patrocina's treatments of Doña Paula's rheumatism. We also got *chicharrónes*, or pork cracklings, a delicious Mexican delicacy, each of the three times Don Casimiro, the hog-raising neighbor, butchered in the summer; and I knew that the gift was payment for Doña Patrocina's treatments. Thus, we could live a long time without cash because of a mango tree and an herb woman. Chico, however, tuning in on the modern world as he did, needed actual money.

He used money in the permanent shops of Oaxaca, rather than in the Saturday market stalls, to buy rice, macaroni, sugar, coffee beans, lye for the cooked corn, soap, and chocolate. (Don Martín was selling all these things for cash or trade by 1954, of course.) Neither Doña Patrocina nor Esperanza could write, so Chico never took a list; they would both stand talking out by the burros as he packed them (and both talked excitedly) and tell him the things they wanted. I surely admired Chico, for he never seemed to forget anything; at least they never scolded him. Often he did errands for neighbors, or we would buy an excess of sugar or coffee which neighbors would pay for with eggs or (while I was there to be fed) with tomatoes and avocados.

When Chico took his wood to Santa María Asumpa, where the

pottery kilns were, he would sometimes bring back clay pots and dishes in exchange for wood. Once he bought a large, new, flat tortilla griddle for Doña Patrocina. It seems hard to see why a smart man like Chico never thought of exchanging a whole load of wood for a whole load of pots, those big baking dishes and water jars made from the red clay of Santa María Asumpa's river bed, and then selling the pots at a profit to the housewives up and down the trail. But I guess there was no profit motive. Perhaps if Chico were to have been the harbinger of fine new things for Santa Cruz that Don Amado wanted, he would have pepped up trade and the use of money; but then, he was concerned just with being successful with things as he knew them.

Doña Rosario, kindly, handsome, middle-aged mother of Chabella, walked down to the San Lorenzo bus from away up the trail toward the sierra in order to go to Oaxaca City and buy a new tortilla griddle made in Santa María Asumpa. Not waiting for the San Lorenzo bus to come home, she took the Etla bus and walked back home uphill through San Pablo. In all that long walk she had balanced the tortilla griddle, twenty inches in diameter, on her head; and when she stopped at Patrocina's to chat of the pleasures of going to market, she stood at ease with it still there. She wouldn't have wanted to cancel the trip and buy pottery from Chico at her own door, and she doesn't want to see changes and improvements come to Santa Cruz which will make it possible for her to do so. Chico is fine as the market liaison, as far as Santa Cruz wants one, but let's not have too much!

Chico was taught to play the fiddle by his uncle, Don Fausto; and in such playing, as well as in general industriousness and responsibility, he seemed to me far superior to the older generation, if his uncle was an example of that. Don Solomón, the teacher who went to the United States as a *bracero,* taught Chico some of the rudiments of note reading and helped the Santa Cruz musicians write out the music in parts. Then they would play eighteen hours at a stretch for some wedding or *mayordomía,* often without pay. The music they had in the house included such pieces as *Sobre las Olas* ("Over the Waves") and "La Paloma," such songs of Oaxaca as *Canción*

Mixteca and *La Llorona,* and a *Canción de la Frontera* which we call "South of the Border." By 1954 Chico had quit music as a partial profession and had left the town orchestra to Don Ceferino Jiménez and his sons. But he still enjoyed playing at home, and he provided four hours of music for a *santo,* a birthday party I went to in honor of Doña Angélica León in 1954. Chico as a person and a civic leader is a success, a credit to Don Amado's plans and to Rosita's teaching.

Then there is the lovely little Esperanza, without whom life in Santa Cruz would have been less fun for me in 1945, and with whom I enjoyed happy hours of visiting in 1954. She seems the epitome of what a young wife should be, and as such she is a necessity in helping to send on Benito Juárezes of the future, if not of the present. Through her I learned much of the marriage customs of Santa Cruz Etla, and through her I came to know that happy marriage is the best thing that can happen in a town.

We had remembered Esperanza as the tiniest, youngest girl in the primary class in 1934, the one in the movies who was always smiling shyly, with a grown person's *rebozo* wrapped round her head and trailing in the mud behind her. This mite of humanity grew into a very jolly, pretty girl who had caught the eye of Doña Patrocina's Chico by the time she was fourteen and he twenty-six. Doña Patrocina had told Rosita in 1944 about the betrothal, a whisper of good news, for Chico was then already twenty-seven, and Patrocina was wistfully hopeful for grandchildren. The wedding was planned for October, 1944. There was to be a fandango, or large circle dance. Rosita was to come. Then Nico and Chico and all of Esperanza's brothers were going to work throughout the dry season making bricks to build Chico and Esperanza a house in Doña Patrocina's houseyard.

The wedding was not held till February, 1945, and no house was built. A few piles of adobe bricks, made by Chico alone, lay stacked behind the house, on the downhill side, until Nico was married three years later. I don't know why the wedding was postponed, but I can guess why the house was not built. Doña Patrocina and Esperanza got along so well together that there was no need then for a second house.

Anyone could get along with the laughing little Esperanza. What puzzles me is how Chico, a shy young man even if he was the town fiddler and secretary, ever got up the nerve to ask for Esperanza at all. Of course he could not marry as long as he was the only support of the family. When Nico was old enough to till the land, Chico was free to make cash as a *leñador*. "Then for a long time I saw no girl to interest me, Doña Elena," he said. Esperanza was busily growing older and prettier all this time. At sixteen she still stood about four feet ten, but she had such a plump little face, such big eyes, and such a merry laugh that she probably caught other eyes than those of Chico. But he had eyes only for her.

"He was interested in many, only afraid to ask for them," teased Esperanza. We were all sitting on the ground in the "kitchen" in the candlelight.

"Then why did he have courage to ask for you, Esperanza?"

She broke into gales of laughter. "Why, Chico, why? You had looked at me first four years ago."

Chico only laughed too, and began playing a tune on the fiddle. It sounded so popularized and familiar that I asked him the name of it. *La Muchacha de mis Sueños*, he answered, "Girl of My Dreams." He had learned it from a street player in Oaxaca City.

There does not seem to be much "dreaming" or romancing in the matter of betrothals in the Etla Hills, although a man like Chico can pick and choose. Rosita told me in detail the customs of betrothal. A young man takes candles and fruit to the family of a marriageable girl, often ten or twelve years his junior. If the family accepts the candles, the boy can come again and ask the father if the gift was "agreeable." Within two or three weeks, the boy's parents take a second gift, fruit, eggs, and cheese. Finally, a month later, a third party, usually the boy's godmother, goes to ask the girl's parents, definitely, for the hand of the girl in marriage. The father will either refuse the request or consent to ask the girl. If the girl accepts, her parents give a dinner with chicken or turkey *mole* and ask the boy and the go-between. A month later the boy's parents give the actual betrothal party, an all-day affair for the girl's parents and cousins and godparents, and the boy's cousins and parents. At this public affair, the girl's parents must ask, "When do you wish the wedding?" The boy names a date, about four or five months ahead, depending or whether a new house must be built and adobe bricks made and dried for it.

All this formality and secrecy seems absurd in a community as small as Santa Cruz Etla. Surely everyone would have known that Chico had his eyes on Esperanza. He told me that he had first asked for her with candles when she was fifteen. His go-between, that San Pablo godmother, Doña Socorro, for whom the Virgin of Carmen was given the party, was refused by Don Melitón Arroyo. Esperanza was too young. As the only girl she was needed at home. "Meanwhile, I turned down others," said Esperanza, interrupting the conversation.

Somehow she got across to Chico the message that he should ask again when she was seventeen. These *palabras primeras* or first words made by the godmother had started in May, 1944. It must have been a better corn year than 1945, for Doña Patrocina and Chico's godmother paid for all those *mole* dinners of hot chile and chicken, to say nothing of the cost of the wedding.

A wedding is a three-day celebration and the whole town comes. Chico and Esperanza hired Don Féliz León's oxcart and went into Oaxaca on a Saturday for the official civil registration. Don Melitón, who was doubtless sorry to lose his only daughter, took her to a photographer and had a peso picture taken of her in her white-satin dress. I never saw the picture because Don Melitón kept it, and I was never actually in his house.

On Sunday, the oxcart was decorated with flowers from Doña Paula's garden, every upright on it twined with garlands. "Flowers were even stuck in the wheel spokes," said Esperanza. Chico and Esperanza rode in this cart to the church in San Pablo Etla, having perforce chosen a Sunday when the *padre* would come on horseback from Etla. This attendance at mass and blessing by the priest made all San Pablo part of the ceremony, which doubtless was hard on Doña Patrocina's entertainment budget.

A bride is called a *novia*, which is also a common word in Mexico for girlfriend or sweetheart. Old-fashioned brides wear long, white dresses, in the same full-gored style as Doña Estéfana's everyday dress. Don Julio's Juanita and Eduardo's Rafaela had worn short, white satin dresses. Esperanza asked her father for such a short, modern dress and got it, but she has been too shy to wear it since. It lies neatly folded at the bottom of her chest. The bridal veil, made of white net, was provided by her godmother, as well as the chest in which she brought all her things to Doña Patrocina's. Doña Patrocina paid for the oxcart, the flowers, and the bridegroom's new white cotton clothes. She also bought bright-colored paper from which she made paper chains to festoon the house inside and out. Remnants of these paper chains still hung from the rafters inside the house the following summer when I lived there.

The procession back to Santa Cruz Etla went across the ravine to Don Melitón's house near the San Lorenzo ridge. As the bride's father, he provided the turkey *mole* for everyone's dinner that first day. I don't see how they got an oxcart across the ravine and up to Don Melitón's; I am afraid Esperanza with her flowers and her white satin dress had to walk. But even on her wedding day she did not have to wear shoes. Congratulations and pulque drinking went on all day Sunday at Don Melitón's, but the bridal couple came home to Doña Patrocina's at nightfall.

They had to be up early Monday, because the second day of the celebration is the most important. This was the day of the fandango, the group dance. I have never seen such a dance, and I could not quite understand from Esperanza's description just how they do it. But the fact that Chico, the groom, was one of the main musicians for the town created a problem for the wedding. Finally his godmother from San Pablo hired four of the San Pablo Etla musicians to play all day Monday for the fandango and all day Tuesday for the smaller-scale dancing and eating that goes on the third day. It must have cost her forty pesos.

It seems to me that being a godparent in the Etla Hills is a pretty expensive proposition. When a child is baptized, the godparent pays for the christening robe and the dinner party. When the child dies, the godparents pay for the funeral party. When a girl marries, there is the problem of the chest and the veil. And when a boy marries, expenses mount up doubly. So many children are born in Santa Cruz Etla, many of whom survive long enough to have a baptism and godparents, and there are so few families, that people have to be godparents just as often as they are parents. Many a good corn year's profits have gone into the celebrations for a godchild. Rosita was a godmother to two children while she was at the school, and she had to provide funerals for both of them before she left.

Doña Patrocina paid for the food served at Esperanza's wedding the second and third days. She had to do most of the preparation because Esperanza did not help her with tortillas until things settled down after the first week. Doña Patrocina also bought cloth for two dresses for Esperanza and new cotton outfits for herself and Nico, as well as one for the bridegroom. All her ready cash was spent on the food and decorations, evidently, and she borrowed money in Etla for the clothes. Three times during the summer of 1945 a young city man came on horseback from a "commercial house" in Etla and collected three silver pesos. Doña Patrocina always had it ready. I did not like to ask, but it looked as if the bill collector went on across the ravine to Don Melitón's for an installment of the wedding expenses at that end as well.

A marriage is called a *casamiento*. The whole idea is taken very seriously in Santa Cruz Etla, and a broken marriage is so seldom heard of that I am still surprised (and maybe all of Santa Cruz Etla was, too) at the thought of Don Julio's new family. One day at Patrocina's I lay sick on my *petate* and listened to the chatter of a gossiping little man, second cousin to Doña Patrocina, who came to visit from San Luis Ocotitlán. The juiciest story he had to tell was about a girl in that town who ran home after eight days of marriage. She would not eat her mother-in-law's cooking. The wizened little cousin thought this story very funny, but I heard Doña Patrocina repeat it in a shocked voice to Doña Estéfana when she came to see me the next day. I have also heard Doña Pastorcita, Don Martín's wife and my hostess in 1954, tell of the scandalous behavior of people in "those valley towns" who only register their marriage with the civil authorities and never go before the *padre*. "Many people in the valley live like that. They are not really married," she said.

Esperanza and Chico seemed just as happy together as high-school sweethearts in the United States, even though they did not "go steady" through school; and Chico was already a member of *Los Policías* and was a young *leñador* when Esperanza was in the first grade. They laughed and teased and joked and chased each other around the houseyard like two ten-year-olds.

In public they were very decorous. At the *mayordomía* at San Pablo Etla, that day of the Virgin of Carmen, Chico did not play the fiddle with the San Pablo musicians, but sat around with the young men and pitched coins at a line drawn on the ground. Esperanza, dressed in the long, pink-flowered dress that Doña Patrocina had given her, sat primly among the women on the *petates*, under the chins of the red oxen. Neither one danced all day.

On the way home, I asked Esperanza: "Is it not the custom for a young bride and groom to dance together at a fiesta?"

Esperanza answered: "It would be the custom if we wished. We did not wish."

I had wondered if Doña Sofía and the *bracero*, Don Pablo, went through all the rigmarole of asking with candles, a go-between, a request to parents, and so on, when they were married, both in middle age and both for the second time. Doña Estéfana had been surprised when I asked. "How else could a man ask for a woman, except to give candles and food to her parents?" she said. "Of course Pablo had to ask me for Sofía."

"But didn't Sofía and Pablo know each other well and make up their own minds?" Doña Estéfana would not answer this. She would not admit that there was one marriage in which she, the parent, was not very important in the decision.

Doña Patrocina told me another time, though, that she and her little old mother had gone to see the widowed Doña Buenaventura, aged at least forty-five, to ask her to receive presents from Don Fausto, the guitar player, only brother of Doña Patrocina. "She kept us waiting for an answer two months, though she was surely lucky to get Fausto, and she knew it," Doña Patrocina remarked in a tone of voice that sounded a trifle catty. However it happened, it didn't last, and Fausto in 1954 was back living with Patrocina in her crowded house, while Buenaventura and her children kept their own counsel over in San Sebastián. How Don Julio and his two different wives fit into all this elaborate pattern of marriage is hard to figure. But I am supposed to be writing about Esperanza, and about how she, as a happy little wife, is just as good a product of Santa Cruz Etla in the second generation as Benito Juárez might have been.

It was a good thing she was happy; surely she worked hard. In Doña Patrocina's household the newest bride is the "hewer of wood and the drawer of water." At least, she certainly drew the water. On her return from the mill in the morning, she got an *olla* or clay jar full of water from the ditch to start the coffee. She was able to eat her own breakfast only after everyone else had enough tortillas. Then she had to go back and forth across the trail to the ditch ten times for *ollas* of water, four for the large jar in the "kitchen," six for the large jar provided in front of the house for washing. On days clothes were washed, this ten-gallon jar had to be filled again in the course of the morning. Both boys washed their faces and hands with water from it after breakfast, using a gourd dipper to dish water into a flat clay bowl. Drinking water came from the large jar, too. I have never heard of these large "storage" jars being washed, and it is easy to see why dysentery, the "water sickness," sometimes lingers on from dry season to the rainy, and back to the dry, collecting its annual toll.

Three days a week Esperanza washed. She herself, being a new bride, owned at least five cotton dresses and the white satin dress. But I doubt if Doña Patrocina had three faded, patched, cotton dresses for daily wear. The people of Santa Cruz Etla do try desperately to be clean, but their muddy trails, their close quarters with the livestock, their dirt floors and lack of chairs, all make it difficult to keep light-colored clothes clean. Esperanza washed, Doña Patrocina ironed, Esperanza did the mending. Nothing was discarded until it was as threadbare as Crescencio's shirt.

Esperanza did not learn to sew in school with Rosita, as did Chabella and Juanita. She had been brought to school in 1934 at the age of six by an older sister aged eight. The summer we knew her then was her only term in school. In the fall of that year her sister died. Esperanza's mother already had three sons younger than Esperanza, and the latter stayed at home, taking on at seven the jobs of hauling water and running to the mill. Four more boys were born to Don Melitón Arroyo and his wife; of the seven, five survived, many boys' mouths for Esperanza to fill with tortillas. It is easy to see why she was gay at Doña Patrocina's; the work there was so much lighter. The two older brothers, Juan and Hipólito, came by the house often to say hello to their sister, and there was still a strong family affection among them. A boy I didn't remember at all stopped me on the trail in 1954 to tell me he was Humberto Arroyo, one of the younger brothers, now grown almost to manhood. I should have recognized him; all of Esperanza's brothers look so much like Esperanza; and there was an unmistakable one in the fourth grade at school in 1954, just two years ahead of Esperanza's own little boy.

I have still a friendly feeling for the smiling Hipólito. Once when La Abuelita and I were alone at Doña Patrocina's that long summer of 1945, all three burros got loose at once. It was only the sudden arrival of Hipólito which saved the day. The grandmother and I could only chase one burro each. Hipólito could chase all three at once, it seemed, for they were quickly rounded up.

In September of 1945 Esperanza left the tortilla-making at Doña Patrocina's for a week to go home to help her mother. Don Melitón's wife gave birth to her tenth child, the first girl-child in eight births. This girl seemed healthy and happy in 1951, a chubby carbon copy of Esperanza in her own first days in school. She was named Juana Petra, and she had to replace Esperanza who was given to Chico. "You don't know how glad my mother was to have this last one be a girl, though it will be a couple of years yet before she can make tortillas," said Esperanza. Sadly I noticed in 1954 that Juana Petra was out of school, like Esperanza before her, and at home making tortillas, though the next older brother was in school.

Don Melitón has been *alcalde* of the school committee, but neither he, nor Esperanza, nor Hipólito, nor any save this young brother, has ever learned to read. Chico teased Esperanza into going to the literacy classes for adults with me in the early afternoon, but she sat around and laughed and chatted and would not study. She remembered most of the alphabet from her year with Rosita and made a great show at home of reading the letters out loud for Chico, but she never would take a pencil in her hand to write anything. Hipólito came sometimes for help from Nico, in the night school, but more often came by Doña Patrocina's when I was helping Eostolia and Esperanza on our portico. As we worked at the letters, all four of us, Doña Patrocina, herself illiterate, called us the "López School for Beginners." Hipólito never got beyond "Lalo," however, and could not be called a "literate one."

The only thing Esperanza missed about school was the chance to learn to embroider. Under Doña Ofelia the three girls in the fourth grade sat primly on the school steps and embroidered altar cloths, blouses, and tortilla warming rags. Two girls were making a table runner ten feet long to use when the town council ate at the school on September 16. The design was of floral baskets and was done in bright thread. It would take months of work. Esperanza would have liked very much to be helping them. She yearned to work with colors.

I suggested she get Chico to buy her a cloth and some colored thread in the market, and I would draw her a design on the cloth. When the cloth came, plain unbleached muslin, she asked for butterflies, *mariposas*. It was easy enough to draw large groups of butterflies hovering above garlands of flowers; but Chico had brought only pink, green, and blue thread, no yellow, nor brown, nor black. The project had to wait for Chico to make another trip. The yellow I had to buy for Esperanza myself, finally, when I went to Oaxaca on the horse. Of course, it was another week before the embroidery got started; when I left only one butterfly was done. Esperanza had to use most of her time in the daylight to wash and mend and make tortillas. I felt rewarded for my butterfly design in the long run, however; the cloth, all four corners worked, is spread over a little stand to hold Chico's fiddle and music in the new house they have now.

I remember an incident of another cloth, one which showed Esperanza's sense of humor. One day in 1945 when I went sketching down to San Pablo Etla, I stopped to talk to the teachers there and got back after dark. Chico was not yet home from market. Doña Patrocina had been called to a sick bed, and Nico had gone with her. La Abuelita went to bed when the sun set. Only Esperanza greeted me, sitting sad and alone in the dim light of the charcoal fire.

"There is no *cena*, no supper, Doña Elena. My mother-in-law is gone; she left no instructions. There are no beans remaining from lunch. All the tortillas Nico took to the poor family where the mother is sick. There is nothing. *¡Qué lástima!*"

She got up by and by and lit a candle in the large room. Soon she called me in there to "see her embroidery."

She had taken the table back into the sleeping room and had spread it with a clean cloth and a fancy supper, much more "style" than I ever had sitting alone at lunch. There was the white cheese of which I was so fond, that we had not had for a week; there were eggs fried like a Spanish omelette; there was chocolate made with milk and foamed up in the Spanish fashion. It was the best *cena* in many days. Esperanza herself sat down with me, the first time she had ever sat in a chair to eat at a table covered with a cloth. She pretended to be very grown up and serious, asking if that were the way ladies, *damas*, acted in my country. But we could not contain our laughter. When Chico drove the burros home from the market, coming in cross and tired, we could not explain to him why we were so merry and "stylish" at the same time.

Esperanza was always amused at my bathing in *el río*, for she was the one who went with me. She had gone with Rosita and me and three other little girls from the school when I bathed in *el río* in 1934. That was the first time I had ever seen the "river," and I had expected that to bathe in the river, *bañar en el río*, meant to go swimming. Rosita and the children had taken soap and towels in a bucket. It had been a "good year" with much water, and *el río* ran two feet deep. In order to "bathe," we found secluded places along the stream and all sat down in the water. It had taken patience and much pantomime for Rosita to explain this to me.

But with Esperanza, by then a young lady, and with La Abuelita along for the walk, I searched up and down *el río* for any place deep enough to bathe in the dry year, 1945. The "river" was almost dry at the oxcart trail crossing on the way to the San Sebastián ridge. We went up it a quarter of a mile trying to find a deep, clean place. Then we met the young daughter of Don Fausto's Buenaventura. "There is a *pozito grandote,* a little well, very big, near here," she said, "and others near it." Esperanza and the little grandmother left me at the first pool while they found a place further down. At my "bathtub" there was a deep, natural well, filled with underground spring water. It overflowed in a narrow place of the river, making a clear pool below the spring about three feet deep and five wide. I was able to wash my hair as well as to take a refreshingly thorough bath in the clean, cold water.

Esperanza found her pool too muddy to wash her hair, and she came down to join me at mine. She may have laughed at my shyness at bathing in the river, but I laughed at her clumsy method of washing the long braids. I helped her undo them and soused them thoroughly with lather from my own soap. Since Esperanza had very long, thick hair and washed it only in cold river water with crude washing soap, she could never get rid of the lice, no matter how hard she tried to catch them individually with the comb.

But who am I to criticize Esperanza for having vermin, when I was so criticized myself on one occasion right at the *pozito grandote?* I went to bathe there often through the summer, after that first time when I washed Esperanza's hair. I would take my clean change of clothes and wash out my dirty ones, often playing an hour or so at the cool little sheltered pool in the heat of the day. The people from our ridge knew I went down there, sometimes with *el caballo,* and they never disturbed me. But undoubtedly the spring just above the pool had the best drinking water for a mile around. I tried not to show surprise, therefore, one day as I sat naked on the edge of the pool, when two men going in to market from the San Sebastián ridge searched out the spring. Coyly I turned my face away and rapidly washed clothes. They stopped at the spring to look at me in astonishment. *Mira, es la gringa,* (look, it is the foreign woman) said one. "How white she is!"

226

Pobrecita, said the other sympathetically, *¡qué la han picado las pulgas!* (poor little thing, how flea-bitten she is!), and they both trudged off down the ravine.

Esperanza in 1954 had neither fleas in her house (at least I picked up none in several afternoons of visiting) nor lice in her head. Perhaps following my own explanations, she now washes her hair in hot water, heated in an *olla* and then poured into the big clay washing tub, and she uses Castile soap bought in Oaxaca City. Her little boy seemed by far the cleanest, neatest, best-combed little boy in the first grade at school.

Because of endless chatter with Esperanza, my Spanish improved more during my summer at Patrocina's than in any other year of my Latin American adventuring. It is easy enough to use the *usted,* or formal "you," forms of Spanish verbs. But between co-godmothers and relatives, and soon between myself and Doña Patrocina, or Esperanza, or Doña Estéfana, we were using *tú,* or "thou," where Rosita had always used *usted.* This called for forms of the verb not so commonly learned. La Abuelita called everyone *tú;* I don't think she knew the *usted* at all, even to address the saints. Since I have never really studied Spanish, but merely picked it up on many trips to Mexico, I do not know the preterit, or past, tense very well. The *tú* forms of the preterit were completely strange words to me, spoken rapidly in the midst of Esperanza's laughter. The rules for verbs and the list of verb-form changes, which I had with me in a formal Spanish grammar in 1945, were of great interest to the literate Chico and Nico. Though able to read well, they did not realize the existence of formal grammar rules in their own language.

I learned other typical expressions from Esperanza. Wild trees and plants are *furios,* as opposed to the garden variety. Raw meat is *crudo.* The commonest expressions Esperanza used were *eso es,* "that's it," "that's the thing," or "that's the way it should be," and *¡mira no más!* which really means "look no more" but is surely as sensible an expression as "just look!" Esperanza, who was never impatient about the water-carrying or the tortilla-making or the embroidery or the literacy lessons or anything, always said every night, *Mañana es otro día* (tomorrow is another day). She also very often said, *Sigan las mañanas,* which perhaps means "bring on your tomorrows," or "let more tomorrows come," or something like that.

The way she and La Abuelita, and even Doña Estéfana, used laughter as conversation confused me, too, until I heard everyone, even the men, laughing out loud at the long, heavy rain they needed so badly that year. They laughed, not with scorn, but with delight. They didn't laugh at me on the horse because I looked funny, but because they were pleased to have me come riding by to chat. When they saw my finished oil paintings they laughed right out loud. Then I knew they liked them as much as they liked the rain.

"Esperanza has not yet been touched by any 'sorrow of life,' and it will not make her very sorrowful when it comes." So I, the sociologist, wrote in 1945. I remember one rainy morning watching her making tortillas. Whole chunks of pine wood are usually used to speed up the fire in tortilla-making. This time Chico had cut up young growth, and the wood was too green to sell to the pottery kilns. It made a very bad smoke, which was forced back to the ground by the rain. Esperanza, close over the smoking fire as she ground tortillas, could not keep the tears from running down her face.

Quick to see "sociological significance" or to try to bring in history, I was reminded of a "Mother's Lament" which some old Spaniard with Cortés had heard in the ancient Mexico City and had translated from the Aztec. I don't remember the words, but the mother's son has gone to war against some Aztec enemy. She does not want the rest of her family to know she is grieving, but she cannot help crying as she sits silently making tortillas. She tells her critical family: "Green the wood is, much it smokes and makes me cry." I have remembered this song every time I have heard Jerome Kern's "Smoke Gets in Your Eyes." And now here was an Indian woman, descendant of the ancient people akin to the Aztecs, and the tears streamed down her face as she made tortillas over a green-wood fire. Esperanza herself spoiled the whole poetic idea. She kept laughing every time she took a corner of her *rebozo* to wipe the tears away.

228

But Esperanza was surely "touched by the sorrow of life" in the second decade I knew her. In 1951, though in Santa Cruz Etla for only a few hours, I ran up and down the trails from Don Martín's visiting everyone. Delighted to know that Nico was married and to see his little daughter, I went bungling right into Doña Patrocina's house. There on the *petate,* where I had slept as a member of her family six years before, lay a little ghost of an Esperanza, sick for two months after a miscarriage in the spring. She could still smile, although she was hardly able to force out a weak little laugh as she lay in the dark room and squeezed my hand. But playing around Doña Patrocina's door were Esperanza's two fine children, a boy born in 1947 and a second born in 1949. Because of Esperanza's long illness, all the family, Nico's half as well, was living still in Patrocina's crowded rooms.

Today Esperanza is laughing, and her pictures show her as pretty as ever. But her face is lined, and her laughter is a trifle less spontaneous. The boy born in 1947 succumbed to the "water sickness" a few months after Esperanza was well enough to get up, and she has never conceived again since her serious illness. Now she and Chico have only the one little boy, the frail and sweet-faced little Ramón, who entered in the first grade in 1954. How Doña Patrocina must have grieved at her own helplessness, the failure of her herb remedies, in the face of Esperanza's own illness and the death of the child!

Now Nico's wife fits quietly into the family and has given birth to two fine and healthy children. Chico's little family has moved across to the other side of Patrocina's house lot, into the house they all built on the site where they had first stacked the adobe bricks before Chico's wedding. Still Esperanza's subdued attitude has left a little grayness over the house. Never again would she or I recapture those gay moments at Doña Patrocina's in 1945.

But she has brought Chico happiness. He wears some store-bought clothes, acts as dignified as did Don Amado himself in the 1930's, and shows every evidence of being head of the best-ordered family in Santa Cruz Etla. Don Amado would find no fault with their progress.

I KNOW DON AMADO would have thought of Chico first of all those older fellows who learned to write in Rosita's night class, because Chico was chief assistant secretary to the town council before Don Amado's death. Maybe he had hopes also for Esteban. I never found out whether it was Don Amado or some of the other older men who had first launched Esteban, oldest and cleanest of Doña Paula's ragged brood, in a career of public service and politics. But he was one of those whom I myself saw learning to read under the Coleman light in the evenings at the school in 1934, when Chico had already known how to read and write for more than a year. Why Esteban, of all the younger men who might have been president? He seemed the least prepossessing of all, though he was older than Chico. Of course, there were few others who had become literate, and it was evidently Don Amado's idea to have the literate young men assume public office. Don Bartolo, the Illiterate One, did not achieve the presidency until Don Amado was too near death to stop it.

At any rate Esteban played the flute and he was surely a dignified and courteous president in 1944 when Don Luis Varela came to visit. Was it Esteban's fault if Don Solomón was a weak teacher and neglected the school, and thus precipitated all that confusion about the "problems" in 1944? Esteban had had some apprenticeship in government, working on the committee of public works; and he had served as chairman of that committee, so I understand, just before his presidency.

At any rate, the death of his wife in childbirth, that lovely young daughter of Doña Angélica and Don Féliz León, embittered him more than I ever saw any other rural Mexican man embittered by a death. Usually they are philosophical about death. Esteban left the community and went to work as a peon, or agricultural worker, on land south of Oaxaca City, living almost like a migrant, with no roots in any land. I have never seen him again. Don Máximo, the second brother of Crescencio and husband of the conscientious and responsible housekeeper, Elodia, told me in 1954 that Esteban was working as day laborer in a new agricultural community in the valley called Pueblo Nuevo, but that *él tiene ni familia ni tierra* (he has neither family nor land). I don't know what good it did him or Santa Cruz Etla either for him to learn to read and write under the Coleman light. At any rate, he missed the chance to do something fine for Santa Cruz Etla or to be a second Benito Juárez.

An opposite story can be told of Panfilo, who learned under the Coleman light before I came to Santa Cruz the first time and had already left home in 1944 because Don Marciano had so many sons. When the Pan American Highway began to creep over the mountains from the north, Panfilo was there working on it, part of the construction crew. He became a foreman. The road wound on down to Tehuantepec, and Panfilo with it. Then he came back to Oaxaca City and worked as a foreman in charge of a group of stonemasons busy there with the many new buildings that were going up in the new Oaxaca. In 1945 he was making four pesos a day and sending ten pesos home a month, as well as a sewing machine. When I heard about him, though I hardly remembered him, I was prone to consider him an important "specimen" from Santa Cruz Etla and to draw all sorts of conclusions about the dawning new age he symbolized. He worked set hours, nine a day, including time for a midday siesta, and earned twice as much as the *leñadores* his age made in the sierra above Santa Cruz Etla in a twelve-hour day. He wore store-bought clothes the three Sundays he walked up from Hacienda Blanca past Doña Patrocina's to his father's house. "Here is Panfilo," I thought, "who has left Santa Cruz Etla. Soon other young men will follow him and everything will be different." But the third time he came on Sunday, I happened to be walking along the trail and met him. He fell in step with me and asked me how I liked to ride his father's horse.

"And how do you like the hills of Santa Cruz Etla, señora?"

"Don't you like Santa Cruz Etla yourself, Don Panfilo?" I asked.

"But how not? It is my *tierra*, my land."

"But you do not live here now yourself."

"Why, naturally I do. Next year I will come back here to marry. Then I will stay in my *tierra*. How else can one live?"

So Panfilo spoke with warmth and loyalty of Santa Cruz Etla. He did marry in the hills, a daughter of Doña Buenaventura who had been a toddler when he was a young man in Rosita's night classes. Don Marciano's land did not have room for them all, however, and Panfilo did not stay on his *tierra*. His heart and his loyalty did, though; in a lull in his work as stonemason, he came up to help his younger brother build the fine new adobe and cement house for his parents to replace their little bamboo shacks. When I asked Don Féliz how Santa Cruz men could have built the new chapel without good plans and skilled help, Don Féliz said enthusiastically: "Remember Panfilo? He was here to act as foreman for us, to help us at every step."

Though Perfecto had drawn the sketch of how the church should look, the façade, so to speak, it was Panfilo who laid out measurements for the walls, constructed the arches, made the whole thing possible. He quit his city job for two months in order to do it. Then, at the May festival, when the church was first used, he came up with his growing family in tow, and presented Don Féliz with a hundred pesos as his *gasto* for church and fiesta. Panfilo is prosperous, for no such construction worker today, with any skill and any foreman's responsibility, gets less than three hundred fifty pesos a month. I am surely sorry not to have talked to Panfilo in 1954, to compliment him on his great services to Santa Cruz and to his father's family, on the manner in which his heart has stayed in Santa Cruz Etla. I am sure that Benito Juárez never went back to the sierra of Ixtlán in his maturity to do as much for his people. Wouldn't Don Amado have thought a stonemason as fine as a lawyer, a doctor, or a teacher, if he had lived to know about Panfilo and the church?

Eduardo el *Mecánico*, son of Don Julio, had learned to read and write from Rosita at night, two years after he hurt his hand that time with the sickle. He must have been eighteen or twenty when his father bought the gasoline mill to grind the corn, and he took complete charge of the machinery. He seemed to me to be a natural-born mechanic; the mill broke down only the one time that I ever heard of. In an era when all of Mexico was going mechanical, in-

232

dustrializing so rapidly, there was such a demand for people with a mechanical bent and the know-how of machinery that, on the face of it, I would have picked Eduardo as the "one most apt to succeed" away from home. But Santa Cruz Etla needed him, as did his father, and he stayed.

In 1945 he had been married for four years to pretty little Rafaela, who was quite modern, and wore a short store-bought gingham dress. She put on a knee-length white satin dress to have her picture taken with her husband and the babies. She owned even a pair of slippers, so Esperanza said, though I never saw her wear anything on her feet. Eduardo's little house, set on the back of Don Julio's old house lot at the mill, was built in quite a modern fashion, much more so than the two rooms which Chico finally finished for Esperanza. It had a wooden door with a knob and with hinges. There were even windows with shutters, but of course no glass.

I heard that Eduardo had wanted to build his new house on the last bit of land Don Julio owned, before he acquired all that land with his second marriage. This bit of land was in a beautiful place, way up the ravine above Don Martín's, heavily shaded with trees— oranges, lemons, avocados. La Abuelita had had a cousin who had once lived there and had sold the land to Don Julio twenty-five years before. There was a thatch and adobe hut still on it. Nico told me that Don Julio forbade Eduardo to go there and then sold the land. Don Julio did not want Eduardo so far from the mill. I saw the wooded place up the ravine, passing it on horseback, and I understand how the pretty young Rafaela would rather have lived there than under the stern and watchful eye of her father-in-law.

In 1954 I ran by chance into Don Julio's new family the second day of my visit, going to see the young Doña Refugio and finding that she was then the mother of Don Julio's young children. I was entertained there, drank a small tequila, and accepted two fresh eggs after I had photographed the children. Perhaps bad news travels fast, and this seemed bad news to Eduardo and his mother. At any rate, I saw Eduardo only at the mill, busy and gruff as his father had been a decade before. Though I offered to take photos all around again and urged him to bring his younger children up to

Don Martín's for pictures, I did not see him socially, nor Rafaela, nor Doña Fecunda his mother, during the visit. Chabella and her mother-in-law Pastorcita, my hostesses in 1954, simply laughed indulgently when I tried to find out if I had offended Eduardo by visiting his father's new family first. Eduardo had been a good friend in 1945, had danced with me at an *angelito* and at the *mayordomía* in San Pablo, had helped in the campaign against illiteracy, and I have been sorry ever since if I did the wrong thing socially!

As far as improvement for Santa Cruz Etla through Eduardo *el Mecánico* goes — well, perhaps the ball-playing comes via Eduardo. He was fond of ball; and, his family having cash money, he had been indulged by his strict father in that one thing alone. It was on Don Julio's land the fellows played ball. It was Eduardo who bought the first ball, and he probably still buys any new ones. In the 1940's it was a hard two-inch rubber ball, or *pelota,* and they either hit it in a kind of handball game against a low adobe wall they built at one end of the "field," or played a type of volleyball with it.

For this latter game, they drew a faint, almost imaginary line through the middle of the hard-packed field. Whoever came to play on Sunday afternoon (I watched them many times) lined up, one by one, on opposite sides of the line. The best players had purchased leather palm-guards, and they took the hard rubber ball and knocked it as forcefully as they would with a bat. The boys like Nico and Joel, who worked in the fields and had little ready cash, wrapped their hands in red bandanas, and they seemed to hit it just as hard. After the hit, the ball was knocked back and forth across the line as in our volleyball game. It was returned on the bounce, but when it bounced twice the point was lost.

No one ever seemed to keep very careful score; no one had loyalty to any one team or captain. I used to cheer for Cassiano or Nico or Don Bartolo (a vigorous player), but I never saw any of them on the same side two Sundays in succession. Sometimes Eduardo and Chico and Don Martín's Miguelito and others would go down to the fine field behind the San Pablo Etla church, where the ball bounced off the church wall when hit too hard instead of being lost down the ravine. Esperanza and I went to watch Chico play at San

Pablo one Sunday and found Santa Cruz men lined up with San Pablo men on each side — of all things! when Santa Cruz spent its life trying to beat San Pablo at everything it could! But the men play always for the love of playing, never to win for any one side.

I had seen young men play basketball and baseball in larger Mexican villages; but none of the boys I asked at Santa Cruz knew anything about baseball, and the basketballs cost thirty-five pesos apiece. When Don Amado received the plans for the school building in Mexico City, the building instructions included plans for basketball goals. In accordance with the blueprints, Don Amado had them constructed; but there were no metal hoops for baskets and the two backboards stood for twenty years without use or explanation, merely a part of the scenery to anyone under twenty-five.

I was delighted, then, to see a group of men, from eighteen to forty years of age, actually playing basketball around these goal posts in front of the *municipio* on both Sunday afternoons I visited in 1954, and to hear that Eduardo, now a devotee of that game, had provided the baskets and the ball for it. Don Bartolo and the older followers of *pelota*, still wearing their leather hand-guards, were down on the little handball field. Don Féliz told me that Don Julio and Eduardo, when the family split up, had decided to give the handball court outright to the town. So Santa Cruz Etla, thanks to Eduardo's interest in ball, now has *two* athletic fields of its own. Would Don Amado, whom I never saw playing ball, have considered this a sufficient public service from one of the new generation who learned to read and write? Even though Eduardo himself, evidently made antisocial by all the trouble with his father, remains entirely aloof from Santa Cruz service committees and politics?

❧ 4 ❧

Don Pablo Bautista was the oldest person who learned his letters by the Coleman light, and so perhaps would not count as one of "the new generation which can read and write." He learned after

Chico and Esteban, during Rosita's last two years in Santa Cruz Etla, after he had married Sofía and had come up from San Pablo to live in Doña Estéfana's family in Santa Cruz. He agreed whole-heartedly with Don Amado about the need for improvements in the hill villages, and he sat talking with us those evenings at Doña Estéfana's in 1944. He was talking about another kind of improve-ment, though, and kept saying, *Debemos ser más modernos* (we must be more modern). A man of about forty years of age in 1944, with a drive and a restlessness foreign to Santa Cruz Etla, he was curious and concerned about the rest of the world, impatient with the burros on the trips to market, angry at the oxen when he plowed in Doña Estéfana's fields. The *matrimonio* who taught in San Pablo all those years had painted a mural on the outside wall of the school showing farmers plowing corn with tractors, a subject of mystery to the people of Santa Cruz Etla. Many of them had asked me if that really happened in my country. "How can machines do the farm work? What do the machines understand compared to an ox?" But Don Pablo was more intelligently interested; he was im-patient even in 1944 at the slow methods of farming, the shallow furrows of the wooden plow. He had learned to read in the hard night class with the younger men in order to find out more about such things.

His was the only mention I ever heard made in Santa Cruz of the possibility of electric light. Over on the San Lorenzo, or south, ridge, about two miles from the Santa Cruz school, runs an electric power line strung on poles. For some reason the line runs along the ridges, instead of through the valley, from the city of Oaxaca to the large valley town of Etla. This line could be seen from many houses, but no one seemed to know or care anything about it. That night in 1944, while lighting me home from the mass meeting Rosita called about the "problems," Don Pablo carried a flashlight (the only one I have ever seen in Santa Cruz Etla, by the way). He spoke then about the electric power line. Every house in Santa Cruz Etla could be as light at night as the round spot of ground below the flashlight—and he focused it to emphasize his point—if only the government would allow extensions from the line and provide copper wire. The people should form a *Cooperativa*. If San Pablo Etla would join, they could all share the expense and the work of building the line. But no one was interested.

"Only I, Pablo Bautista, realize what electricity would mean to the village," I quoted him in my 1944 diary. "We would have lights at night; women could even make tortillas at night in the harvest season when they have to work in the fields in the daytime. School could be held at night all the time."

Strange that the only use of electricity which Don Pablo knew about was light. I asked him also about his flashlight. It had cost twelve pesos, about $2.50 at that time, but a great sacrifice for one of these people. The batteries cost sixty centavos apiece, but he did not begrudge the money. "Too much money is spent on fiestas here in Santa Cruz Etla which could be used for practical things," he told me.

Then he went to the United States, where flashlights seem to grow on every tree. The United States government, during the World War II years, arranged with the Mexican government to bring in Mexican men as temporary farm laborers. Agents of the United States government made speeches in plazas the length and breadth of Mexico in 1944, drafting such workers. Thousands of city workers, farmers, and hill village people volunteered to go. The men were to stay six months or a year. They were called *braceros*, a name coming from the word *brazo*, or arm. Perhaps it is something like our word "field hand." I never heard the word in Mexico in any other connection, but everywhere I went during the war years people expected me to know all about the *braceros*. Labor was scarce on the farms of the United States. The armies of the Allies had to be fed. Mexican farmers are strong men, accustomed to many hours of hard manual labor in the hot sun. The money paid them in dollars by the farm contractors of the United States seemed very big money when sent home and changed into pesos.

Because so many workers wanted to go, by the second summer every state was assigned a quota. Certain provincial capitals provided the required workers each month. Oaxaca's turn came in

April of 1945. Three thousand Oaxaca men could go. Three hundred had gone the year before, including two men from San Pablo Etla. Even Rosita's young cousin went, a boy in teacher training school. He worked at repairing railroad track in upper New York State. He wrote home about the cities, the cold, the automobiles, the strange food. Rosita's family was very worried for fear he would never come back, but he did, happily enough, and is today teaching in Oaxaca City.

The wages paid to the *braceros* in the United States averaged sixty-five cents an hour in the war years, so the official reports said. All the Mexican workers on any one farm lived and ate together, sharing expenses and Mexican-style food. They could not understand the people around them in most places where they were working—the vegetables gardens of Maryland and New Jersey, the wheat fields of eastern Washington and Oregon, the fruit orchards of California, and other places. They did not spend very much money. For some it was possible to save three or four hundred dollars. Three hundred dollars would have been almost fifteen hundred pesos in 1945, a gold mine in any village where an acre of corn was bringing in seventy-five pesos a year, and rural schoolteachers got sixty pesos a month.

In 1945 I was asked in Santa Cruz Etla, again at a dance in San Pablo, and among Rosita's friends in Oaxaca: Do the *braceros* work well? Are the Americans pleased with them? Do they learn the American ways of working? On a train that summer of 1945, an unknown man who saw I was from the United States crossed the car to lean over and say to me seriously: "Pardon, señora, but in your country, the *braceros*, my countrymen, have they worked well?

I wish I could report, for both the United States and Mexico, such happy circumstances for the *braceros* in the 1950's. Urged to go to work in the United States during the war, the *braceros* found the wages good; in return, most American farmers found the *braceros* good workers, if perhaps too docile and too willing to work for very low wages in American money. Many who went during the war years wanted to go back again; American farmers in the southwest still wanted their type of workers, one who was pleased with sixty-five cents an hour for "stoop" labor in the Imperial and Salt River valleys of Arizona and California and the Rio Grande Delta at Brownsville. So the *braceros* continued to go, and the farmers continued to hire them. The treaty arrangements of wartime ran out, and no long-term, completely satisfactory new treaty was made. Some *braceros* continued to go legally with approval from the United States consul, but most of them crossed the Rio Grande illegally and became "wetbacks."

I cannot write about this situation with any firsthand knowledge, for I found no one in the whole Etla Hills region who had gone back to the United States as a wetback. But it is true that Rosita's relatives believe from talk in Oaxaca and from stories in the city newspapers that the United States "mistreated" the wetbacks, "rounded them up like criminals," that the United States government made them unwelcome while the farmers continued to hire them by the thousands and thousands. In 1954 no one in Mexico was asking me if the *braceros* were doing a good job in my country; I was embarrassed by questions as to why we no longer wanted them, why we paid them so well (in terms of pesos of course) and then "drove them back across the Rio Grande like cattle." I am only glad to be able to say that no Santa Cruz Etla man had come to the United States under these difficult illegal circumstances.

Don Pablo, the practical Don Pablo who wanted to learn so much about the world, took advantage of the treaty arrangements during World War II and of the Oaxaca "draft" to go to the United States where he could get all his questions about machine methods answered. Don Rafael Pérez of San Pablo Etla, who had gone a year before the Oaxaca draft, had brought home a thousand pesos in the spring of 1945. He had bought a new team of oxen, five hundred pesos for each ox, *la yunta de Rafael Pérez;* people spoke about the team with awe. "How could anyone spend five hundred pesos apiece for oxen?" asked Patrocina. (Perhaps the high prices returning *braceros* were willing to pay had something to do with it, but one reason Cassiano went to work in Mexico City in 1954 was because he could not then buy a new ox team for less than 1,200 pesos.) Don Enrique Mejía of San Pablo had done other things with his money—sporty clothes, room in town, months of idleness around the Oaxaca plaza after he returned. But they both went back under the Oaxaca quota in 1945.

It was easy for them to persuade Don Pablo to go. With him went Don Solomón, the young, fiddle-playing schoolteacher who had been so unhappy with his wife. Even a rural teacher could use a thousand pesos. Doña Sofía did not know what Don Pablo would want with a thousand pesos. One thing she was sure of, they would put a tile roof on the house Don Pablo had built her, to replace the thatch. This could be done for one hundred pesos. Then what? New oxen? Doña Estéfana had two fine teams she raised from her own stock, better than any expensive, valley-bred oxen. A cart? One could be built for perhaps fifty pesos. More land? Surely Doña Estéfana had enough for all. The electric lights? Don Pablo's thousand pesos could light all the village, but it could not begin to bring the line into the town.

When I arrived in 1945 and stood talking on the school steps, the day Don Bartolo was "ill," many questions were asked me about Don Pablo's presence in the United States. Hadn't I seen him? Could he learn my language as I had learned theirs? Why couldn't he learn it from two printed lists of corresponding words, as they had seen me studying a Spanish vocabulary, for he could read? How was the climate where he was? How was the corn crop there? They knew we plowed with machines. How was this possible? What about the bean crop this year in the United States? They had been amused in other years when I told them we did not eat the rich, red beans every day. What then did Don Pablo find to eat? Did the use of machines on the farms leave time for woodcutting?

Don Pablo sent a letter to Doña Sofía while he was in the United States. Since there was no mail service then, not even to San Pablo, he had written to Santa Cruz Etla, as I always did, in care of Rosita in Oaxaca City, asking her to send it up to the hills by any charcoal seller she saw in town. Don Pablo said he had been in Mexico City; only Don Amado of all the hill people had ever been to Mexico City at that time. Then he was sent to Washington to work in an orchard. Rosita saw the letter and thought it meant

Washington, D. C. "He is in your capital," she told me excitedly. The postmark was illegible, having been through so many hands, but my guess was Washington State, perhaps the apple orchards of Yakima Valley.

I tried to imagine Don Pablo in Yakima, that beautiful little farming valley. And yet a world away from Santa Cruz Etla! In Santa Cruz a few families have apple trees in their houseyards, and they eat the sour little apples while they are still hard. In Yakima Don Pablo would have seen acres and acres of big red apples and helped to harvest them by the ton. In Santa Cruz Etla nothing can be grown when there is no rain; the people suffer for water through the rainless season of December, January, February. In Yakima he would see ditches full of irrigation water; the floodgates would be lifted and the orchard land six inches under water overnight. No crop would die for lack of water. But, ah, the winter, the "winter" when Santa Cruz Etla has the dry, hot dust—well, I hope Don Pablo did not stay through January and February in Washington State.

If the Washington where Don Pablo worked lay in the western part of the United States, why hadn't I seen Don Pablo in my country of California? This puzzled all the people who chattered with me on Doña Estéfana's portico when I went there to chat that summer of 1945. They couldn't understand then why I hadn't seen him, though in 1954 they would think it perfectly natural that I should not find the Santa Cruz people who were in Mexico City, on my way through the capital. They *know* Mexico City is a large and confusing place. "But my country is bigger than the whole state of Oaxaca and Mexico City combined," I had to tell them in 1945. "In Oaxaca City, at the market, Rosita sometimes cannot find any of you for three days together, in order to give you the photos I take and send her by mail. How could I see Don Pablo in a crowded place like my country?"

Then they would ask: "How far away is it? How many days would he go on the train to get there? How is it possible any place is that many days away?"

I was sorry not to be able to tell them that I had seen and helped Don Pablo. Rosita had written down my Los Angeles address when he came through Oaxaca and told her good-bye, but the wartime *braceros* were moved in groups from one job to another, their fares paid in advance. When their work was done, they were sent directly back to Mexico City. I knew he would never have been able to see me in Los Angeles.

Doña Patrocina's Chico, who had worked briefly with construction machinery on the Pan American Highway, understood, so he said, how a machine could plow; but he surely wanted to ask Don Pablo how machines could harvest corn. Machines did not have sense like an ox, and certainly no ox could harvest corn. Chico sounded pretty scornful of machinery in general, and his scorn perhaps helped him to be contented in Santa Cruz Etla.

A good thing he was. I saw in San Pablo at the *mayordomía* for the Virgin of Carmen the discontent that work as a *bracero* had created for Don Enrique Mejía, Enrique *el Alto*, the tall one, as they called him, who spent his money on ease and luxury in Oaxaca before he went back to San Pablo. Don Bernabé brought him over and introduced him to me, as we were both special guests. He had on flannel slacks, high leather shoes, a red and black lumberjack shirt, a leather belt, and a black felt "store" hat.

Immediately he asked me to dance. I inquired about what part of the United States he had visited, and he told me the Salinas Valley of California. When I asked, "What did you do there?" he answered that he had been taught to *limpiar las betarragas*. This puzzled me at first; the only thing it could mean was "clean the beets." But I knew well the Salinas Valley of California, and I had only to stop and think. There are many acres of sugar beets; the seeds are planted close together; the plants grow in clusters. They must be thinned out across straight rows. Many young plants are hoed out and thrown away so that the strongest may live. The *braceros* had been taught to "clean" the rows and leave the strongest shoots to grow. He said also that he had lived with other Mexicans and had eaten "fine Mexican food, very rich; the tortillas there are made by a machine, in the town of Salinas, señora." He added: "No one here believes that that is true. Will you tell them that it is possible in your country?"

Don Enrique *el Alto* had learned more than that in the United States. He had learned to dance as no hill Indian ever danced with a woman. He had rhythm and grace; he glided and turned. The others always shuffle forward and back, barefooted or in sloppy sandals on the rough ground. He was the finest dancer I ever danced with in Oaxaca. In the United States he would be called a "hot number." He knew all the "cheek-to-cheek" techniques.

I did not like to keep dancing with him for fear the people would be offended at his style. But they were interested and amused. He had told them he had learned English, and they thought we were gaily talking to each other in my language. However, I was merely gasping out answers to his confused mixture of Spanish and English words. The people cheered our dancing; it was quite an event.

Doña Sofía wondered if Don Pablo would have learned to dance like that. Don Enrique's dancing, his manner, his clothes, his whole attitude are foreign to Santa Cruz Etla, things which forebode too much change. Personally I hope Don Pablo did not learn to dance like that.

Doña Estéfana's whole household was certainly anxious to have Don Pablo come home. She had said sadly to me, *Somos todas gallinas aquí en la gallinera, sin gallo* (we are all hens here in this henhouse; there is no rooster). Joel, Cassiano, and Aurelio did not yet count as roosters in her estimation; Don Amado was dead and Don Ignacio, her son, was living in San Pablo.

It would almost have been worth a special trip to Santa Cruz Etla to have seen Don Pablo when he first came back in 1946. Then I would have asked him the questions: how did he like harvesting with machinery, irrigating from a ditch larger than the main river of Oaxaca Valley, turning on the electricity in his bunkhouse, etc. I kept thinking about those things the Mexico City authorities wanted their groups of traveling rural teachers, the cultural missionaries, to do. After his experiences in the United States wouldn't Don Pablo have wanted to do some of those things on the list?— plant fruit trees of diversified types (Don Florenzio had long since done that); introduce new crops; build small reservoirs for

243

year-round irrigation; study crop rotation; establish hatcheries. A season of picking apples or thinning beets would hardly teach the know-how of all those things. "Electric connections" is not listed, as most villages to be visited by any such missionary groups were much more remote from electric lines than was Santa Cruz Etla.

Don Pablo was still full of the idea of the electricity and had spoken to Don Martín and Don Féliz about it in 1953. There is the new *seminario,* a training school for the Jesuits, on the same level of foothills not far away, built in 1952. It has both electric lights and a telephone, so the wire between Etla and Oaxaca City has been tapped for local use. Don Martín, at Don Pablo's urging, went to the electric light commissioner's office in Oaxaca to ask about it. He did not understand their answer well enough to explain it to me, but evidently he was told that a local generator, run by gasoline, would be as cheap as bringing the line down into Santa Cruz. This answer made my scientifically-minded husband snort in disgust. "Politics in the woodpile, somewhere! They just don't want to bother with meters and bills and collections from so many little users." At any rate, Don Pablo clung to the idea of the electric line even more strongly when he returned from the United States.

But he gave up all his other ideas about farming. Evidently he stayed at home with Doña Sofía through the harvest season of 1947, then he went off to find work in Oaxaca City. He came home on Saturdays with the San Lorenzo bus and returned on foot and by train on Sunday night. He turned his money over to Doña Sofía, and she bought the tile roof and then clothes and dishes for herself, though these latter were not quite up to city fashion. Then when the bright little Leopoldo, only child of Sofía and Pablo, was through the four grades of the Santa Cruz school, she sent him, in store-bought clothes, down to the fifth and sixth grades in San Pablo.

When Leopoldo was in the sixth grade and almost ready to pass the examination for completion, Don Pablo, tired of a small-town job and anxious to work out a future for his son in the city, went to the national capital. There he found work in a factory making glazed tile for fancy, new city floors. Three months after Leopoldo finished school in 1953, Don Pablo took time off from his job and came home again. When he returned, Leopoldo went with him. Doña Estéfana was already ailing; and though evidently Don Pablo was willing and anxious to take his wife to Mexico City, she felt she could not leave her mother. In 1954 Sofía sat in the dark adobe house and waited on the childish little old invalid, while her menfolks, her "roosters," made good money in the city.

"Oh, yes, I will go to Pablo in the city, when *la mamacita* dies, Doña Elena, what else?" she said. "Naturally, I will have to go. What does one do in the city? How does one make tortillas without wood from the hills? I hear there is no houseyard there, no room for the *animalitos*. I surely wish, Doña Elena, that Pablo had never gone to your country. Then he would have been happy farming here in Santa Cruz Etla." Leopoldo, in touch with me occasionally by letter from Mexico City, writes that his mother has never yet left Santa Cruz Etla, that month after month, season after season, she has found an excuse to stay alone in the empty house on Doña Estéfana's back acre.

Probably Don Amado would have discounted Don Pablo, when he came to consider all those who got some education through the school. Don Pablo is intelligent and aggressive, and he has made his son Leopoldo a modernized white-collar worker in the city. But Santa Cruz Etla is no better off because of him.

꒰ 5 ꒱

TRYING TO LOOK through Don Amado's eyes, I had thought about the boys who had learned to read and write, as young adults, from Rosita. No one in Santa Cruz ever learned to write any better than either the happy stay-at-home Chico, or the dissatisfied wanderer Pablo. Yet neither of them is what Don Amado hoped for. Those whom I taught myself in the *campaña contra analfabetismo* are even less so.

When I looked again in 1954 to see what a little learning had accomplished for the Ramírez brothers, Elijeo and Eliseo, they

245

were not there to look for. I knew that they had one of the worst pieces of land to work in all the Etla Hills and that they really depended on the woodcutting. With that source of income becoming more and more difficult to tap and with no children to hold them on the land, all three of them, the two men and Eostolia uprooted themselves and left Santa Cruz Etla after the mother of the brothers died of old age. Strangely enough, they went to Etla town. Being near the Pan American Highway, Etla has had something of a boom after three sleepy centuries, and now it has some permanent refreshment booths in the little church plaza. Here, according to Chico, Eostolia was able to get a license to operate a concession because she could prove she was literate — thanks to those lessons I taught her at the "López School for Beginners" in the drowsy afternoons at Patrocina's. Now she and Elijeo buy ice from the one ice-cream store in Etla, spend hours shaving it into slush, and then sell the slush in cones, covered with raspberry or other juicy-colored flavoring syrup, a delicacy called *raspada*. Evidently Eliseo does not stay in the booth; he hawks the cones up and down the plaza.

They had sent thirty pesos up to Santa Cruz for the new church building, which implied that they were not doing very well. Only Eliseo had come home for the May fiesta in 1954, because over the *Cinco de Mayo* Eostolia and Elijeo could sell many *raspadas* in Etla town. I am sorry not to have looked them up in Etla, since I had felt so idealistic about teaching them to read nine years before. At least when they had to leave their *tierra*, because the land itself did not treat them well, their ability to read and write helped them get into something else. Young and forward-looking, they easily put down roots in some new place. Don Amado would have been disappointed in this and would have expected more from the *campaña*.

Don Ceferino Jiménez, who always knew how to read music, who was something of a "masher" and more than willing to dance with his "literacy" teacher when he broke his bass viol at an *angelita*, showed more promise for Santa Cruz Etla. In 1945 he had an eight-year-old boy in the first grade and a ten-year-old boy in the second, who came to school so seldom I hardly identified them. Father and

The Eleanora who
promised to bring
many sons into the
world, with all her
children in 1954

Chico, 1945

Esperanza, 1945

Esperanza and her
little son Ramón,
1954

Nico in 1945

Esperanza drawing water from
the brook in 1945

Nico shaping the wooden plow
with the adze

Nico's little
daughter Eloisa
in 1954

both sons followed "intellectual" careers, however. They succeeded also in accomplishing something else Don Amado wanted, recognition for Santa Cruz Etla at the expense of San Pablo.

Whenever music was to be hired for fiestas, it never used to be the Santa Cruz band, which had so few good musicians. Don Martín had hired the San Pablo musicians for the first *angelito* we ever attended; the orchestra from San Luis Ocotitlán always came for the May fiesta, I had been told. I was pleased, therefore, to find five musicians with modern instruments, a good set of drums, and real music stands, summoned quickly by Don Féliz and ready to play for us on the school steps that day in 1954 when we had the oxen pull us out of the mud. This was Don Ceferino's own family orchestra. Giving up the bass viol, he himself always played the fiddle and acted as "conductor." One son played the slide trombone, another the clarinet, instruments he had purchased for them and probably had taught them to play. With a nephew at the drums and another at the cornet, Don Ceferino had a well-trained little group with a big repertoire. Gone were Don Ceferino's sly sallies at things feminine; his hair thinned, his face lined, he looked twenty years older, now that his sons were grown. (But of course, so did his "literacy" teacher.)

Santa Cruz Etla was proud of the Jiménez orchestra, though. Chico, with no ill will since he no longer plays the violin outside the family circle, bragged about them. "They were hired for three hundred pesos to play for the San Pablo fiesta in honor of Saint Paul, Doña Elena, isn't that *magnífico?* There never was a band in San Pablo which knew as many pieces as they." Don Ceferino had given a hundred pesos of this money to the Santa Cruz Etla fiesta fund, though he and his sons, then seventeen and nineteen, had each already paid the church-building fee of a hundred pesos.

"I have always been obligated to you that you taught me the letters, so many years ago, Doña Elena," said this new Don Ceferino, very formally. (It wasn't so many years ago, though, Don Ceferino, not as the years go for Santa Cruz Etla, nor for you or for me, either.)

When he came again with his troupe to play all day the Sunday we left, and Don Ceferino told me he would take no money from the town funds because his gratitude to me was still so great, I took courage to ask him: "How have you used the reading and writing, Don Ceferino? Often and with ease?"

"Oh, not with ease, Doña Elena, I have nothing to read and nothing to write, though I like to see the names of new pieces, and to go into music stores in Oaxaca boldly to write down the names of pieces we would like ordered. But the writing still comes hard, and letters of the alphabet are not so easy to read as the notes of music."

So Don Ceferino, with enough push and persistence to have learned to read and write in his mid-forties, had enough push also to create a band for Santa Cruz Etla better than those of the surrounding towns, and to keep his sons tied to him with a bond of mutual interest and welfare. There seems to be no other connection between the campaign against illiteracy and Don Ceferino's success. Don Amado might have been pleased with the success, anyway.

✵ 6 ✵

PERHAPS IT WAS to be the younger people, those who had been in school in 1934, who were to bring the honor and the improvements to Santa Cruz Etla. Perhaps those who got their education while they were of school age would fulfill Don Amado's hopes.

Speaking of his dream for a Benito Juárez of Santa Cruz Etla, he had said on one of those long evenings at Doña Estéfana's: "The council should pick a boy and send him to school in Oaxaca with corn money from *la parcela*. We must give at least one of our young people the best education, in the years below twenty. The years between ten and twenty are the long ten years. These ten years begin a man's real life; after that, ten years, any ten years, are wasted and nothing."

It had been Rosita's idea, at the time of my first visit to the school, that some boy from Santa Cruz Etla would be chosen on the Oaxaca State scholarship program and sent to the teacher-training school, as young El Maestro had been trained, so that he could be returned to teach in his own community—the scientific agricultural teaching of the cultural missions program. Whenever Rosita spoke about this idea, it was Doña Pastorcita's Nico she had in mind.

Every time I mentioned him in my 1934 diary, I said: "Nicolás López, the brightest boy in school." He was in the fourth grade then. Our movies show him sprinkling down the tile floor of the school porch, superintending the moving of chairs and tables, ringing the bell. One movie sequence shows all the boys, Joel, Aurelio, and even Crescencio, at work in the school garden. It is certainly amusing to run the movie over and see them, "frozen" forever as boys of primary-school age, and then to know them as they are now, fathers of the community. But in those movies of the garden, it is always Nico who is working. He waters the roses; he plants the beans; he digs furrows round the corn and spinach. His serious little face is always turned toward the work, never toward the camera. We have thought of Nico through the years as looking just like this.

He was a very good student also, the best boy at reading and writing and arithmetic. Often Rosita had him teach the beginning classes; he sang the folk songs and danced the folk dances to show off the school. In short, he was a model pupil and would do justice to the honor of Santa Cruz Etla in any scholarship program.

The Oaxaca teacher-training scholarship program ended up by serving only non-Spanish-speaking, primitive Indian communities. In order to go to school in Oaxaca on his own for the teacher-training program, a boy would have to have rural school classes through the sixth grade, which was possible even in San Pablo only when there were four students who wanted to go so far. Nico was needed so much at home; Rosita went to teach in Mitla; Don Amado had waited in vain for a good corn year and could not send on even his own son. I remember saying whenever I showed the movies of Nico gardening: "That is the boy who is going to be sent on scholarship to learn to be a teacher among his people"; but it was never to come true.

It was evident in 1945 that Nico did not mind then, if he ever did. He had exactly the same boyish facial expression as at thirteen, and had grown only a little taller. His talk still had a boyish lisp. None of the boys looks his age, anyway; a Santa Cruz Etla man is often in his mid-twenties before there is any hair on his face.

Beard or no beard, Nico learned early to assume responsibility. During my summer at Doña Patrocina's, in 1945, he worked harder at the farm work than did any of his neighbors. However, Don Amado had had no interest in, nor patience with, farm work. Would he think that one of the most successful farmers in Santa Cruz, the best farmer of all the younger people who had gone to school, was doing enough for, and in, Santa Cruz Etla to balance missing his chance at being a Benito Juárez?

Nico got up at dawn and led the animals one by one across the trail to the brook for a drink. The cultural missions list includes "constructing buildings for animal shelters." Rosita did not teach Nico anything about sheds for the bigger animals, though she kept the school's rabbits in hutches. In 1945 there were no rabbits in Santa Cruz Etla, and Nico still kept his animals tethered in the yard. But the climate is mild there, and the animals were surely well cared for. When Nico tied them up again after the morning drink, he would hurry with a large burro pannier to the little patch of an alfalfa field beyond the mango trees. He would cut enough of the green alfalfa to fill the basket, making quick short strokes with the sickle. One full pannier fed the two oxen, a second the two gray burros, a third the brown burro and the pig.

Already Esperanza would be coming back from Don Julio's mill with the corn; Doña Patrocina would have the fires started under the beans and the tortilla griddle; and La Abuelita would be out feeding the chickens and turkeys with handfuls of black corn. Chico was also up early to get the burros harnessed with the packs and ready to start for hills or market, and the two young men would have the first hot tortillas.

Then Nico would bring up the old black and white ox and get out the yoke. The yoke was four feet wide, carved out of one big timber, with spoon-shaped places for the backs of the oxen's necks. Nico would lay the yoke over the black and white ox's neck right behind his horns. When it was thoroughly tied with rawhides, he placed a little basket made of woven hemp over the poor ox's mouth, so that he could not eat or drink all day.

The black and white ox was always very docile throughout all this. He would stand alone, pulled uncomfortably sideways while the empty half of the yoke dragged the ground. The brown ox was not so mild. Nico twisted the hemp rope around his nose when he led him up to the yoke. As soon as the brown ox was standing beside the black and white, he would quiet down; but Nico often had trouble with him. One day he got away during the harnessing process and ran across into the schoolyard. I was afraid for the roses growing next door at Doña Paula's, and since I was the only one unoccupied, I helped give chase. I am sure this ox did not like me, anyway; he always glowered at me when I went by him to pick mangoes. This time, just seeing me chase him made him all the more anxious for freedom, and he set off down the ravine and across to the San Lorenzo ridge. Nico, much faster at running through cornfields than I, was far behind him. The ox got all the way to the house of Don Melitón Arroyo before we caught him. The oxen of the Etla Hills are seldom that wild, though; remember the time I sat under the nose of a strange one all through a social afternoon in San Pablo.

Nico was not usually delayed so much in going to the fields. He would attach the long wooden tongue of the plow to the center of the yoke with more rawhide and go over the brow of the hill to plow. It must have been nearly eight then, on most mornings. Nico himself could always tell time by the sun. When my watch ran down and I had no time, I set the watch on Nico's advice. I did this on the morning the Oaxaca Department of Public Health came to vaccinate everyone, and I found my watch only one minute wrong when compared with the doctor's.

Nico knew when to quit for the midday meal; he and the oxen all knew without looking at the sun. In the harvest season, he told me, he came home and ate hurriedly and returned at once to work in the fields till dark. In the plowing and planting and weeding time, most of the men worked from seven-thirty or eight until about two-thirty. Nico would then unhitch the oxen, lead them one by one to water, and finally come in to his own dinner. After dinner, every day that I stayed around in the afternoon, he was busy with his "yard work"—making a new wooden plow, shelling corn to help the little grandmother with her turkeys, making new padding for the donkey packsaddle. He did not stop work till almost dusk, when it was time to cut three more baskets of alfalfa and to lead the oxen and the burros (if they were home yet) down for another drink.

There is no real twilight in Santa Cruz Etla. It is too far south of the Tropic of Cancer. The sun goes down, and bang! it is dark. In the brief light before *cena*, Nico and the León boys would play like schoolboys. One evening I lay napping under the mango tree on the edge of the green alfalfa field. Suddenly I looked up and there were the three friends, all "mature young men on the police force," standing on their hands not six feet from me. They were as surprised to see me as I them, and we joked about it many times afterwards.

The main problem of the farm is to decide when to do what. Nico must think of when to plant, and how much seed it will take per acre. This seed he must have saved out from the crop of the year before. The chickens and turkeys must be fed corn the year round, also. All this corn must be set aside from that apportioned out for tortillas for the family. Many families have to buy corn in a bad corn year, but never Doña Patrocina's, if Nico can help it.

It was he who decided to take in the grandmother's turkeys when she came to Doña Patrocina's house to live. "They eat a great deal of corn, Doña Elena, but they make such a good *gasto* for the fiestas and *mayordomías*," he said. I had to have someone justify the presence of these vicious, loud-voiced turkeys who made so much noise and took such a violent dislike to me. If they helped Nico, I would accept them.

The alfalfa to feed the other animals had to be replanted every third year. Nico had done it three times since he had been in charge of the farming. It gets green in May, as soon as there is a little rain, and stays green, growing up over and over after it is cut, until the last of January. This is a fine thing, for there is usually no rain at

252

all from December to May. When the alfalfa is no longer green, the oxen must eat corn fodder. "February and March is a sad time, *un tiempo triste para los animalitos,*" said Nico.

Corn is planted usually the last of May. Nico puts beans in between the rows of corn in the plot nearest the house, and squashes and chiles in the plot second nearest. Doña Estéfana planted *garbanzos* in two acres of her land in 1944; we had chickpeas cooked in meat juice several times at Doña Patrocina's for dinner, so perhaps Nico had planted them the year before, also. Don Féliz León has often planted wheat, *trigo,* on his steep hillside quarter-hectare; he sold the wheat in 1944 for fifty pesos, a very good return on a quarter-hectare in those days.

There was so little rain in 1945 that many families were still planting in the last of June. Nico had plowed and Chico had stayed home with him to help with the planting just a week before I came the last of June. Halfway through the summer, Nico was finishing the first plowing to clear weeds, done six weeks after planting. But over on the eroded San Lorenzo ridge, which I could see from the portico at Doña Patrocina's, men were plowing and women were planting after them, silhouetted against the sky, as late as the middle of July. What a contrast in 1954, that good corn year! By the time I came in the middle of July that year, everyone's corn was already lush and green.

Twelve weeks after planting, Nico began to plow again. The corn would be harvested in October, toward the end of the rainy season. "A fine time of year, a great harvest festival," said Doña Patrocina. "Then the rains have lessened. All rain ends by *La Navidad,* the Christmas time. The trees stay green but the grass turns brown. Everything is dust. It is the time of the very warm days but the very cold nights."

I have never been in Santa Cruz Etla except when it is green and beautiful and flowers are everywhere. I would miss the banks of beautiful, white cumulus clouds which roam the sky all day in the rainy season. I am told that the sky is clear, hot, blue, all through the dry months. I know I don't want to be in Santa Cruz Etla when it is any colder. I was never really warm there at night.

Although Nico works as hard as possible, rainy season and dry, he makes just enough for the family to eat—his family, Chico's, Doña Patrocina, and Don Fausto—for Chico still brings in the cash money and Nico does the food-producing for all. In the 1940's a good corn year produced enough to bring seventy or eighty pesos a hectare when sold for cash, fifteen or sixteen dollars in United States money. In the 1950's, with the higher prices all over Mexico, and the devaluation of the peso, Nico's corn lands brought two hundred pesos' worth of corn a hectare, he figured (though this had about the same dollar value). Of course, since he didn't sell it, it had the same value as always for him—food for the family, fodder for the cattle, seed for the next year. In the 1940's I gave Doña Patrocina a peso (then twenty cents) a day to buy tidbits for me and the rest of the family while I was there, so the hectares of land did not have to support the summer visitor. I sat down to eat with the combined families twice during my 1954 visit, and neither time did they have anything like the fancy fare they had when I provided the peso's worth of dainties.

I see in my 1945 notes that I had worried about the expansion of the family in the future. "Esperanza and Chico will have children," I wrote, "Nico will marry; in five years there will perhaps be many more mouths to feed. Even then there will be no more land, and neither Nico or Chico can leave to work elsewhere as they are both so busy with the work at home." Crops were better in 1954, prices were higher, but there were four more mouths to feed. Both young couples and the three little children had more store-bought clothes, and Nico had a factory-made jacket he bought for the May fiesta. He showed it to me with pride, saying, "Now, Doña Elenita, I never need wear a *sarape* again, this is so much lighter all over and keeps my arms warm too." So there were signs of prosperity in 1954, but no change in the kind of food or the amount each had to eat.

No change in the equipment of house or farm, either. Nico made in 1945, and still does make, all the wooden things which the family uses. The boys had some metal tools, a pair of pliers, a sack-sewing needle, an adze, a chisel, an axe, and a machete, that long, all-purpose farm knife used by so many Indian peoples in the semi-tropics.

Nico and Chico had no hammer; they used a homemade wooden mallet for pounding.

With this limited equipment they fashioned all the wooden things they used; ox yokes, plows, hooks for saddle cinches, roof beams to replace the sagging ones, and even the chair and table. There was always a large stack of firewood in front of the house, ready to be sent to market. For a small thing like the saddle cinch hook or a new mallet, Nico would merely take a likely looking block of wood from the pile and hack away on it with the machete. I marveled at how smooth and finished everything looked.

In the middle of the six-weeks' plowing that year, the old plow wore out. A wooden plow seldom lasts a season. Chico inspected the old plow, and the next night he brought back only two burro-loads of charcoal from the hills. Dragging behind the third burro was tied a section of young tree trunk about a foot in diameter, material to make a new plow. Next day Nico plowed with the old one till noon and then spent the afternoon hacking the bark off the log with his adze. I guess that last day was just too much for the old plow, because it was never even brought home, and Nico stayed in the houseyard working on the new one all day each day until he had finished it.

When the log was free of bark, he cut it square on each side with the axe, like the railroad ties which Santa Cruz Etla men sell at Hacienda Blanca station. It took him all the rest of the day to get one end of it narrowed to a point; to do that he used the adze with accurate, quick strokes. Chico went to town with firewood on the second day and returned with a new metal plate and four screws for the point. To figure the exact place where the wood should be grooved for the metal and holes dug for the screws, Nico measured with a little splinter cut from the rough adze handle. "The iron point costs two pesos fifty; we have not had to buy one for three years," he said.

Now the point, the share of the plow was made, while Nico worked all day in the houseyard. He had to make the slot in which to fit the long tongue leading up to the yoke, the tongue which ran between the oxen. There was another slot to be made above the top of the metal plate, in which a wooden handle must be fitted. Both these slots were carefully cut out with the chisel. He did not even measure these slots, nor make any mark with a pencil, but the tongue and handle from the previous plow fitted them exactly.

Nico needed to nail these parts into the slots, but he had no nails. So he just took his machete and carved out four wooden pins. His wooden mallet broke in two when he started pounding on the pins. In half an hour he had made a new mallet from another stick of firewood, perfectly shaped, with no loss of temper on the shaper's part, as far as I could see, inasmuch as Nico himself kept on singing one of the songs Chico plays on the fiddle, while the mallet broke and he made another. With all the enthusiasm in the United States today for "make-it-yourself" kits and projects, the "make-it-your-selfer" has a great deal to learn from Nico in improvising tools, in fitting things with accuracy without any measuring implements, and in maintaining serenity through every process.

He worked a whole day making the slots and putting the parts of the plow together. The next morning he took two hours more smoothing all the rough places with the adze. It was then too late to hitch up the oxen and plow, so he chose a large stick of wood and started to make something else. "What is it this time?" I asked.

"I will need a new little plow, an *aradito,* for the second plowing, when the corn is high and the rows are too narrow for this one. I will work on it now, for I do not like to see the tools lying idle around the houseyard, Doña Elenita." (Only Nico and Doña Patrocina call me Elenita, "little Helen," and they both so tiny. I stand six inches taller and weigh at least thirty pounds more than any one in Patrocina's family and my hair is much whiter than La Abuelita's was when she died.)

None of this fine farming, this careful use of the old tools in the old ways, this following of the seasons with the same crops grown by the ancient Mixtecs—none of this that Nico does is what Don Amado had in mind when he hoped for such heroic developments to come from the establishment of the school. Don Amado was never in his lifetime as good a farmer as Nico was at eighteen; he would be disgusted that I took all this time to describe Nico's farm-

256

ing in the middle of a section about the students who might parallel Benito Juárez. But the cultural missionaries, the rural school program-planners in Mexico, intended to do more with agricultural teaching than with any other field. "Modern methods of planting" should be taught, and "plowing done so as to control erosion," and "the best corn saved during harvest to be used as seed," and "both plants and animals are to be improved by careful breeding." Nico may still be using the methods his father used, the methods scorned by both Don Amado and Don Pablo, but his acreage and his crop bear witness to his efficiency.

I notice what I wrote in 1945: "Nico will make a girl a fine husband. He is so good natured and jolly, works so hard, and has so much sense. Twenty-four is young to marry, but I teased Nico about it." Teasing was fun in that happy family.

"Esperanza and Chico are so happy," I remember saying to him one evening, as I watched him cut alfalfa. "Surely you must want a wife also."

To my surprise, he answered in a very natural tone of voice, "I have picked one out already. When you come to live with us again I will be married."

"Who is she, Nico?"

"I will never tell you, Doña Elenita. You would tell Esperanza and my mother, for women can never keep secrets; they will tell others, who will tell the girl, and all will be spoiled. Even now I do not know if she would want me."

"Will you bring her back here to live?"

"Where else?"

"But suppose Esperanza doesn't like her?" said I, a great enthusiast for Esperanza.

Debe (she'll have to).

"And if she doesn't like Esperanza?"

Debe también (she'll have to, also).

It seems to have worked out as simply as that. Doña Patrocina and two daughters-in-law live happily around the same houseyard, in three separate "apartments," but often sharing meals, and with the same limited amount of household equipment. Nico's wife

257

Manuela is certainly not as gay and pretty as Esperanza, and looks much older, though she is three years younger. She has the mark of the pure Indian in her face and is a niece of Don Marciano's raw-boned, Indian-looking wife. But she and Nico are as devoted to each other as Esperanza and Chico. And in 1954 their lovely little girl, Eloisa, showed promise of being the model child in Don Alfredo's school.

⇜ 7 ⇝

Turning from Nico who was Rosita's best student in 1934, the discouraged Don Amado might look next to the boy who was then her worst student. Crescencio typified to me in 1945 all the young woodcutters, as Nico typified all the young farmers, and Don Amado certainly did not want the products of the fine school to stay wood-cutters all their lives.

For Crescencio had learned to be efficient and conscientious, though not yet tidy or literate, by the mid-1940's. When we drove up in front of the school in the rural director's station wagon in 1944, I saw a tall, eighteen-year-old boy watering oxen at the brook in the schoolyard. He had a thatch of uncombed hair. His clothes were tattered; he did not have even the sandals on his feet that most men wear. I knew immediately that it was Crescencio. Strangely enough, he recognized both my husband and me; and when he saw Rosita in the front seat, his face lit up and he came up to shake hands. The whole time I was there in 1944 he had to be very much in evidence, because Don Esteban, his brother, was president. At the festivals for the rural director he stood right behind the town council with Máximo, the next older brother. He was clean, but still uncombed, on these occasions. And he certainly had nothing to say.

During the summer of 1945 he was more friendly, and often in the evening he came over to Doña Patrocina's, just acros the alfalfa field, to see what I had painted during the day. He asked after my husband and wanted to know about Rosita's kindergarten. I tried to

258

persuade him to come to the classes for illiterates, but on the mention of such a project he would shut up like a clam. Some evenings he came, said a quick *buenas noches,* and as quickly melted away into the shadows. At least, he was no longer a comedian.

As a woodcutter he did the "production end" of the charcoal-burning business, and let Chico do all the selling. It was a sort of partnership. Crescencio would rather cut wood and watch the charcoal burning all day long alone in the woods than ever go to market where he would have to talk to people. In fact, I don't think he had been to Oaxaca City before he was twenty.

I remember one evening when Crescencio was stitting with us on the "kitchen floor" after *cena,* I was telling again of my rides to the sierra. I asked questions about the whole woodcutting business through which so many Santa Cruz families had always made their cash money. I cannot remember just the conversation and who said what, but I know the boys were surprised at my stupid and detailed questions.

"Isn't there a charcoal-burning business in your country?" Chico, usually the best informed about things foreign, asked. "Then how is it possible to cook? Does everyone cook with plain pine wood?"

In 1945 city folks in Oaxaca, even the wealthiest families, were still cooking over small metal braziers or on tile stoves, using charcoal as the only fuel. Housewives bought it in the market, or at corner stores, or from boys at the door, at three pesos for two kilograms in those days. All this *carbón* was brought down from the surrounding mountains on burro-back by hill-dwelling Indians.

Crescencio went to the sierra, up my lovely trail, six days a week. He left as soon as he had watered the stock in the dawn, for it took him two hours to get to the "cutting grounds." On Monday and Tuesday he cut down trees. On Wednesday he cut the trees into stovewood lengths with his ax and machete. On Thursday he piled his wood into stacks shaped like tepees, with leaves, branches, and bark on the outside. The fresh wood inside was allowed to burn slowly, away from the air, until it became charcoal. Crescencio would come home overnight and leave it burning. I never heard of any forest fire in the sierra, though from the schoolyard we could see little smoke-pillars rising high on the mountainside from each separate stack of smoldering wood.

When Crescencio went back on Friday, the fires would have burned out. He took his three burros with him then, their backs carefully covered with packsaddles which Chico had made out of old *petates*. The charcoal was loaded into hemp nets and tied securely to the burros' backs, three netfuls of charcoal on each burro. Each netful, nearly two kilograms, sold for three pesos. With three burros, each loaded with three nets, Crescencio could make twenty-seven pesos a week, of which Chico got nine when he took it to Oaxaca as the middleman. This meant three or four dollars a week for Crescencio by the 1945 exchange rate.

Chico never burned charcoal, but on the days when he was in the sierra, he cut wood in special lengths for the pottery kilns in Santa María Asumpa. He could cut enough in two days to load the León boys' oxcart on a third day for the trip to the kilns. Such a load got twelve pesos in Santa María Asumpa in those days. Sometimes Chico took burro-loads of firewood into Oaxaca at a peso a load, but more often he sold Crescencio's charcoal, letting the León boys across the ditch sell his cut wood. They in turn spent what time they were in the sierra cutting railroad ties and roof beams, which were dragged behind burros one by one to the station at Hacienda Blanca. When many ties and beams were ready for transporting, all nine or ten burros from all three families were driven to the sierra at once, perhaps every two or three weeks.

I was interested in this division of labor. Why did Crescencio make all the charcoal, the León boys cut the ties, Chico the kiln wood, yet no one actually took his own product to market? "One does that part of the work to which his family has always been accustomed," Chico told me.

In all this description of Crescencio and the woodcutting processes, it is necessary to use the past tense. Both Crescencio and the woodcutting business have changed. Where the boys used to ride or walk with the burros two hours to get up to the woodcutting sierra, gradually, since the days of the *guerrita* with San Felipe de Agua, the trip has been lengthened till now more than three hours each way are necessary; to that extent they have cut out the wood and "eaten of their own substance," so to speak. Now it is no longer possible to go through the whole charcoal-burning process in the Monday to Friday week in time to meet each Saturday market. True, the prices are higher, but so are the prices of the things they have to buy. True, they can meet the schedule of a two-week cycle, and have four loads ready every second Saturday instead of three loads every Saturday, but that means more burros for hauling and less total profit. About half the number of young men are still cutting wood for charcoal as before; not one is making the entire living for his family by it. Besides, the hotels and many newly built, modern-style houses in Oaxaca are using electricity or butane for cooking. Of the four boys in the "wood and charcoal" cooperative effort centering around Chico in 1945, only the León boys still work at it regularly. Chico and Nico together farm both their own land and La Abuelita's old acreage, as well as half of Don Fausto's. Chico often takes wood to market for the León boys; but, as he told me in 1954, "I have not been up the sierra myself for more than five years, Doña Elena."

So what of Crescencio? This seems unbelievable as I write it, but Crescencio is in the Mexican army. Máximo, the only one of Doña Paula's sons still at home, worked with the public works committee in getting our car out of the mud when we came unannounced in 1954, and immediately I asked him about Esteban and Crescencio. All Máximo knew was that Crescencio had enlisted. Don Féliz said later that pressure was brought to bear on the Santa Cruz municipality to send someone to the army, as no one from Santa Cruz had ever gone, not even during the activity of World War II. Single, discouraged about the charcoal business, not essential in the farming of Doña Paula's acres, and just one more mouth for Elodia to feed, Crescencio had gone off to Oaxaca and joined up. Probably it was only the third or fourth time he had ever been in to the city. Máximo did not know where he was with the army, or how long he would have to stay. Since everyone left at Doña Paula's is illiterate, and of course so is Crescencio (will the army teach him to read, I wonder), his family had had no word.

When I saw Cassiano in Mexico City in September, 1954, he told me that at Doña Paula's request he had very recently got in touch with Crescencio through the army, and that a literate fellow-soldier had written for him to Cassiano and through him to all the Santa Cruz people. The short message said that Crescencio was in a corporal's guard riding the freight trains from Tepic to Mazatlán and then on to the north up the Pacific Coast. What a strange life for Crescencio, down out of his sierra and away from his burros! The train runs along the palm-lined seacoast right across the Tropic of Cancer. Every Mexican train carries a token guard of soldiers, a reminder of the days when train travel was endangered by bandits forty years ago. The guards loaf along the train, sit on top of the freight, chat with the second-class passengers when there is a passenger car at the end of the train just before the caboose. If Crescencio has his furloughs in Mazatlán, a nice tropical town as different from Santa Cruz as towns on the French Riviera are from villages in the Alps, he at least has had a chance to swim in the ocean and to watch the sunset out over the Pacific. No one else in Santa Cruz Etla has ever seen either the Atlantic or the Pacific, except perhaps Don Pablo in Seattle. I wonder if Crescencio will go back to Santa Cruz when his enlistment is over, a spruce, tidy, well-lettered young man, talkative about his adventures, a good catch for even a San Pablo girl. If so, then how will he live, what work will he do? Would Don Amado be pleased at what Crescencio learned in the army?

What of the others who had been school children in 1934? There were the boys in Doña Estéfana's family, Aurelio and Joel. Both of them are today good farmers, and either would probably provide just as good a description of farming methods as did Nico. They both had so much more land than Nico to work with, Doña Estéfana's broad acres which are in a good location and have eroded so little. Aurelio and his father Ignacio farm about ten acres of the old lady's best land; Joel works the five acres that belong to Sofía and a small plot that Don Pablo had owned, and helps his father-in-law as well.

In 1944 and 1945 Joel had been a particular friend of mine, and

The sons of Don Amado
Martiniano, Cassiano, Margarito, 1944

Leopoldo, an unidentified
first grader, and Martiniano
in Doña Ester's class in 1945

Margarito, Martiniano, and Cassiano
in Mexico City, 1954

Leopoldo in Mexico
City, 1954

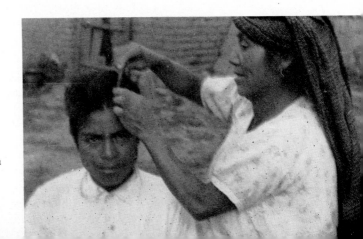

Cassiano, while Doña
Patrocina fixed up
his hair before
posing for my
snapshots in 1945

The citified public
health doctor
vaccinating children
on the school steps
in 1945

Don Ceferino with
his family orchestra
in 1954. The two
young men to his
left are his sons.

Margarita and
the author, 1954

I had preferred him above Aurelio, whom his grandmother so favored. Aurelio had always seemed serious and stuffy; Joel was a jolly pet of ours in the 1934 school. As a young man he spent many hours talking to me of those "days of Rosita," of the fun he had in school. I wrote of Joel in 1944: "He is so fond of his mother and grandmother, and plans to bring a wife there to live. He scorns any girls he knows now, but then, of course, as he himself says, he has not seen just the right girl. All the girls his own age who went to school when he did are married now to older fellows."

Thus, like all serious young Santa Cruz Etla men, Joel bided his time, waiting for someone younger to grow up, someone who had been toddling round the houseyard when he was already through school. If Joel was ten in 1934, he is long past thirty today. He was married at about twenty-six to the smart Teresa of Don Marcelino. She was about twelve in 1945, therefore sixteen or seventeen when she married Joel. By 1954 they had two little boys, and Joel had built a new house for them at the farthest end of Doña Estéfana's acres, under a mango tree at the head of *la zanja*. He was not at home himself when I came to call and get a photo of his babies; after three years' service on the public works committee, he was already *alcalde* of public works and was busy with the ditch in that year of heavy rain. There was also the problem of the road repair so that we could get our car up again for Don Féliz' fiesta. When the road was repaired and the fiesta in honor of our last departure was held, Joel was busy playing handball, *pelota*, too busy to have his picture taken with the committee, just as much a boy as ever about the ball game. I think Don Amado would have been pleased with Joel, though. He is literate; he helped teach in the campaign against illiteracy. He is a good farmer, has built a new home in the community, has used his education to work in the service of the town, and still is the same happy extrovert he always was.

Both Aurelio and Joel were Don Amado's cousins; both stayed in Santa Cruz Etla when his own sons did not, though their material inheritance was so much better that they had every incentive to stay. Aurelio, the serious and stuffy, born dignified and grown up, has lived most of his life in the shadow of Doña Estéfana's personality. His pleasant wife, a San Pablo girl like his mother, was sick for a year after the birth of their only child; and Don Ignacio's wife from San Pablo, who had so antagonized the old lady, came to care for her daughter-in-law. All three generations were living with Doña Estéfana in 1951. In 1954 only Aurelio's little family occupied Doña Estéfana's historic old house, while she herself lay slowly dying in Sofía's hut at the back of the houseyard. Don Ignacio, who lived again in San Pablo and spent Sundays with his mother, said her great delight was in Aurelio's little son (I was asked to take a picture of him wearing his baptismal dress); she remembered to ask for the little boy every day and spent a half-hour lulling him to sleep on her cot. With Leopoldo gone to the city, this child is the principal heir to her house. Aurelio will prosper because Doña Estéfana's land will remain the best in Santa Cruz, uneroded among the trees, producing enough corn for three generations of her descendants. Don Amado would have felt, however, that there was no progress for the town in the picture of Aurelio's placid life.

Who else of the children in the "days of Rosita"? Adolfo Soto is working in Oaxaca City. Ordón, the stodgy but beloved only son of Doña Enriqueta, works his father's farm and supports his mother, while his father rests, and now Ordón has his own young wife. The León boys, Francisco still shy and retiring and Felicito newly married, work with the railroad ties and will inherit their father's five acres between them. Carmita, unkind daughter of the deaf old Doña Carmen, now lives on that nice acreage left by her mother and has her husband's land as well. Augustina is in the high hills, as lost to Santa Cruz Etla as any young man who went to work on the highway or enlisted in the army. Refugio, a sallow, thin, be-goitered child in 1934, has founded a new family for Don Julio. Perhaps Don Julio's Juanita, that pretty little dancer in 1934, would please Don Amado, with her own pretty little daughter and her well-kept, plastered San Pablo house; but of course, living in San Pablo, she contributes nothing to Santa Cruz Etla.

Since the girls are more apt to stay in Santa Cruz Etla than the boys, many of them contribute more to the life of the town. A fresh-faced matron whom I approached in 1954, that fiesta Sunday, asked if I remembered her, a little girl named Eleanora at school in 1934 from San Lorenzo, who had her picture taken with the dolls. But it seems she had told me, though I had forgotten I had even asked then what the little girls would be doing in the future, that she was going "to bring many sons into the world." I pretended to remember all about this conversation, and wondered why she giggled shyly as she repeated it and asked me to photograph her entire family. Promising to meet them for the photo as soon as she had assembled "all her children," I turned to talk to the other old friends. When she came back and stood her family in a row at the rear of the school building, she had lined up eight *daughters,* the oldest perhaps fifteen, the youngest three. All smiling with their mother, a cheery, happy group, they made me think that the retiring Doña Eleanora, whose very existence I had forgotten, had perhaps contributed most of all to the happy continuance of Santa Cruz Etla. At home again in Los Angeles, I found the unmistakable face of this Eleanora in the photo of the girls who dressed the dolls, and I saw that twenty years and eight children have aged her very little.

When contributions are to be counted, I must think first, though, of my dear friend Chabella, wife of Miguelito, the only son of Don Martín. Chabella was the best girl student in 1934. She was also the neatest seamstress and was allowed to do the embroidery on the dolls from the Isthmus of Tehuantepec. Like Nico, she appears as a model child in the entire sequence of the movie I took in 1934. Did she marry Miguelito for love, Miguelito so meek, so thin, so retiring, so negative a personality in his father's house? He had had two years of school with Rosita before we came, and he had helped his father with the *animalitos* and the planting. When he was twenty-five and Chabella fifteen, the two families, the prosperous widow Doña Rosario, still at fifty as pretty as Chabella, and Don Martín and Doña Pastorcita on their side, had arranged the marriage. If Chabella was dissatisfied, she never showed it. A source of joy and comfort to her in-laws, she was for years the serene mistress of their household, doing half the work of the bakery, keeping the accounts for the store, and supervising the household, always smiling or singing to herself, grown fat through the years but very pretty still. And like the queen bee in the hive, she produced the young, the beloved grandchildren of Don Martín, eight live births of which she lost only two. Her oldest, Margarita, was fifteen in 1954, and she was my friend and companion during my visit that year. Artemio was thirteen in 1954 in the fifth grade of the school in San Pablo Etla. Adela was in the fourth grade at Santa Cruz, Don Alfredo's shining light as Chabella had been Rosita's in 1934. She was named for her Aunt Adelita who was a good student in the fourth grade with Doña Ofelia in 1945, and who died shortly after Doña Ofelia left. Then there was a beautiful chubby boy named Jesús, the only child so named that I ever knew of in Santa Cruz Etla. He had seemed the sturdiest of the brood in 1945, but he and another little sister died of *sarampión*, the measles, in 1947, when so many children had died on the San Sebastián ridge. Don Martín had a photograph that I had taken of him as a baby enlarged and highly tinted and hung up in a gilt frame above his "store counter." The little girl who died was replaced by another, Lupita, the next year. Then came Graciela, and finally, in 1954, there was a six-months-old Guillermo, fat and cooing at Chabella's breast, to replace Jesús.

Kept clean and tidy in store-bought clothes, living in a house with a tile floor and whitewashed walls so that it was easier to stay clean, these intelligent and happy children of the intelligent and happy Chabella, grandchildren of the intelligent and happy Don Martín, seemed Santa Cruz Etla's best hope. Artemio, the third boy in Santa Cruz who went on to San Pablo for the fifth and sixth grades, owned store-bought shoes and wore them most of the time— shoes in a nation in which "those who wear shoes" are sharply divided from *ellos sin zapatas* (those without shoes). I understand Don Martín had to fight to get Artemio willing to stay in this "upper class" of society, but as of 1954 he was winning out. And as for Margarita, only Don Martín's death prevented her from going on to the highest education Santa Cruz had ever known. When Chabella's husband became the master of the family and moved it to the city, on Don Martín's death, Chabella herself had to leave Santa Cruz, and with her most of the children. If they today are receiving greater opportunities in Oaxaca City than Santa Cruz Etla could give them and are going on to make names for themselves there, they would still be a disappointment to Don Amado because they did not stay in Santa Cruz.

OF ALL THE BOYS IN SANTA CRUZ, Don Marcelino's Perfecto is the only one still living there who ever went to school in San Pablo Etla for the fifth and sixth grades. This gave him the status of an intellectual. Though not a student of Doña Ofelia, having finished the fourth grade even before Don Solomón's time, he was the only person in Santa Cruz of whom Doña Ofelia really approved, the only bookish intellectual she found there. Moreover, he could draw, when he could get pencil and paper, and could make pictures of almost anything. "This importance has not spoiled him," I wrote in 1945. "He works quietly with his father and helps with the plowing. His father tells me he is *muy delicado,* very delicate, and they are just waiting for a good corn year to send Perfecto into teacher-training school in Oaxaca." This was exactly the kind of thing Don Amado had hoped would happen. Meanwhile, Perfecto stayed in Santa Cruz, went to school in San Pablo for the advanced work when it was later offered there, helped teach the classes for illiterates, and often wrote the town records for Don Bartolo and subsequent presidents. He it was who decorated the walls of the municipal building with geometric designs, as a public offering apart from work done as laborers by his father and himself. Then when the idea of the church began to materialize, Perfecto made a front-view pencil drawing of what it should be, quite accurate for a person with no training in rendering; and with Panfilo's plans, it was a guide in the entire building project.

I asked Perfecto about the fifth and sixth grades in San Pablo, taught by the husband member of the fine, public-spirited *matrimonio* who ran the school there. This man would teach the advanced classes on his own time whenever there were four or more pupils from all the surrounding communities interested in going on. The students had to buy expensive books, an outlay of fifteen or twenty pesos in 1945, books on world geography, formal grammar, arithmetic through square roots and percentages, natural sciences, and Mexican history. The teacher, who taught thirty or forty San Pabloites in the third and fourth grades every day, could give these advanced scholars only a few minutes out of every hour to recite lessons. Really they taught themselves from the books. The boys would take two years to each grade level, finishing with the equivalent in subject matter of the eighth or ninth grade in the United States, or more often falling by the wayside after a year or two when the families needed them at home. Perfecto had finished both classes in a single three-year period. "Perfecto should make a good rural teacher, and will do well if he ever gets to the Oaxaca teacher-training school," I wrote in 1945. In 1951, when Don Marcelino, was municipal president, Perfecto came down in an oxcart to meet us at the highway, and then he assumed responsibility for our entertainment throughout the day's visit, rounding up people we asked to see, helping Don Martín's family serve us food, and driving us back down at dusk to our waiting car. He was very quiet for such an erudite scholar, and really I never saw in him Don Amado's idea of another Benito Juárez.

He and Don Marcelino gave up early any idea of his ever leaving Santa Cruz Etla. Don Marcelino broke his leg in 1953, and it did not set straight. Now Perfecto and his brother-in-law Joel, who married the little sister Teresa, must work Don Marcelino's land. Accepting this future philosophically, Perfecto married a girl whom he had first seen as a little first grader in San Pablo when he was ready to "graduate" from the school there. He watched her grow up and asked for her with the usual formality, education or no. Still excited about the fine wedding he had, he condoled with me in 1954 for not being able to attend. He would have liked to have waited for the church he designed to be finished, but his wife's people wanted the wedding held in San Pablo. That would not have pleased Don Amado, and the "waste" of Perfecto's education wouldn't have either, though that old idealist would have been pleased with the drawing of the church.

I had hopes in 1945 for Isaías Pérez and Gerónomo and Aurelia, those good students in Doña Ofelia's fourth grade. Isaías Pérez works as a woodcutter, one of the few boys in the younger generation who still do, and sells his own charcoal in Oaxaca. How long will he stay in the woodcutter's trade when he goes in so often to the city, sees so many phases of "the new life," and has an increasingly hard time making a living in the charcoal burner's life? I did not get to talk to Isaías long enough in 1954 to ask how he felt about this; I could only notice how clear his eyes were (a credit to Doña Patrocina's treatments) and how fast he was at basketball on Sunday.

Gerónomo remembered me very well, having come to see me as soon as he heard I was at Don Martín's. He wanted to know how often I had ridden a horse in the United States in the years since he had helped me that first morning we went to ask Don Marciano for *el caballo.* He had heard that I could drive the car myself, and he wanted to make sure, for none of the Santa Cruz Etla people, no matter how often they went to town, ever saw a woman driving in Oaxaca. Gerónomo was a leader in *Los Policías,* wore store-bought clothing and a Yankee-style dungaree jacket on Sundays, and owned a pair of shoes. With all this modernity, he seemed very immature as he talked to me about cars and horses, not half as serious as Nico or Joel or Perfecto had been at twenty-one or twenty-two. Like Don Bartolo's son, he works as a goatherd a great deal of the time, or helps his father with the hogs, and perhaps has not rubbed against life enough to be concerned about it. "A *casamiento* for me, Doña Elena? Why I am not yet a man, to plan on a household," he said, laughing, in answer to my teasing question. No hopes for Don Amado's Benito Juárez in Doña Ofelia's fourth graders.

There is still Leopoldo, however, who was a first grader with Doña Ester in 1945 when I helped her make models for the children's writing. Also a grandson of Doña Estéfana, the only child of Sofía by Don Pablo, Leopoldo always showed promise in school. I took pictures of him, eager and interested in the schoolwork, in that first-grade year. After Perfecto and before Artemio, he went

269

on to the fifth and sixth grades in San Pablo, his books and his store-bought clothes purchased with the outside money Don Pablo sent home. Leopoldo had finished the San Pablo school in 1952 when he was fifteen.

He has written me recently, incidentally, that his class was the last to do so at San Pablo Etla, that the erosion of the soil on the bare San Pablo hillsides had driven so many people to find work away from the land that there are now not enough children to keep two teachers busy in the school there. The *matrimonio*, after nineteen years in San Pablo, has gone down to found a new big school at Pueblo Nuevo in the valley, where some of the San Pablo people have taken up land. So Santa Cruz Etla won on that score, in the long run of two decades. The Santa Cruz school still has two teachers and a larger enrollment than it has ever had, and Don Alfredo told me he would give the fifth and sixth grades himself if he stayed in Santa Cruz. This is surely a victory for Santa Cruz, an eventual solving of one of those "problems" we presented to Don Luis Varela in 1944; and it would have been a source of pride to Don Amado.

Leopoldo, another of Don Amado's cousins, would also be a source of pride to him, though not in terms of Santa Cruz Etla. Don Pablo came home to get him when he had finished school and took him to Mexico City. There Rosita helped him to find a job as errand boy in the office of a big clothing store. It is surprising that Leopoldo learned his way around the city so quickly. Rosita says that the clothing-store office manager, a friend of Rosita's doctor husband, speaks very well of Leopoldo. Told on the phone that a *profesora americana* wanted to talk to Leopoldo and to arrange an afternoon off for him to meet old friends, the office manager was loath to let him go, not because he disliked granting the boy a favor, but because he was "afraid the *señora americana* was planning to take Leopoldo off to the States." "If he only had a little typing and bookkeeping training, he would move up rapidly in the commercial field," the manager told Rosita.

"Why can't Leopoldo have such training?" I demanded when Rosita told me. "Aren't there commercial high schools free here in Mexico City? Leopoldo has had the fifth and sixth grades," I added, knowing that a diploma for these last two years is necessary for any secondary school work in Mexico.

Such an idea had not occurred to Don Pablo, but it had to Leopoldo. He had inquired through others in his office and had found an *instituto,* or secondary school, in the neighborhood which gave commercial classes at night. He was unwilling to leave his good daytime job, at which, as a little "apprentice," he made a hundred twenty pesos a month. In 1954 this was about ten dollars. Don Pablo was also unwilling to have him stop working but glad to have him "keep occupied in the evenings in this big city." The *instituto* night classes are free, but there is a fee for the practice on the typewriter, and there is the cost of books and paper and beginners' bookkeeping kits. Still, five dollars from me is more than sixty pesos for Leopoldo, and fifty pesos was all that Leopoldo needed to enter the *instituto* when a new monthly registration took place September 1. As of the present writing (1958), he has needed no further five-dollar "scholarship," is making rapid progress, and should get a diploma of secondary commercial-technical education in another year. He also learned some English and has written me a few careful letters in it. I was impressed with Leopoldo when I saw him in Mexico City. He is short and slight like the Mixtecs, and he has the Indian countenance, which still works against him in Mexico City; but he is very ambitious and has the drive and will to succeed. Doña Sofía, shy product of the Etla Hills, would be lost with these two grown men, fifty-five-year-old Don Pablo and twenty-year-old Leopoldo, in their sophisticated Mexico City environment. I am glad that Leopoldo is successful, but this commercial "get-ahead-yourself" advance is not what Don Amado wanted.

9

I HAD ASKED DON AMADO, one of those evenings at Doña Estéfana's in 1944, what would happen if each family had many sons survive. Wouldn't the people outgrow the land?

"No, it is not more land we need, but more sons," he had replied. "Few of us have had more than two sons survive. A fortunate man who had many sons survive could work with them all, tilling all the land together, not dividing it three or four ways. Thus, he could get several crops in a good year, corn, and beans, and then sometimes beans again. We do not have enough workers now, Doña Elena. A people without many surviving sons is a poor people—and a poor people will always remain a poor people." What a strange prophecy for his own family!

He himself fathered three fine sons, intelligent, eager, idealistic, all three. But Don Amado died before the youngest son was old enough to go to school at all. At the time of his death, Don Amado left three acres of very poor land, a thatched house (three sides made of adobe, one side made of bamboo and wattle), a team of very old oxen, and two burros. And he left Margarito, aged six, Martiniano aged nine, and Cassiano aged sixteen. Cassiano as a person is worth many, many teams of oxen and hundreds of acres of land.

Cassiano is not handsome like Aurelio and Perfecto, nor gay like Nico and Joel. He is just good and honest and smart and sincere. In 1945 he was the only one of the older boys who came regularly every night to teach the illiterates, and this after a hard day's work plowing with his father's oxen in his father's fields. When the work on the three acres needed no attention, he went to cut wood in the sierra, one of the youngest boys to do so regularly, and Don Martín would take it into Oaxaca to sell for him when he took the oxcart. After he finished the fourth grade in the Santa Cruz Etla school —he had been in Rosita's last primary class before she went to Mitla—he had waited two years for a good corn year so that he might go to the fifth grade in San Pablo Etla. Then his father had died, and he had shouldered the burden of the weedy three acres—and his shoulders were not yet seventeen years old. In addition, he helped in the *municipio,* working with Chico keeping records for Don Bartolo, for he wrote a very fine hand.

He was determined in those years to be like his father, to stay in Santa Cruz Etla and to do all he could to improve the school and the community. He said to me one day, walking along behind his

272

burros as I led Don Marciano's horse: "My father was the best educated man in all the hills. He spent much time with me, helping me to be serious. The greatest pity is that he is not here to help my little brothers."

I recorded this conversation in my 1945 notes, and added: "Cassiano will help his little brothers; he will help everyone while he neglects himself." In those days he never even combed his hair, and he looked as neglected as his father before him. Just before I left in 1945, he came to see me at Doña Patrocina's to have his picture taken as a souvenir for me. She, motherly soul, got out Chico's wooden comb and tried to make his cowlicks lie down. "Give him twenty years, and he will be Santa Cruz Etla's absent-minded professor," I wrote then.

I notice that I concluded those 1945 notes on Don Amado's family by saying, "Martiniano, aged nine, seems stuffy and serious, but Margarito, who already reads as well as his nine-year-old brother, has his mother's happy nature. Perhaps it is left for Margarito to go on to the fifth and sixth grades away from home, and then to the city for secondary school, so that he can become the second Benito Juárez his father so hoped for." Margarito never got to the sixth grade while in the hills.

Doña Rufina herself, the boys' mother, died in the spring of 1954, just a few months before I came to visit. If she had lived, all might be different for the sons of Don Amado. Her gay spirit hushed, the house empty, Cassiano did not know which way to turn. He had hoped to marry a pretty little cousin of Chabella named Marta, so he told me later. How could he bring her home to an empty house, to the heavy cooking for three men, to a life on such poor acreage? The oxen had died, and Cassiano could not replace them for less than 1,200 pesos. He did not want to work the farm through another season by borrowing Joel's team. Money from the sierra came in very slowly by then for the charcoal burners. What could he do for his little brothers, for naturally he thought of them first?

He told me in Mexico City that his mother, knowing for several days that she was going to die (no one in Santa Cruz could tell me what it was she died of), had asked Cassiano to look again through

273

those letters and papers of Don Amado which she had shown me ten years before. Among them was a letter from the family of the soldier friend of Don Amado's grandfather, the one who had taken Don Amado to Mexico City when he was young. Evidently on the last trip the "sage of Santa Cruz Etla" had made to the city to get the town's official papers, he visited with the family of this old friend. Then letters had come from this family before Don Amado died. Cassiano wrote to the still-living widow of the old family friend and asked for advice about coming to the city. The old *comadre* had written in return to say, with the usual courtesy of the old-time Mexican families, that her house was his house. Meanwhile, Don Pablo had been home for the May fiesta and had promised to try to get Cassiano a job in the tile factory where he was working.

Cassiano stayed in Santa Cruz long enough after his mother's death to finish a double stint of work on the new church, since he did not have a hundred pesos to pay into the church fund. Martiniano, then eighteen, worked also, mixing concrete and laying bricks. Then after the May fiesta, which Cassiano celebrated "with tears in my heart, Doña Elena," he and the brothers prepared to leave. Cassiano sold his two burros, gave Doña Sofía what little supplies he had left in his empty house, and closed the house door.

He had just enough money to pay for three fares to Mexico City on the second-class train. He and the younger boys had nothing but their white, countrified clothes and their worn old sandals. The old *comadre* in Mexico City, probably none too happy that these far-distant country "connections" had taken seriously her offer of hospitality, had sent them to other relatives of hers who rented out the whole top floor, the *azotea*, of a downtown tenement building. Here in a garret room the boys laid down *petates*, and they have stayed there since, four staircases up, without being asked for rent. I did not see the place, but I have seen other *azoteas*, rabbit-warren rooms in the tenements of Mexico City; and I know in my heart that Cassiano and his little brothers, or anyone else for that matter, would be better off in the meanest adobe hut in Santa Cruz Etla.

Don Pablo, true to his word and to his loyalty to all the relatives of his mother-in-law, Doña Estéfana, had been able to persuade his foreman to hire this country cousin in the tile factory on the night shift. Building is booming in Mexico City; building-material factories work twenty-four hours a day, seven days in the week. Cassiano's job is from ten at night to six in the morning. He has one day off a week, a different day each week, but never Sunday. Factory laborers are strongly unionized in Mexico City, and he is sure of social security in the way of health services and accident insurance. He puts in only a forty-eight hour week, and in 1954 he was receiving a standard eighty pesos a week in wages. But the factory was across the city from the *azotea;* he could not be around in the daytime to watch and help the younger boys. He saw the temptations all around for them and was sorely troubled.

Martiniano, less stodgy than he had been as a child, went with Leopoldo and Don Pablo to a small restaurant where they always ate supper, having no woman to make tortillas for them. Here Martiniano arranged to clear the plates and wash the dishes in return for two meals a day. Occasionally people tipped him, and the restaurant owner gave him money to buy a real Yankee-style, collegiate, red corduroy jacket. Martiniano felt that Cassiano should be very pleased with him and not worry any more, for he got good meals and had some new clothes. As of this writing he is a waiter in a much bigger place.

There remained the problem of Margarito, who had so far found nothing to do save join the throng of little boys—and he seemed a little boy with his very short stature of the Etla Hills people and his childish, open face—who rush up to every parking motorist in Mexico City and offer to watch the car. Less aggressive than the city boys, he seldom got any cash for doing even this.

Rosita had helped Don Pablo and Leopoldo when they first came to Mexico City, since she had once been a *comadre* of Sofía for the child that had died. However, once Leopoldo was placed in a job, Don Pablo had hesitated to bother her further with the problems of other Santa Cruz Etla "exiles." And that is why Cassiano had been in Mexico City six weeks when I came to Mexico in the summer of 1954, and Rosita did not know that he was there, did not know even that Rufina was dead.

I went to Santa Cruz Etla in July, visited with Don Martín, painted pictures for Don Féliz, held Doña Estéfana's hand in the dark hut, and asked for Rufina and Cassiano. Joel thought I should have already seen the boys in Mexico City, though Don Martín, who had been there within the past year, knew how hard it is to find even people you are definitely looking for, once you get to the metropolis. At any rate, Sofía had a postcard from Leopoldo with a "develop while you wait" photo on the back of it taken in Chapultepec Park the Sunday before Cassiano went to work, when Leopoldo was taking pleasure in showing his country cousins around the city. There in the photo stood Cassiano, Martiniano, Margarito, and Leopoldo, all very grown up and serious. I determined to reach them all through Rosita when I returned to the city, get some photos myself, and ask about their seeming new prosperity.

Rosita, with her usual concern for Santa Cruz Etla people, stirred in addition by fond memories of the little Cassiano when he was in her primary class, immediately contacted Leopoldo's employer by telephone, and through Leopoldo got in touch with the other boys. She and I sent a taxi around to collect them and bring them to Rosita's from the *azotea*, from the restaurant, from the tile factory, from the clothing store. They all came, even Don Pablo briefly, to pay respects to me and my husband and to greet Rosita and her family. Then we took the four boys out to dinner near the great church of Guadalupe and ordered fancy steaks for them.

This last was a thoughtless kindness on my part. Leopoldo, the sophisticated one, could eat skillfully with knife and fork; but the boys from the country, so recently away from sitting on the ground and eating with hands and chunks of tortilla, were lost with the knife and fork and could not cut the steak. I plied Cassiano with questions, inconsiderate in my requests that he tell all about his mother's death, his trip to the city, the decline of the charcoal-burning business, the cost of a new team of oxen, his plans for the future. Though twenty-six years old, he was deeply sensitive, and he was trying to choke back his tears. He could not at the same time choke down his steak, especially when he did not know how to cut it up, and hesitated to pick it up in his fingers. Margarito and

Martiniano wolfed theirs down, Martiniano with some help from the knife and fork due to his experience in the restaurant. Cassiano, hungry as he must have been for good, rich meat, did not actually eat one bite; and I never thought of the explanation for it till my husband called it to my attention afterwards.

Naturally, Rosita thought of fewer questions and more helpful plans. She had another friend with an errand-running job up her sleeve for Margarito, though this friend, a medical-supply man, wanted only boys who had the diploma for completion of the sixth grade. Still, in the free night school, about which we had made plans earlier in the evening for Leopoldo and the business-practice classes, there were also night school classes in the fifth and sixth grades; so many Mexico City employers want that higher standard of education, so many adults want to get that diploma so they can attend evening *institutos,* or secondary schools. Again there was the problem of fifth-grade books for Margarito, but I did not even have to offer another five dollars since Rosita has access to many such books that Margarito could borrow. Few problems are solved so easily. Since Rosita sponsored him, the employer took Margarito without the certificate and promised to pay him more as soon as he finished the fifth-grade work. By October he was enrolled in the night classes, and Cassiano was delighted that Margarito was busy all the time. His pay of twenty pesos a week, a dollar sixty United States, has been a great help to Cassiano.

Of all the Santa Cruz Etla people, Margarito has written to me most often. Finished with the fifth and sixth grade and in possession of a diploma, he has been attending the *instituto* at night and has taken classes in English. His letters in English are much better than mine in Spanish, and it is my fault at this end when our correspondence lags. No longer a mere errand boy, he finds his increased knowledge an asset to his employer; and he now owns three corduroy jackets and a black business suit as well. I am afraid his letters imply that he would much prefer a life in Los Angeles to one back in Santa Cruz Etla.

In the long run, the success of the two younger boys in finding work in Mexico City only complicated Cassiano's own life. If he could save twenty pesos a week out of his own wages of eighty, he would soon have two thousand pesos in his savings. With this he could go back to the beloved hills and the graves of his parents and resume the position Don Amado meant for him to take in Santa Cruz Etla. If prices do not go up, he could buy a new team of oxen and two acres of land which Don Martín's family offered to sell him. He could improve his house, put tiles on his roof, fill in the fourth side with adobe, whitewash the house, and bring into it a Santa Cruz bride. Then he could assume again the job of town secretary, work for the school committee, and (though he did not say it) hope eventually to be president. All chances of his own further education having vanished forever, he philosophically said: "I can do what my father hoped for in Santa Cruz Etla. I cannot do these things he planned if I stay in the city without education and without future. I must go back within two years. I surely must get back." Two times two years have since gone by, and Cassiano is still in Mexico City, living in the same *azotea*, working in the same tile shop, while Martiniano and Margarito become prosperous young men about town.

"What about the little brothers, *mis hermanitos?*" he asked Rosita and me in 1954. "My mother and my father entrusted them to me. Already they are much happier in this large and terrible city than I will ever be. How can I leave them here? How can they ever be the leaders of the Indian people that Benito Juárez was? How can I answer to my mother and my father that *los hermanitos* did nothing with their lives but live and work, work and live in the big city?" He let the problem of his brothers worry him even after they were both doing well; and he stayed in the city to "watch over them," though Margarito writes that at every new planting season he lays his plans to "go home."

At least I could ease his spirit by taking photos of them all there in Mexico City and sending copies of them to Doña Sofía. I sent also each of Don Amado's sons an enlarged copy of the photos of Don Amado and Doña Rufina which appear in this book. Each year I have been waiting to hear that it is a good corn year in the Etla Hills, that Rosita has encouraged Cassiano to shake off the responsibility of the younger boys in Mexico City, to take his two thousand pesos and go home. Then he can "lay Don Amado's ghost" by getting his roots deep again in the Santa Cruz soil and represent Don Amado and Rosita there for the rest of his life.

~~⛪ IO ⛪~~

I HAD HOPED somehow to help fulfill Don Amado's dream of bringing honor to Santa Cruz Etla and improvements to the hill people, and when I left there in 1954, I had laid a plan myself to "send on a Benito Juárez." It was to have been not a boy, but a girl, Don Martín's smart little granddaughter Margarita; I thought there was a chance to give her an education in nursing or medicine. By this means we would have been able to improve the health of Santa Cruz, a problem that Don Amado did not even know could be tackled.

Don Martín had visited Rosita in Mexico City in May of 1954, right after the spring fiesta, before the planting season and just before Cassiano came to the city. Don Martín had arrived with his wife Pastorcita and his *comadre* Doña Rosario, the mother of Chabella, through whose distant Santa María Asumpa cousins now in Mexico City they had all had a place to sleep. With this trio of the dignified older generation from Santa Cruz had come the pretty little Margarita, Chabella's oldest child. The purpose of Don Martín's visit was to ask the advice of Rosita and of the Santa María cousins about further education, citified or otherwise, for Margarita. She wanted to be a nurse, or a doctor, or a something which helped babies live longer. Don Martín knew that Rosita's husband was a doctor. Through him they could find out if a career in the field of public health was a fit thing for a woman, if country girls could ever do such a thing.

This idea for Margarita was not as far-fetched as you might think. Every teacher—poor and indifferent as the Santa Cruz teachers had been during Margarita's work up through the fourth

279

grade—every teacher who had known her had considered her intelligence unusual and had spoken to Don Martín about it. She had finished the fourth grade just when Don Martín, acting at the request of the town council, had occasion to contact church authorities in Oaxaca City about building the church. Though Santa Cruz received no financial help and no supervision from city church leaders, several of them were interested in the community effort, including the teachers at the seminary which was just then being built on the hills within sight of Santa Cruz Etla. When Don Martín brought up the subject of his bright little granddaughter and asked advice of the seminary teachers about sending her on foot to the San Pablo Etla school, where no Santa Cruz girl had gone before, these church authorities made arrangements for her with a convent school for girls in Oaxaca City which offered the fifth and sixth grades.

So Margarita, beginning in the March term in 1952, lived with the kind nuns in the convent, away from her family in Santa Cruz; and in two years of hard study she passed both the fifth and the sixth grades. Convent-bred children have a chance to study harder and longer than Santa Cruz children, and under better supervision, and they are expected to finish one grade every year. This instruction was not free for Don Martín; he sent thirty pesos a month to buy her food and provided books and uniforms at untold expense. The store had been prospering; the family made every other sacrifice; the church fee of a hundred pesos had to be paid in installments, even though Don Martín himself was the chief instigator of the church project.

Margarita was thus the first child from Santa Cruz Etla who ever finished the fifth and sixth grades by going away from home to school. Inspired by this very unusual opportunity, she studied harder than ever, and the nuns had the same kind things to say for her possibilities as had the teachers in Santa Cruz Etla. The next steps would not be so easy. Even if she got a tuition-free scholarship to a Catholic secondary school in Oaxaca—and such a thing is seldom offered—the nuns in Oaxaca told Don Martín that it would still cost him a hundred pesos a month to keep Margarita in the boarding school where she could get high-school credit. That would be for three years. Then nurses' training, which is not free either, would be three years more.

Rosita had few helpful suggestions for Don Martín about training in Mexico City. Her husband could get Margarita into nurses' training there, but not before she had finished the secondary school. Already Rosita was helping two young cousins from Oaxaca finish their education in the capital; she could not take on in addition the responsibility for a fifteen-year-old girl from Santa Cruz Etla. Perhaps when her youngest girl cousin, who lived in Rosita's flat, finished the secondary school near Rosita's home, perhaps next year —well, Rosita surely hated the fact that she could not offer to help, but she could only tell Don Martín to wait a year and to keep in touch with her. Don Martín, the patient and philosophical, seeking only advice and not expecting financial help, took his feminine following back to Santa Cruz Etla, all of them having enjoyed the city with its sights and lights and famous shrine of Guadalupe.

Rosita told me of Don Martín's visit when I saw her on my way south in early July of 1954. "I should have told Don Martín right out that the whole project is impossible," she sighed, "such a long training period, so much difficulty in getting the high-school education first. I mean to help all the Santa Cruz people I can, but to see a girl through nurses' training is just out of the question for us now. I see so many children every day in the kindergarten here who need help worse; I just have to put the needs of the Santa Cruz Etla people out of my heart. However did a girl as isolated as Margarita get the idea of public health nursing, or the study of medicine?"

I knew exactly how Margarita, or any other girl in Santa Cruz Etla, got that idea, and it was partly because of Rosita herself. And now it is worth going back again to the "days of Don Bartolo" to describe one more incident.

"Remember that Don Bartolo claimed to be sick with the *paludismo* that day we came in 1945," I reminded Rosita. "You yourself believed him, took the whole matter so seriously, and reported malaria in Santa Cruz Etla as soon as you got back to Oaxaca and could go to the *Departimiento de Salubridad*."

When she had made the report, the doctor at the Health Department had asked her: "Have the people been vaccinated against smallpox, *la viruela?* There is smallpox in Tehuantepec, and with the Pan American Highway going all the way through there now, people from Tehuantepec come to market in Oaxaca. We have new funds to vaccinate everyone in the villages. A station wagon can get up there now, can't it? Then we will send a doctor to help the malaria cases and three nurses to vaccinate the people. They will come on Thursday of this week." Rosita didn't remember his exact words to this extent, but I have them in my old diary notes as she had told them to me.

She had sent the words to me at Santa Cruz in a letter via Chico. "You must tell the community to be ready," she wrote. When I told Doña Patrocina about it, the wise old lady said: "That is more serious than *paludismo.* One sees many faces marked with it in Oaxaca. When I was a child, we had it here in the hills, and many died, including the brother of Don Martín. He had it himself, Doña Elena, I remember, and you can see the marks still on his face. We will all be fortunate indeed this time that you and Rosita came, if it can be prevented." This from the cure woman who by all reports should oppose modern medicine.

She sent Nico to get Don Bartolo. I read him the letter. He "prepared the community" by talking to the children at the school on Wednesday. He was by this time recovered from the "malaria" and was his old self again. Even in front of the serious little school children lined up to hear him, he could not help saying, "We shall have a happy day, perhaps the nurses will be pretty."

The children all came to school the next day in starched, clean clothes, the little girls in pink, white, blue, or yellow dresses down to their ankles; the little boys in clean, white "pajama" outfits. Don Martín, with his pock-marked face and his lifelong fear of smallpox among little children, sent Chabella to the school with the little ones, Margarita (then almost six), Artemio, Adela, and the baby Jesús, all of them as clean and starchy as the children already in school. Other mothers brought their baby children, and when the station wagon arrived, a *camioneta* just like that of the rural education director, children and mothers were lined up out in the road.

I have never seen anything in Mexico done more efficiently and thoroughly than was that vaccination. Heading the expedition was a citified doctor about thirty-five, in a business suit. He it was who "brushed off" our short, insignificant-looking little president, Don Bartolo; but I liked the patient way he dealt with the children. Don Bartolo was disappointed in the nurses. Only one was really pretty, but the second was fat and jolly and the third exceedingly business-like. I am sure every little girl in school was very impressed with the glamor of the nurses.

The efficient one stayed at the schoolhouse. The little primary teacher, Doña Ester, listed every child's name for her on a long official blank. Doña Rosario's Adelita and Don Lalo's Aurelia helped swab a clean place on each child's arm with disinfectant solution. The children knew their own ages and told the nurse as they came by for the quick scratch of the vaccination. No one was afraid; no one cried, at least not at the school.

The other two nurses started out, Don Marcelino's Teresa with one and Dona Paula's Alicia with the other, the pretty nurse to the south ridge, the fat one to the north. They went into every house; they vaccinated every member of every family. Mothers were told to wake the tiniest babies, to call men in from the fields. I heard later that the pretty one had gone into the mill to catch every young woman who was waiting there for corn to be ground, probably making a disturbance for Don Julio. When the efficient, snappy nurse finished at the school, she went to the nearby houses on the central ridge, catching Esperanza and Nico and Doña Patrocina at our house. Even La Abuelita, calling on the blessed saints under her breath to help her against this invasion of modernism, submitted without too much cringing.

Meanwhile, the doctor talked on the porch to the teachers, the mothers, and Don Bartolo about malaria and left instructions to cover open stagnant water with oil, to report any large numbers of mosquitos and any cases of "heats and colds." He told about the *sarampión* raging in valley towns beyond Hacienda Blanca, and warned the Santa Cruz mothers to keep children warm, rested, and away from the light if the *sarampión* came. The *sarampión* did come in a very virulent form, in a later year when I wasn't there, and it hit the family of Chabella and Margarita hard, taking Chabella's sister Adelita, Chabella's youngest girl, and the baby Jesús.

The vaccination incident ended as do all such affairs in Santa Cruz Etla; there were long speeches by the municipal president, the visiting dignitaries, the teachers, and the Mothers' Club members. The doctor thanked Don Bartolo for the cooperation. Don Bartolo thanked the doctor and the nurses for the *salubridad*, as he said, the "health." There has never been *viruela* in Santa Cruz Etla since, although all this "'vaccination day" happened much longer ago now than the seven years it takes a vaccination to become ineffective. Only Don Martín and two of the other older Santa Cruz Etla people were ever pock-marked.

Doubtless this whole incident, which had so impressed me, had impressed the bright-eyed little Margarita even more. After all, most of the work had been done by the three woman. I remember that on that day Chabella, as a leader among the young mothers, stayed on the school porch in the thick of it all day with all her children. Margarita remembered a great deal about it when I chatted with her in 1954. In the crowded room at Don Martín's she slept in the bed with me, and I had a chance to talk to her often of her days in school.

All through the years I had been depressed at the unsanitary conditions of Santa Cruz Etla, no worse than other rural mountain villages in Latin America, but surely no better. There was the dysentery we got in 1934 when Augustina washed all our dishes in the ditch, the water sickness which hit me again so very hard at Doña Patrocina's when we used the old wells, the little attack again in 1954 from Chabella's luscious, white, goat's-milk cheese, in spite of the preventative pills I was taking then. Such water sickness causes the death of many little children in Santa Cruz Etla, and it will take a long program of education, a large expenditure for a purified water supply, to get it stopped. Rosita as a young teacher in the school had been provided with an enema can, a hypodermic needle, and a clinical thermometer as part of the equipment for a rural teacher in those early days; but she had no bandages, no antiseptics, no other medicines, and of course no skill or training in using even what she had. Though she would doubtless be horrified if I reminded her of it now, she washed the hypodermic needle in the brook herself and used the enema can to keep chalk in. Doña Patrocina knows no scientific way to prevent death in childbirth, of either mother or baby, and she is still the one who delivers the babies of Santa Cruz Etla.

The Mexican government's health program, separate now from rural schools and cultural missions, can help in all these things when and if the communities ask for help, and when the small staffs of the health service can reach the communities. Don Martín knew all this; he knew of the *viruela* which marked him when he was a boy, of the *sarampión* which took his pet grandchild Jesús, of the deaths due to bad water, of the loss of all Pastorcita's children save Miguelito. He wished with all his heart that he could dedicate Margarita to helping in public health work; but "Oh, Doña Elena, the hundred pesos a month for the secondary school alone! Some months we can be sure of it, but other months no. And in a bad corn year, the store and the bakery suffer with the rest of Santa Cruz Etla. It would perhaps be a mistake to send her away, build up her hopes, and then not be able to continue such an expensive plan." Don Martín knew enough arithmetic to figure that three years of high school plus three years of nurses' training makes more than seventy months, and seventy months at a hundred pesos a month is seven thousand pesos, more than the church itself cost the whole community.

Meanwhile I visited at Don Martín's, became attached to the sweet little Margarita, took her with me to visit other houses, condoled with her about the impossibility of further education, answered her questions about girls growing up to be doctors, as well as nurses, in the United States. But still no thought on my part that here was a possible answer to Don Amado's hopes for a Benito Juárez.

We went back to Oaxaca City in time for the *Lunes del Cerro*,

285

that big fiesta of regional dances honoring Benito Juárez which is held there in mid-July every year. We reported at Rosita's old "townhouse flat," in the down-at-the-heels colonial mansion divided into housekeeping rooms where she used to keep her mother, her uncle, and her aunt, and where Aunt Mercedes and Uncle Octaviano live still. Doña Mercedes and Don Octaviano went with us in our car to the top of the hill to see the dances, and I chatted with them about things as they are in Santa Cruz Etla today.

"If only I had a young person in the house with me," said Aunt Mercedes. "All the young nieces and nephews are gone; the youngest preferred to go to secondary school in Mexico City with Rosita rather than live with me and go to the Oaxaca *Instituto*. I wish some little girl from Santa Cruz Etla—they are such fine people up there—would want to go to secondary school and live with Octaviano and me. Well, it's impossible, I suppose. No girl will have finished the fifth and sixth grades, and I would at least want a high-school-age girl. Besides, it would cost fifty or sixty pesos a month to feed her; I could not afford just to hire her to work for her board, food for a young person is so expensive, and we cannot ask Rosita for any more than she sends us. No one in Santa Cruz Etla could afford to pay for a child's board, I suppose. Still it would surely be a gladsome thing to have a pretty little girl from Santa Cruz, unspoiled by town ways, to keep us company."

Thus the old Doña Mercedes rambled on, while Uncle Octaviano nodded assent; and I watched the plumed Indian dancers jumping around on the *Lunes del Cerro* stage, hardly bothering to think through the meaning of Doña Mercedes' Spanish, as I busily snapped pictures on Kodachrome film and adjusted the lens to the changing light.

Suddenly the light snapped on in my head. A pretty little girl from Santa Cruz Etla? To live with you and go to secondary school, Doña Mercedes? There is no one who passed the sixth grade? Oh, yes there is!

"How much did you say it would cost to keep a girl with you, Doña Mercedes?" I asked aloud. "Sixty pesos a month would pay for everything?"

Sixty pesos a month was then less than five dollars. In the East Los Angeles Junior College I was teaching a class of young would-be social workers, most of them themselves of Mexican ancestry, and sending them out to do practice work in boys' clubs and social centers. The children they worked with were sometimes but one generation removed from the Santa Cruz Etlas of many parts of Mexico. I have talked a great deal about this service to the Los Angeles under-privileged community, but the actual truth is that I got more than five dollars an hour extra for the four hours a week I put in supervising the social-work students in the evenings. How could my conscience rest easy, when Margarita could go to secondary school a whole month with only one of these easily earned five-dollar bills? The money could be sent in an international bank draft every month to Doña Mercedes in Oaxaca for a ten-cent fee.

Doña Mercedes and Don Octaviano, close friends through the years to many of the Santa Cruz Etla people, were delighted at the thought of taking Margarita and sending her to the *Instituto,* only three blocks from their "flat." Fortunately, Don Martín had brought most of his family to the *Lunes del Cerro* on the special San Lorenzo bus. They stopped by, at the end of the festival, at Doña Mercedes' apartment, having arranged to come there and bid us one more good-bye before we went. Don Martín, Chabella and Miguelito, and Margarita herself in charge of the baby Guillermo, all came by.

If I had expected exuberance at my plan, I would have been disappointed. Don Martín was deeply appreciative, but he did not want to feel obligated to me. Chabella looked at Miguelito, a glad hope in her eyes for her oldest daughter. Miguelito looked at his father, for Don Martín was then head of the family and made all its decisions. None of us felt Miguelito's own opposition then. I looked at Margarita and saw her eyes full of tears for fear that her grandfather would say no.

Don Octaviano broke the long silence. It would be a favor not only to Don Martín, but to them as well, the old relatives of Rosita. Rosita herself would be distressed to hear that Don Martín had refused to let them have this gay young companion. Surely they had

287

another few years to live; the girl would finish secondary school while they were still on earth to enjoy and take pride in her. Still Don Martín hesitated; any young girl is more responsibility than she is help. Finally I had to make a little speech, reminding them of the pride we had always felt, all of us there, in the young people of Santa Cruz Etla. We should all have been inspired by the old Don Amado ten years before to do something which would bring special honor to the town. Now here was Margarita, the best student the Santa Cruz Etla school had produced, and her family was trying to withhold from Santa Cruz the honor of her further education. I told them that if Margarita was ambitious, she might be able to become a woman doctor, for there was one already then working for the *Departimiento de Salubridad* in Oaxaca. Of course, it would take nine years altogether for Margarita to get such training. But Don Martín should know that nine years is nothing; already it had been twenty years since he, as municipal president, had first welcomed me to the porch of the Santa Cruz Etla school. The amount of money involved even for medical school, which is tuition-free to the best students in Mexico, would be a very small amount of United States money, stretched out through the years.

Stirred by such oratory, Don Martín swallowed his pride for the sake of his greater pride in the town—the free, successful, independent town of Santa Cruz Etla. The arrangements were made; Margarita entered happily the Oaxaca *Instituto* in the new term; Rosita sent letters full of praise and congratulations. And if any of the hundreds of my own splendid students of Mexican ancestry in East Los Angeles who heard about this wondered why I was sending money down to Mexico every month, from 1954 to 1956, when the need for funds for medical education are just as great among *them*, I could only answer sadly: "Find me a way that I can send a Los Angeles city student of Mexican ancestry through any American medical school at a total of five dollars a month, and I will surely do it."

So I left Oaxaca in the fall of 1954 smugly pleased with my plan. Then I threw myself into my own busy life, traveled elsewhere in the summers, wrote in a dilatory fashion when I sent the monthly pittance of money, and answered such letters as I received from the other Santa Cruz people. Chico was being considered for president, Don Féliz served again as the public works chairman, Leopoldo and Cassiano's little brothers did well in the city. Eventually I kept an old promise to myself and began the preparation of this manuscript. When it was almost finished, I received two letters in black-bordered envelopes, one from the town council, one from Chabella writing in Miguelito's name. Both announced the sudden death of Don Martín while at work on the spring planting. Miguelito's letter ended by thanking me for all the help to Margarita, then in her fifth term in the secondary school, and saying how tragic it was that her grandfather's death ended her career.

A subsequent short, sad note from Margarita herself hinted that her father, long the minor member of the family, had always opposed her education and now meant to concentrate on sending her brother Artemio on to be a lawyer. After all, Benito Juárez was himself a lawyer, product of Oaxaca's own law school. Thus, Artemio whom I had never known well, who was at school in San Pablo Etla in the fifth grade the year that I lived at Don Martín's on my last visit, whom I had always considered rather badly spoiled by his sisters, as well as by his grandparents and parents—this Artemio was to be the one to get the highest education of all the youngsters of Santa Cruz.

This will undoubtedly come true, for Miguelito has moved most of his family to Oaxaca. Having sold the farm land Don Martín owned in Santa Cruz Etla piece by piece to other farmers after the harvest in 1956, he took the money and set up a bakery booth on the edge of the Oaxaca City market. Here he bakes bread and Chabella stands at the counter persuading the *tonto* Indians from the high sierra to try wheat bread when in town. Pastorcita, his mother, with the two youngest of his girls, runs the bakery in Santa Cruz Etla in the whitewashed house where the *tonto* hired man still makes the bread, though surely she will not keep this up many years into her old age.

After a term of absence from school due to all these changes in her life, Margarita was allowed by her father to go back and finish her last term at the *instituto,* so that now she is a high-school graduate. But as of this writing, she is kept most of the time waiting in the bakeshop. Artemio, on the other hand, with no chores to do, no stock to feed, is kept in a very fine secondary boys' school in Oaxaca City, though I am afraid he has none of the enthusiasm for it that Margarita would have had. Rosita writes me not to worry too much about this, since Doña Mercedes, her aunt, has been ill a great deal and has needed more care than Margarita could have given her. As soon as a really good year comes in the bakery, Rosita says, Miguelito can be persuaded to send Margarita and her younger sister Adela both on to teacher-training school or into nurse's training. But with the whole family, now that Don Martín is dead, having set up headquarters in Oaxaca City, I do know that neither Margarita nor Adela, whether as teacher, public-health nurse, doctor, or even happy housewife, will ever go back to serve Santa Cruz Etla.

⇜꙰ I I ꙰⇝

As I FINISHED this little manuscript on Santa Cruz Etla and read it through a last time before sending it to the publisher, I felt disturbed at the sour tone it left in the air. The forest has been overcut; the soil is eroding; the peppiest, most progressive young people are in the city. My own contacts with the town grow fewer through the years, as everyone, myself included, grows older. If I were to go back in 1964, I say to myself, how many other old friends will be gone, besides Don Amado and Don Martín and Doña Estéfana? The young matrons in 1964 with whom I would have to live will be those who were older girls in school with Don Alfredo in 1954, whom I scarcely got to know. Where would I now find the old, warm welcome?

And much as I wanted to see the community improve when I first went there at twenty-five, now at forty-nine I dread change almost as much as did La Abuelita. I do not want to know if the bus comes to the main ridge, if everyone is wearing "store clothes," if the *tonto* pipers have never again played at a *mayordomía*. I hate to see the ending of all that was "quaint and picturesque," subject alike for camera and for water-color sketch pad.

What a selfish attitude! How often have I lectured about the great improvements in the Mexican nation as a whole, its rapid advance in the modern world. And now comes to my hand the *Américas* magazine, official publication of the Pan American Union, for October, 1957. Its lead article (by Carl C. Taylor, pages 3-7), called "The Awakening Village," is writen by a rural sociologist in the employ of the United Nations and of the Ford Foundation who has studied village life all over the world. In particular he writes of grass-roots improvements in India, where he has "seen the same national spirit and idealism" as "in Latin America." Change is "inevitable and necessary," he writes, "and national leaders must insist that the program develop from the bottom up. . . . To build a new society in any country, we must build from the ground up. This means building one sound community after another by arousing the people to work for undertakings that benefit them directly and that indirectly contribute to the country's development."

It is partially because the Santa Cruz Etlas of Mexico have been "awakening villages" that Mexico's modernization has been so rapid. That Margarita works in a better bakery in town, that Leopoldo and Margarito have white-collar jobs in the city—these developments that I have deplored have "indirectly contributed to the country's development." All Mexico will be better off when the Cassianos who live on eroded land can work for guaranteed union wages in the city, when the Artemios wear shoes and go to secondary school, when the Chicos and Nicos who stay home can afford to wear store-bought jackets, when all the young fathers of the community can take time off on a Sunday afternoon to play basketball with a factory-made ball thrown through factory-made hoops.

Not any one individual was doing exactly what Don Amado had hoped a second Benito Juárez would do, but Santa Cruz Etla as a whole was helping to accomplish what Benito Juárez himself had wanted for the Mexican nation—the elevation of a whole people.

Thus I have come full circle to realize that change is as good a thing as I thought in 1934 that it would be. I have also come to

know many other things from my years of contact with this particular "awakening village." I have learned that people, at heart, are
the same everywhere. The people of Santa Cruz Etla longed for
knowledge for their children, for prestige for their community above
other communities, for material improvements in their lives, as
would the people of Paris or New York or Mexico City or Los
Angeles. Only they do seem to have built their lives around these
longings in a so much warmer and friendlier way!

Scale
Approximately
3 inches = ½ mile

N E
W S

El Rio

Carmen

Bathing Pools

Enriqueta

Marciano

Abuelita's Old House

Spring

Margarita Rivera

San Sebastián Loma

Buenaventura

Hand Ball Field

El Rio

Lalo

Scho

San Sebastián People

Isaías Pérez

New Church

Zanja

Municipio

Féliz León

Zanja

Oxcart Road

La Coo

Sierra

Los Tortos

Scale.
¼ inch = 1 mile

San Felipe de Agua

San Luis Ocotitlán

Santa Cruz Etla

Etla City

San Pablo Etla

Oaxaca City

Pan. Amer. Highway

Hacienda Blanca

To San Pablo
5 miles

Refugi